WIN

35 WINNING STRATEGIES

FROM TODAY'S LEADING ENTREPRENEURS

Published by CelebrityPress™, Orlando, FL
A division of The Celebrity Branding Agency®

Celebrity Branding® is a registered trademark
Printed in the United States of America.

ISBN: 9780983340447
LCCN: 2011930491

This publication is designed to provide accurate and authoritative information with regard to the subject matter covered. It is sold with the understanding that the publisher is not engaged in rendering legal, accounting, or other professional advice. If legal advice or other expert assistance is required, the services of a competent professional should be sought. The opinions expressed by the authors in this book are not endorsed by CelebrityPress™ and are the sole responsibility of the author rendering the opinion.

Most CelebrityPress™ titles are available at special quantity discounts for bulk purchases for sales promotions, premiums, fundraising, and educational use. Special versions or book excerpts can also be created to fit specific needs.

For more information, please write:

CelebrityPress™,
520 N. Orlando Ave, #2
Winter Park, FL 32789

or call 1.877.261.4930

Visit us online at www.**CelebrityPressPublishing**.com

WIN

35 WINNING STRATEGIES

FROM TODAY'S LEADING ENTREPRENEURS

TABLE OF CONTENTS

CHAPTER 1
THE MÉNAGE À TROIS:
KEY TRAITS TO COMPEL A WINNING LIFE
BY WES PITTMAN, ESQ... 13

CHAPTER 2
LEARN FROM THE MASTERS
BY DR. VERONICA ANDERSON 29

CHAPTER 3
TAKING CALCULATED RISKS
BY GRACE DALY 39

CHAPTER 4
SWEAT EQUITY
BY DARYN CLARK 45

CHAPTER 5
YOU CANNOT HIT A HIDDEN TARGET!
BECOME A MASTER OF TARGETED THINKING
BY MIKE DENISON.. 53

CHAPTER 6
BRAIN TRAIN
BY SUMMER KNIGHT, MD, MBA 63

CHAPTER 7
TRADITIONAL RULES FOR A SUCCESSFUL LIFE
BY PEGGY LUSK 73

CHAPTER 8
WINNING TRUTHS
BY JOHN E. LEDFORD, CFP® 81

CHAPTER 9
GREED AND THE GOLDEN EGGS
BY JIM STACEY 89

CHAPTER 10
**HOW TO PROFIT FROM THE INFORMATION
REVOLUTION**
BY DAVID SCHWAB, PH.D. 97

CHAPTER 11
WIN WITH WISDOM
BY DR. EMMA JEAN THOMPSON 105

CHAPTER 12
SUCCESSFUL FAMILIES –
"SECRETS TO RAISING SUCCESSFUL AND MOTIVATED CHILDREN"
BY MASTER GARY A. SCHILL... 115

CHAPTER 13
THE POWER OF CHOICE
BY MELINDA HUTCHINGS 123

CHAPTER 14
IT'S ALL ABOUT FREEDOM!
BY KATHY WENSEL 131

CHAPTER 15
WIN! WIN! WIN! AN ENTIRE BOOK ABOUT WINNING!
BY SUE FERREIRA 139

CHAPTER 16
STICKY NOTE TO-DO SYSTEM –
UTILIZE STICKY NOTES AND STOP WASTING YOUR TIME RE-WRITING
YOUR TO-DO LISTS.
BY NANCY KRUSCHKE, CPO® 147

CHAPTER 17
TO WIN YOU MUST FOLLOW YOUR PATH
BY HOLLIS COLQUHOUN 157

CHAPTER 18
I TEACH HEALTH ... I DO NOT TREAT DISEASE
BY DR. PHIL SELINSKY 165

CHAPTER 19
CREATE YOUR OWN REALITY
BY LORETTA WASHBURN 177

CHAPTER 20
DELAY DOES NOT MEAN DENIAL
BY DENISE Y. MOSE, PH.D 185

CHAPTER 21
REAL ESTATE – INVESTING TO WIN!
A SHORT COURSE ON GETTING IT RIGHT.
BY MICHAEL MAZZELLA 193

CHAPTER 22
DUPLICATE YOURSELF
BY FRANK LAPLACA 203

CHAPTER 23
LIVING A FEARLESS LIFE BY CHOICE
(HOW 'HAND MEDITATION' CAN TAKE YOU THERE)
BY ANGELIKA CHRISTIE 211

CHAPTER 24
YOU'VE WON BEFORE YOU'VE BEGUN.
BY JEFF PEOPLES AND DAVID ELLZEY 219

CHAPTER 25
MASTERING THE 12 KEY AREAS THAT DRIVE BUSINESS SUCCESS
BY VICTOR HOLMAN 229

CHAPTER 26
KNOW WHO YOU ARE AND DO WHAT YOU LOVE!
BY LAURA TREONZE... 237

CHAPTER 27
HONESTY ... THE FIRST STEP TO SUCCESS
BY WILLIAM GOLD 245

CHAPTER 28
HOW CAN WE EMERGE STRONGER IN TIMES OF CRISIS?
BY FRANCISCO YANEZ.. 251

CHAPTER 29
FINANCING COLLEGE EDUCATION CAN BE A WIN!
BY CLIFF MORGAN/TODD THOMAE 259

CHAPTER 30
SEVEN FUNDAMENTALS OF A HIGHLY SUCCESSFUL FLIP
BY BRANT PHILLIPS 271

CHAPTER 31
HOW TO WIN BY CREATING SOLUTION-DRIVEN PRODUCTS
BY GREG ROLLETT 279

CHAPTER 32
DON'T JUST MAKE A LIVING, MAKE A LIFE!!
– CHOOSE TO LIVE YOUR BEST LIFE EVER!
BY GLENNA GRIFFIN... 287

CHAPTER 33
THE POWER OF YOUR CORE STORY –
HOW TO WIN BY CREATING THE COMPETITIVE ADVANTAGE AND THE
COMPETITIVE DIFFERENTIATOR
BY BART QUEEN 295

CHAPTER 34
NICHING –
MAKE MORE MONEY BY FINDING NEW (NICHE) MARKETS FOR THE
THINGS YOU ALREADY DO.
BY WILLIAM R. BENNER, JR. 305

CHAPTER 35
THE BUSINESS TRIFECTA & THE MAGIC FORMULA
FOR MEDIA SUCCESS
BY NICK NANTON, ESQ., JW DICKS, ESQ, & LINDSAY DICKS   315

CHAPTER I

THE MÉNAGE À TROIS: KEY TRAITS TO COMPEL A WINNING LIFE

BY WES PITTMAN, ESQ.

S tanding on blistering black asphalt under the Phoenix sun in July 1996, I momentarily wondered if the principles that had guided me so successfully to this point in life would do so again. My mandate was to investigate Allison Stanley's death. As you will see, adherence to those easy principles in her case, and in two others that I will describe, again proved decisive in reaching my goals. Whatever your business or profession, they will work for you, too. Guaranteed.

I am an attorney, a personal injury attorney, one of the best in the country according to my colleagues, one who other lawyers turn to for advice about their difficult cases. On this day in the Arizona desert, I was the modern day gladiator, the Samurai warrior for my client, Scott Stanley – tasked by him to determine why Allison, his wife of 36 years, had died in a collision that should have resulted in nothing more than bruises and sore muscles. Fun-loving and still vivacious, she had driven her late model car to town where she lunched with girlfriends.

In the early afternoon drive toward home, she meandered along the peaceful two-lane country road under clear, sunny skies. This north central Florida area was made of rolling hills, towering oaks, and vast green pastures of thoroughbred and quarter horse farms. It was her last sojourn along this serene landscape to the horse and cattle farm that Scott and she had built from the dirt up. Suddenly, from her left another driver failed to heed a stop sign at the intersecting road. The driver, realizing the error, nearly missed her car but struck it just behind the rear wheel. She spun a quarter turn, enough to cause the cars sides to slap together before careening just off the road from the low speed impact. The inattentive driver was shaken but exited his small vehicle quickly and gingerly moved in Allison's direction. He was relieved at first glance to see minimal damage to both cars, but he was perplexed that her door was partially open. When he saw Allison, he was horrified to find that her upper body was motionless, hanging limply between the door and its frame.

He later told me that an eternity passed before the sirens of the ambulance and a sheriff's patrol pierced the air. The ambulance crew determined immediately that Allison had expired from injuries caused by her door opening upon impact and, then, slamming on her partially ejected body as the sides of the cars made contact.

Why was Scott's wife, driving at slow speed, wearing her seat belt, killed instantly in a low force collision? My job was to find out. Believing that thorough preparation is a key to success not only in the law but in most things in life, from my Panama City, Florida office, I immediately arranged to secure Allison's vehicle in the wrecker yard for inspection. Understandably, Scott's call to me came days after the tragedy, so I traveled there as quickly as possible to view and photograph the scene and the car. No time is like the present in the investigation of an injury or death case, because critical evidence can be lost during unnecessary delays. If winning a meritorious case is required of me, as I fervently believe it is, I insist on viewing the scene and all available evidence. My convenience is not a consideration. So many times, I have found bits and pieces of evidence missed by others in cursory inspections. Sometimes it was because they looked at a wrecked vehicle or a road scene from only one direction, took a few photos, and left. My approach yields more clues, and those clues tend to become evidence that is admissible in court for the benefit of my clients. I scan a scene from every direction, and I do it as the light changes. Maybe the others don't know that the grain of the pavement in changing light makes a difference in finding tire marks. And tire marks, for example, are pieces of evidence that, if preserved in photos, build the foundation for the testimony of accident reconstruction experts. In other words, persistent attention to detail from the outset is of paramount importance. If facts are lost, those facts being the bits and pieces that we refer to as evidence in a court of law, we cannot hope to develop a winning theory or theme of a case. An open mind, considering all the possibilities raised by those valuable details, does indeed arrive at winning theories, themes, and strategies. One of my favorite law professors was fond of chastising his students from the lectern every time we missed an analysis. I remember his saying in a nasal Wisconsin twang, "Ladies and Gentlemen, what are the facts? What are the facts? Look for them, because the facts make the law." Indeed they do, so finding every scintilla of evidence, every fact, leads to successful analysis and, ultimately, winning. That's the way it is in my profession, the law. It's the same in other endeavors in life whether one's work happens to be architecture, construction, marketing, accounting, or anything else.

My stint that day outside Phoenix was to continue my investigation into Allison's death. I had been to the scene and to the wrecker yard to meticulously inspect and photograph both. The inattentive driver, still shaken, had been interviewed and gave the details I mentioned before. My inspection of Allison's car confirmed the rear driver's side strike and the "witness marks" comprised of small dents and scratches with paint transfers from the other vehicle. It had been disturbing to see the door still agape in the wrecker yard, held to the B-pillar by a bungee cord. The A-pillar is the post to which the hinges are attached. The B-pillar holds the latch receptacle that receives the bolt from the door itself. Close inspection of the bolt through a magnifying glass was at first unrevealing, but when my gaze was redirected to the latch, I noticed a minute, almost imperceptible, deviation of the cusps of the latch that grab and are supposed to hold the bolt firmly, even in a major collision, so that the door will remain closed to safely package the occupant. I quickly looked again at the bolt but through a more powerful magnifying lens, and my heart skipped. The smallest of striations, that is, scratches where the bolt exited the cusps during this low speed impact, were now visible. It was enough for me to realize that the manufacturer of Allison's vehicle had failed to design a safe car for her.

A car maker has an obligation to its paying customers and passengers to design and build a reasonably safe car, knowing that a certain number of them will be in collisions ranging from fender benders to massive wrecks. Cars and trucks cannot be made perfectly safe for the entire range of impacts they can experience, but logic indicated that Allison's car, her transportation package, if you will, miserably failed to meet reasonable standards. Her door should have remained closed during the minor wreck. I filed suit against the car manufacturer, a Detroit giant.

It in turn, as auto manufacturers routinely do, denied my allegations and commissioned an "independent" company to crash test an identical car under duplicate conditions, speeds, angle and position of impact, etc., to demonstrate to me and, ultimately, to a jury that its door latch would not fail under those circumstances. The company was hardly independent. It made millions a year from the manufacturer by supplying engineers to always testify on its behalf and by performing crash testing that, miraculously, always seemed to support the manufacturer's position that it built perfectly safe vehicles. Always. Further, the company's reputation was that it's crash-testing, analysis, and testimony were highly suspect. As a result, those of us who do auto product liability cases frequently referred to the company as Fake Analysis Associates or FAA for short.

The test vehicle had been crashed by FAA using test equipment to duplicate the parameters of the actual collision. In later depositions, I confirmed the validity of the testing, but on this fateful day under the blazing sun, as I've said before, I was there to inspect FAA's crashed test vehicle. A hundred yards away, its air conditioned warehouse was an oasis that would have been welcomed for the inspection, but its officers and the manufacturer's had decided to put the vehicle on the black asphalt without shelter from the sun for one reason. To make me so miserable that I would hurry the inspection. Despite the 115 degree temperature, I did not hurry. Dropping my camera bag beside the damaged car, I slowly walked around it to get the big picture. In all, the damage fairly mimicked the damage to Allison's car except for one crucial thing. The door was scratched and bent, as Allison's had been, but while the top of the door frame was bent open enough to see down to the door latch, which clearly still held the door bolt, the door on this test vehicle just as clearly remained closed. My first impression was that the crash test supported the manufacturer's claim that it had designed and built a reasonably safe door latch. However, I had learned from many prior experiences that first impressions, if relied upon, often lead to disaster.

Resisting the temptation to find air conditioning somewhere else, I began the slow and exhausting process of finding and photographing every scratch, gouge, dent, paint transfer, wrinkle in skin, and broken glass that existed. I was perplexed. I saw nothing that would support Scott Stanley's case. The door, in what seemed to be an identical crash to Allison's, had remained closed. Was her event an isolated occurrence, one that would not hold up in court as being caused by a manufacturer's bad design? I pondered, applied more sun screen, and pondered some more. Slowly during the next hours of reviewing every clue, a question formed in my mind. The top of the door frame was bent open enough to reveal the latch, but witness marks on the bottom of the door frame indicated that the forces applied by the impact there should have had the same effect on the lower part of the frame. So why wasn't the bottom of the door frame bent outward, too? I reached into my camera bag where I always carry a small mirror attached to a long telescoping rod. Feeding it down the small space between the upper door and the B-pillar, I was able to wiggle it below the latch. Shining a flashlight down the same path, I slightly rotated the mirror just enough to see a bolt. This bolt was not a part of the automobile itself. It had been inserted before testing by FAA to hold the door in place during the crash test. In essence, it provided double the holding power to keep that door closed so that the door latch would not fail during the test like it had failed during Allison's fatal collision. I will never know whether it was FAA or the manufacturer that bolted the door together before the crash test, and whether the culprit forgot to remove it or just thought I couldn't possibly find it.

Nevertheless, meticulous attention to detail in the first phase of investigation and continuing pursuit of every fact, every clue, every shred of evidence until conclusion of the case was a highly important key to success in Scott's case. When the manufacturer learned that I found the bolt, indicating that it or it's expert consulting firm was fraudulently creating false evidence, it called for negotiations which resulted in its payment of a handsome settlement for Allison's death.

As important as attention to detail is, it does not itself comprise the so called gold standard for achieving success in legal cases or in any other endeavor. I will explain. For many years, I have been a passionate aviator of high performance multi-engine and turboprop aircraft, a hot air balloon, and as a bird of sorts when I used to sky dive. As a conscientious pilot who read reports of accidents in order to avoid them, I learned an important fact from National Transportation Safety Board investigations. Rarely does only one error in flying lead to disaster. Typically, as it is expressed in pilot language, "a constellation of events terminated in a fatal crash." A late night before a flight and a less than perfect decision to fly through a line of thunderstorms might have been survivable, but when the white-knuckled distraction of a failing engine is added, the end result is predictable. Similarly, in my experience, a successful person cannot point to just one trait to thank for success. *Superior performance stems from "a constellation of key traits."* The French term "ménage à trois" comes to mind.

Ménage à trois, in the classical sense, has a sexual connotation, certainly not what is intended here. In literal translation the phrase means "house of three," a reference to three people who are romantically engaged occupying the same residence. One famous account from Sweden in the mid-1700s began when a count was supposedly hired by the king to assist him in the consummation of his marriage with the queen. His part was to serve as a sexual instructor for the royal couple. The "aid" rendered by the count reputedly resulted in the birth of the future king, Gustav IV Adolf. Likewise, in the 1969 film *Paint Your Wagon,* Ben married Elizabeth, but she fell in love with Partner. They decided that if a Ben could have two wives, then, a woman could have two husbands. My reference to Ménage à Trois, now purposefully capitalized, is to refer to the well known wine of the same name. It means a blend of three grape varieties, a threesome designed to achieve a pleasant and harmonious balance of flavor that the juice of one grape alone cannot attain.

Having set the stage for sharing my secrets of success by introducing one grape of the Ménage à Trois, i.e., meticulous attention to detail, a trait with which the characteristics of the other two grapes are blended to arrive at a successful experience over and over again, I can now more comfortably reveal the other important grapes. They are (1) building the right team with which to formulate strategy and provide powerful testimony and (2) reducing complex matters to simplicity, because without simplicity, communication suffers, and in the end, persuasion requires good communication. Ménage à Trois of success in the law, as well as in the success of an endeavor, is attention to detail, building the right team to deliver the meaning of the details, and, finally, the effective communication of the idea to the ultimate buyer, in my case, a juror or an insurance adjuster. In other words, this combination in pilot-speak is the "constellation of key traits" that leads almost inevitably to success. It works in my field and in every other. Think about sales, for example, which requires knowledge of the facts. The salesperson must acquire the details about the product to know it inside and out to determine selling points, to compare it to a competitor's product, and to meet the customer's objections. An effective sales team devises strategy based on the product's performance or aesthetic details. Finally, the sale is dependent upon the effective presentation of the product's most important advantages to the prospective buyer. How does this Ménage à Trois of key traits for success work in other professional fields?

Consider a veterinarian seeing a badly-injured dog for the first time. The first minutes are consumed by attention to detail, perhaps by feeling the animal's leg to determine if it is broken, then by analyzing x-rays to further define the degree of damage. Once the damage is known, the successful veterinarian will enlist the right team to solve the problem. I'm thinking of a dog of mine for which the vet called in a highly experienced orthopedic veterinarian who in turn had a local medical school make an acrylic model of the leg from CT scan images to better plan a surgery. Finally, the best communicator of the group sold me on the procedure despite its high cost by explaining the proposed complex operation in understandable terms, the bottom line being that the painful condition this young dog was in could be alleviated by following their proposal. I was sold. I had been impressed by their attention to detail, the team's knowledge, and by their simple, straightforward communication.

Although my personal injury work is the representation of victims from a multitude of serious trucking accidents, car accidents, nursing home and medical malpractice, and train, bus, and air transportation mishaps, most of my cases, of course, stem from everyday, but hardly mundane, car accidents. Nevertheless, I will use another example of my work from the product liability aspect of accident law to prove the key importance of the second Ménage à Trois grape in our analogy, building the right team, because that case illustrates the point so well. The wreck was near Atlanta. An eight-year-old girl seated in the front passenger seat of the family's car suffered brain damage when her seat belt failed to hold her in place in a moderate-speed collision. Her head struck the dashboard of the car. Her eleven-year-old sister, sitting behind her, slid under her own lap belt and suffered paralysis from the stomach down, when the belt compressed the soft tissues of her abdomen and her spinal cord. Their father had been driving them to a baseball game when an oncoming driver lost control of his car and veered head-on into theirs at thirty miles per hour. Horribly, their mother, who was an on-duty emergency medical technician, was in the ambulance crew that responded. She saw her badly damaged children and later, holding her hands up into the air as if reaching for them, told me how she had watched the life-flight helicopter carrying them to a trauma hospital, not knowing whether she would see either of them alive again.

Assuming that a car that packages its occupants reasonably well should not have failed them by permitting these catastrophic injuries, I secured the evidence, as by now you know is my firmly entrenched practice, and began to assemble a team of experts to analyze and present it to a federal court jury. The car was designed by a French auto maker but had been built in a joint venture by it and a big three American automaker. I was convinced that the front and rear seat belt designs were defective and dangerous. I felt compelled to find the best seatbelt expert for these badly injured girls' cases. It didn't matter where. Through considerable research, I learned of Nils Bohlin who had then just retired from Volvo in Sweden. Formerly, he was a Saab Aircraft engineer who designed safety harnesses for use in the military jets it built. When Volvo's vice president was severely injured in a fairly minor auto accident in Sweden, the president of Volvo called Nils and asked him to join Volvo for the specific purpose of designing a seatbelt system for Volvo's cars that would prevent the kind of injury its vice president had sustained.

After about a year of research in the early 1960s, the young Nils Bohlin invented the 3-point restraint system that to this day is worn in cars and trucks worldwide. Clearly, he was the world's premier expert on seatbelt design, so he was the man I wanted. I contacted him. We agreed to meet at his home in Sweden. I carried with me the girls' medical records that showed the points of external bruising and cuts and the internal head and spinal cord damage. From that and from other evidence that I had developed through accident reconstruction to confirm impact speed and angle of impact, Nils quickly expressed the preliminary opinion that the French design was indeed faulty and had caused my clients' terrible injuries. Because of his difficult schedule, we decided that he should not travel to the U.S. to examine the seat belt design in the wrecked car but that we could accomplish the same analysis by finding an exemplar (identical car to use as an example) vehicle in Europe. Since Belgium is next to France, had quite a few of the French designed vehicles in question, and was close to Sweden, we next met in Ieper, a drab Belgian city best known by the poem beginning with the words, "In Flanders fields they lay." The poem was a tribute to Allied soldiers who died in droves and are buried there following the German's use of mustard gas in World War I. Befitting the grim nature of the local history and the tragedy that had struck my young clients, it rained the entire time we were there, and the cold warehouse, in which we secretly did our work to prevent any possibility that word of it would leak to the French automaker, threatened us with pneumonia.

I went ahead of Nils by a couple days to locate an exemplar vehicle that I could rent and take to the warehouse. Under umbrella and raincoat, I walked the streets until I found a father out with his two young daughters who happened to be exactly the height and weight of my clients. For a small fee, the father agreed to accompany the children to the warehouse as needed for the next couple days. Now, I had an exemplar vehicle and exemplar children. Nils was delighted to hear the news upon his arrival. Early the next morning, we began our work by inspecting the car. He quickly determined that the front seat 3-point restraint system was designed so badly that the little girl who patiently sat in the seat for us, like my Atlanta client, would have had a head injury in a frontal impact. The anchor point for the belt on the B-pillar, which by now you are familiar with, was so high that it would have easily permitted her shoulder to rotate out from under the chest portion of the belt after which only her lap belt would have held her. At the full forward position of seat adjustment used by my eight-year-old client, the exemplar child's head easily reached the dashboard.

A case like this has only two possibilities, settlement or trial. Either way, evidence had to be presented to the manufacturer's lawyers or to a jury, so I had also brought another part of the team I assembled. It consisted of a noted film maker and his acclaimed cameraman. The film maker was Bill Buckley, the award winning genius who captured Harry Truman in the series *Years of Decision* for PBS in the 1950s. Nothing less than quality imaging was acceptable. Perfect lighting and correct angles of view were essential to capture this evidence for presentation to whatever audience I later had to convince. We spent the next hours photographing our little model as Nils positioned her from point to point in the rotation out of the chest belt until her head lay against the dash. Then, he taped belt webbing at what would have been the proper attachment point on the B-pillar, somewhat lower on the pillar than it was on the wrecked car, to prevent the injury, and we photographed how that restraint configuration would have saved a brain from damage. The still and video images we got were magnificent to illustrate the point.

Nils turned to the rear bench seat. Under pressure from his hands, it easily collapsed downward. A well designed seat has a pan under it to catch the buttocks as they move forward to prevent the "submarining" of the passenger's body under a belt. This car had nothing of the sort, so my eleven-year-old client slid under the belt which then crushed her spinal cord. Nils also measured the angle of the belt from its attachment point and found that its design violated our Federal Motor Vehicle Standards. As you have probably correctly guessed, more webbing was taped in place to illustrate the appropriate attachment point to obtain a correct angle of restraint, and Bill Buckley and his cameraman documented it.

After suit was filed, numerous depositions were taken, and trial was approaching. The co-manufacturers of the vehicle asked for pre-trial mediation to try to get the case resolved. By then, I had spent another day with Nils Bohlin and the camera crew to get his comments on videotape, some as voiceovers of the still photos he had taken in Belgium. Editing of the tape brought the content down to a tight, hard hitting 6-minute product that at mediation I showed to an attentive group of defense lawyers who were clearly dismayed by its content. The cases settled for multiples of seven figures. My only reason for mentioning the result is to give validity to the concept that assembling the best possible team to analyze and present the evidence – Nils Bohlin and Bill Buckley – is a good investment that provides dividends. Why? Because they gave me, my clients' modern day gladiator, strength in front of the audience by virtue of unquestionable credibility. When you assemble your team of "experts," the same will happen for you. The second grape of our Ménage à Trois analogy now being firmly in hand, I turn to the third, the need to create simplicity out of complexity to enhance communication and, therefore, persuasion.

One Saturday night, a teenager borrowed his daddy's yellow Corvette convertible to take his trophy girlfriend to a high school homecoming game. He arrived at a 4-way stop intersection beside the stadium just ahead of a kind, middle-aged deputy sheriff on a motorcycle to his left. Exercising his right-of-way prerogative, the teen accelerated to make the left turn but cut too tight and hit the deputy with considerable force. The man's leg was shattered by the car's front bumper. Following difficult surgery and his many months of physical therapy and recuperation, we arrived at trial. The defendant denied any fault. The case was more complex than one might imagine, because there were so many witnesses due to the proximity to the stadium. Typically, if there are ten eyewitnesses, they will testify to ten different versions of an accident. The matter was further complicated by the layout of the intersection. Instead of being perfectly square, the part of the road the deputy was on was offset to the left, so to make a turn without running into the deputy, who had stopped behind a crosswalk but close to the center line, the Corvette would have to take a more sweeping turn than normal. More important, its driver, who did make that turn, would have had to compensate for the discrepancy in the layout by changing the radius of his turn as he made it instead of gliding through it at a constant radius. After the jury was selected, I gave my opening statement and was followed by the defense attorney's opening. He has always been a little pompous, so the same was expected this time. He performed as usual, stating, "All the facts in this case are like big barn doors that are swung by tiny hinges, so watch for the tiny hinges, the things that you can hang your hat on in making a decision in favor of my client."

Early in my case preparation, I thought that the layout of the intersection might present a problem for my case, but I also recognized that it might offer an opportunity for a win if I presented the evidence just right. I hired a crane and crane operator and hoisted a photographer high into the air over the intersection to take a bird's eye photo of it. It, among many other photos of the intersection, was shared quietly with defense counsel during our mandatory exchange of potential trial exhibits before the trial. I called my client and witnesses to testify after which the other attorney called his witnesses, including the Corvette's young driver. Of course, he testified that he had driven through the intersection perfectly, making his left hand turn just as he should have under good control. I asked him only one question on cross examination. "Once you started your turn to the left, was your turn constant, or did you have to change your path as you made the turn?" His answer: "It was a constant turn; I didn't have to move the steering wheel." Both sides rested. I gave the first part of my closing statement. It lasted about 40 minutes as I reviewed the evidence given by my witnesses and reminded the jurors about the substantial medical care my client had required. The defense attorney then gave his summation. At the end, he reminded the jury about the little hinges that swing big barn doors and said that his evidence had given the jury the little hinges they needed to swing the big barn doors to a verdict for his client. Since the plaintiff gets to open and close in summation, I rose to give my rebuttal to his arguments. In my experience, simplicity is king, because everyone can understand complex matters when they are reduced to the simple. During the presentation of my case, I had introduced into evidence most of the photos of the intersection, including my overhead photo, but I did so without calling attention to the overhead shot. I had also gone to a store where I bought a thirty-nine cent compass, one of those little metal tools that is used in geometry and drafting classes to draw a constant radius arc or circle. One end holds a pencil, but the other end has a point that the student sticks in the paper to station the compass in the center of the circle about to be drawn. I asked the court for permission to approach the jury. Receiving it, I got the overhead photo from the court clerk and put it on the wooden bar in front of the jury. They waited for an explanation. I put the metal point of the compass on the corner of the intersection between the teenager and the deputy and the pencil part of the compass on the approximate point where the boy's left front tire would have been at the 4-way stop. The jurors leaned in to look. I reminded them of the defendant's testimony that his turn was constant once he had started in motion. They leaned in even more, and those on the ends got up to come over. I swung the pencil side of the compass from the boy's position in a constant direction to the left, representing his left turn. In that moment it became obvious to the jury that the teen's constant turn, without his making a correction for the roadway's design, had taken him over the top of the officer rather than into his intended lane of travel. My final words to the jury as I placed the compass on the bar before them were, "And those, ladies and gentlemen, are the little hinges that swing big doors." I sat down. As I walked to my table, out of the corner of my eye, I saw an ashen-faced defense lawyer. The compass remained on the bar a foot from the jury while the judge delivered his instructions. The jury retired to deliberate. During the trial, the insurance company increased the offer to $25,000 and, finally, to $50,000 on the third day of testimony. We said "no" to each offer. After an hour, the jury returned to the courtroom to give its verdict. The award to my client was over $1,000,000.

Simplicity, leading to persuasive communication with that jury, carried the day. Kelly Johnson, who worked for Lockheed, coined the acronym KISS and translated it, "Keep It Simple Stupid." Centuries before, Leonardo DaVinci's take on the same principle was, "Simplicity is the ultimate sophistication." Either way, it's an enduring principle worth remembering.

Now, you have my keys to success. I rarely entertain the thought of failure, because I know they will not fail me. Nor will they fail you. Use them with confidence.

ABOUT WES

Wes Pittman earned his law degree with honors at the University of Florida. Since then, he has become a highly successful and sought-after attorney representing injured people or the families of those killed through the negligence of others. His success is perhaps best measured by the fact that other attorneys and professionals in other disciplines routinely seek his advice, counsel, and representation.

Although based in Florida, he is frequently admitted to practice in courts in other states throughout the U.S. and has represented clients in foreign jurisdictions, including England, Germany, the Netherlands, Switzerland, and Italy.

He founded The Pittman Firm, P.A., which is committed in its entirety to serving the interests of injured people and consumers. His vow to represent people, not insurance companies or corporations, has been upheld throughout the firm's history. His advocacy against the trucking industry for permitting overworked and undertrained drivers to kill and maim on the nation's highways, the medical and nursing home industries for negligently disregarding reasonable standards of care for their patients, and auto manufacturers for their propensity to place profits over safety has earned him a reputation as a "pit bull" of litigation. As a result of his efforts and to the benefit of the public, many of those defendants and others have adopted safety standards that save lives.

Mr. Pittman has lectured extensively at professional conferences throughout the United States, Europe and Asia on matters relating to personal injury and death cases. He has authored numerous professional articles for attorneys practicing in these areas. He appears weekly on WJHG-TV, the local NBC affiliate in Panama City, Florida, to discuss current legal topics and to provide consumer information about automobile, motorcycle, maritime and truck safety, product defects, harassment and discrimination in the workplace, and other diverse matters relating to personal injury and wrongful death.

He has served multiple terms on the board of directors of the Florida Justice Association, formerly known as the Academy of Florida Trial Lawyers, and on its executive committee. He is also a sustaining member of the American Association for Justice and has been a member of its product liability and medical malpractice committees. Mr. Pittman is a member of Million Dollar Advocates, and on a local level, he is a member of The Florida Bar where he has contributed to its Automobile Insurance Committee and its Civil Procedure Rules Committee.

Additional memberships have included the Southern Trial Lawyers' Association and the American Society of Law and Medicine. He is currently a Florida director of APIT-LA, the Association of Plaintiffs Interstate Trucking Lawyers of America, and is a member of the American Trial Lawyers Association, where he is listed in the top 100 Trial Lawyers in Florida.

Mr. Pittman concentrates his practice of law in the areas of personal injury, wrongful death, medical negligence, product liability, and class action as well as multidistrict litigation involving pharmaceuticals and nutritional supplement misformulation, and the negligent design of medical devices resulting in injuries.

He is married to Jan Pittman, and they have three children. His hobbies include flying hot air balloons, airplanes, and helicopters, fly fishing, hiking, and photography. His wife is an avid equestrian who continues to win world championships in quarter horse western pleasure competitions.

CHAPTER 2

LEARN FROM THE MASTERS

BY DR. VERONICA ANDERSON

There's an old Wayne Gretzky quote that I love, "I skate to where the puck is going to be, not where it has been."

~ Steve Jobs

L et me begin by assuming that you probably want to accomplish great things with your life – otherwise you wouldn't be reading this book. That's awesome – far too many people settle for the status quo in their lives (including myself at one point – but we'll talk about that a little later on in this chapter).

One of the major mistakes a person with huge ambitions often makes, however, is trying to reinvent the wheel from scratch. They don't review what people in the past have done – and, therefore, they don't know the perils and pitfalls of the path they've chosen (not to mention the shortcuts to success!). Of course, they believe they're doing something no one else has done – so how can anyone really help them?

That's flawed thinking. To truly succeed, you have to understand that the wheel has already been invented and that someone has already walked the road you're traveling on. And those that have walked the road before you and reached their goals in an admirable manner are people that I like to call "The Masters."

The Masters are a gift to all of us; through them we can learn how to endure tough times and succeed in spite of them. They've triumphed over difficulties in their own lives and, by doing so, have made a difference in the world around them. Their clear-eyed vision and unwavering focus can provide incredibly valuable solutions to dilemmas that might seem otherwise impossible to overcome.

Masters don't have to have done exactly what we're trying to do; they could have been in an entirely different place, period and profession to ours. But they can still impart a great deal of education, inspiration and motivation to those willing to partake. Whatever your objectives, you will face similar challenges to those people faced in the past. The details may be different, but the actual situations can be startlingly alike.

Finally, Masters can be just as important to your personal life as they are to your professional one; this is something I've experienced firsthand. Just as we can feel stymied in what we want to accomplish in business, we can also hit dead ends with our relationships and our worldviews. Masters can help us move beyond these impasses to a more fulfilling future.

MASTERS PAST AND PRESENT

In the past, the greatest Masters were mostly religious and political leaders. I'm thinking of towering figures such as Jesus, Buddha, and Gandhi – and, more recently, people such as Martin Luther King and Nelson Mandela. These are people who inspired millions of followers, changed the way their contemporaries thought, and left a lasting impact on the world. Their words and actions reverberated beyond their specific life struggles.

I'd like to add a couple of names to that illustrious list that, at first glance, might seem jarring. I'm talking about Microsoft founder Bill Gates and Apple CEO and founder Steve Jobs. You don't often think of Jesus and Jobs together – I mean, it's called the New Testament, not the iTestament – but in many ways, Jobs and Gates are The Masters of the 21st Century, especially in terms of who can inspire and teach today's entrepreneurs.

What do they have in common with the great Masters of the past?

Well, they all began with a singular vision that they wouldn't allow to be sidetracked. No matter what controversies swirled around them, no matter what obstacles were put in their way, no matter how many times they were told they were attempting the impossible, they moved steadily forward with a singular focus on what they were trying to accomplish.

Frequently, it was difficult to communicate that vision to others. They often paid a heavy price for their beliefs. The epic struggles of men like Jesus, Mandela and MLK are widely known. Even Steve Jobs was forced out of Apple, his own company, for clinging to his idea of what the future of technology should be. When Apple flailed in his absence, he was brought back in as CEO – and has more than validated his vision in recent years with some of the most popular technological breakthroughs in history.

And it's not just about technology, by the way. There are many geniuses out there with their own hi-tech ideas that could conceivably become game changers. The difference is you may never hear of them or their inventions - because they have no idea how to effectively bring their visions to the marketplace. That's the difference between them and people like Gates and Jobs; those two understood what the public needed and wanted.

Which brings us to one more incredibly important reason that these two men are Masters; *they served the world with their vision.* It doesn't matter that there are people out there who might be more talented or have higher I.Q.'s. If they're not out there changing the world, we unfortunately don't know about them. Again, I know "serving" is a strange word to use with successful business moguls like Gates and Jobs. But, I would argue, it's never just about money with men like them. It's about their vision to *change the world for the better.*

If you listen to Jobs and Gates talk about their products, the language is much more spiritual and religious in tone than the ordinary business person's speech. Let's recall the "Think Different" ad campaign that Jobs put into action once he returned to Apple in 1997. The centerpiece of the campaign was giant billboards featuring portraits of Einstein, Edison, John Lennon, Gandhi, Muhammad Ali – celebrations of The

Masters that inspired Jobs. No mention of actual products – just the visual representation of the Apple philosophy.

Also consider Gates' mammoth charity work since he stepped down from actively running Microsoft. Inspired by past philanthropic Masters, Andrew Carnegie and John D. Rockefeller, Gates and his wife created The Bill and Melinda Gates Foundation, which is now the largest charitable organization on the planet. He's still attempting to change the world, utilizing his fortune and his prominent position to effect that change.

How do Masters like Gates and Jobs accomplish bringing their vision to the world? Through discipline – discipline in all areas of their life. High achievers like them learn they must try something over and over and over again, until they've finally achieved the success and the mastery that they're after.

Critical to this unrelenting drive and discipline is maintaining a level of wellness in body, mind and spirit, which is my focus and my vision for everyone I talk to through my practice, my writings and my radio show. True wellness creates a firm foundation for mastery of any kind of discipline.

FEMININE MASTERY

I believe that Female Masters manifest their Masterhood differently from men. That's because women are unique in that they enable the human race to continue. Anyone who's a mother would tell you that giving birth is a gift – and it creates a different consciousness than men possess.

Women I consider to be Masters carry out their vision in two different ways – some of them are completely out front with their lives, carrying out their vision in a very public way, as a man would; women like former Prime Minister Margaret Thatcher or current Secretary of State Hillary Clinton fit that definition . Others carry out their vision by supporting their partners and helping them to fulfill their roles as Masters; former first lady Nancy Reagan and Martin Luther King's widow, Coretta Scott King come to mind here.

When I mention female Masters in this latter category, I certainly don't mean to be condescending or demeaning; their importance to their husbands' achievements can't be overlooked. I think it's an amazing accomplishment to fulfill your vision without having your name directly attached to it.

For example, when Ronald Reagan was in his second term as President, he was already beginning to feel the effects of his oncoming Alzheimer's Disease. Nancy constantly looked after him, reminding him of important details - and she made sure his staff was handling things the way they should.

Coretta Scott King was already an activist when she met her husband. She has been carrying his torch for over twice as long as he actually spent as a public figure, before he was assassinated at the age of 39; there wouldn't be a Martin Luther King Jr. holiday if she hadn't campaigned for it. We still are very aware of his vision, his triumphs and his ultimate importance because of her dedication and persistence.

And let's not forget our current first Lady, Michelle Obama. I attended Princeton when she was also a student. Even then I was struck by her warm spirit and her generosity to myself and my classmates, even though she was two years ahead of us. When she met her future husband, she was a lawyer and he was just an intern – she had been assigned to mentor *him*. Later on, after they had married and when he wanted to run for office, she was totally against it; she just wanted him to have a normal career. She ended up supporting his vision, however – she became the higher income earner and helped him ascend to the highest office in the country in an incredibly Masterful way.

Michelle Obama, along with our other female Masters, have something great to offer the world in terms of their own visions – but they also combine that vision with motherhood and partnership to create their own powerful Master's triad that's unique to women. Even Margaret Thatcher felt being a wife and mother was just as important as her governing responsibilities – and would interrupt official duties to attend her children's school conferences.

MASTERING OUR OWN LIVES

How do we learn from Masters? How do we even find the Masters who can help us with our own lives?

You have to begin by looking for people who are way out in front of where you are – way out in front of where most others are, as a matter of fact. Your own personal Masters should be those who have gotten to a place you'd like to see yourself reaching; people who know how to get there and who have already made the journey. These can be Masters you personally know – or others, such as the ones I've mentioned, who are more public figures that offer compelling inspiration to your particular situation.

There are three qualities a Master should possess:

1. A SINGULAR VISION

Everyone can't think (or innovate) at the level of a Steve Jobs – but most of us can create and pursue an integrated vision that leads to a more fulfilling life. This can take the form of how we deal with spiritual issues, business goals and more personal relationship objectives. That vision is best combined with the kind of life experience that leads to a more lasting wisdom.

2. A QUALITY OF SERVING

This comes from a mindset of seeing yourself as serving other people or the entire world in some way. It doesn't mean you're selfless or not interested in making money; it *does* mean you see what you do as adding to the world in some way.

3. DISCIPLINE

The above two qualities mean nothing without the discipline and the determination to see it all through; it's what truly makes a Master. You can sit on the couch and daydream brilliantly – but it doesn't add up to much if you don't take it out to the world and try to transform those daydreams into a workable reality.

As I've intimated, Masters don't have to be world famous – they can also be everyday people that do things that are extraordinary. I would like to close out this chapter by sharing how three Masters in my life helped me find my way through a difficult period.

From the age of four, my ambition was to become a doctor. I achieved that goal and I settled in to what was a "normal" life. I was married, I had my own practice and I attended the kind of church I grew up with on a weekly basis. I was doing everything that I was supposed to do, without really thinking twice about it.

And one day I realized I was *totally miserable.*

Deep inside, I felt completely unfulfilled – and I knew there was something bigger that I was meant to do with my life. Even though, from the outside, my life seemed like the perfect package, it was *hard* – and if you're happy and doing what you want to be doing, if your life is really flowing as it was meant to be, it shouldn't be hard.

I knew I had to make big changes – and three personal Masters helped me through those changes, which resulted in me leaving my practice, my marriage and my church; a complete break with the life I had been leading up until then.

The first Master was a woman I met when I ran a marathon. Judy was a yoga teacher – and we discovered that we had grown up in the same town and our birthdays were a mere 4 days apart. Judy, however, was ten years older than I am, and had a lot more life experience. She had been through her own challenging situations and came out the better for it. When it came to my marriage troubles, she told me to think it through before I took any action. She advised me in a totally non-judgmental way, and was more concerned that I didn't handle the situation as badly as a few of her friends had. She was a wonderful friend, and she held my hand through one of the toughest parts of my life.

Bonnie was another important Master in my life. I met her one day at my gym (I tend to meet the people who are closest to me when I'm doing the activities that are the most important to me, which might be the case with you). We began talking in the locker room. She was very upbeat, always smiling and seemed to always find the funny side in any situation – which made it all the more surprising when I found out that she had been through an abusive marriage and she had lost a son.

But she approached life not as a victim, but as someone determined to walk through life with a happy spirit. I saw in her someone who would not let herself be defined by the negative things that had happened in her life. As a matter of fact, the tough times seemed to motivate her to grow her spirit to a higher place – and I let that be an example to me moving forward.

My third Master was Cheri Huber, a Zen Buddhist Monk. You might think a female monk might not have a lot to say about the kind of personal transformation I was going through. But Cheri had been married, has a child and a grandchild and knows what it's like to deal with life, love and motherhood. Her vision has now brought her to a place where, through her foundation, Living Compassion, she works tirelessly to help children in Africa. When I asked her for a phone interview, she took time out of her schedule to meet my request, even though she had no idea who I was.

That interview was the beginning of a wonderful new friendship. Cheri became like an aunt, mother and big sister to me all at once. There was no religious judgment or distance in how she related to me – instead, she was honest, wise and loving, and made me feel like life was filled with possibilities. She was awesome at motivating people; she also helped me realize that I had a vision and I had to take the appropriate actions to make that vision my reality.

She also put me in touch with my loving and nurturing side. Many women try to ignore the fact that we are women in this day and age, especially those of us competing in what has been for centuries a male-dominated world. We fail to realize that our feminine side is something we should celebrate and access in our everyday life.

When I think about what these three Masters have meant to me personally, I am very moved at what they gave me – and it's easy for me to cry with gratitude. They truly helped lead me to a better place – as true Masters do!

It's important to note that these Masters helped me through a personal, spiritual *and* professional journey. One very positive outcome of this journey was that it unlocked my entrepreneurial ambitions, and put me on the road to achieving my business goals. As a specialist in Wellness, I know that all areas of life are linked; if you want to achieve your full potential as an entrepreneur, it's important to align all areas of your life so they're as strong, vibrant and healthy as possible. This gives you the energy and the spirit to fulfill your life's objectives.

One final note about Masters: There is a difference between emulation and imitation. You can follow the example of a Master – but you can't *be* that Master. You must find and pursue your own personal vision, not someone else's.

Ultimately, you are your own Master. Your truth helps you find your path. The Masters are there to help you make your way down that path.

You just need to find them.

ABOUT VERONICA

The new generation of medicine, Dr. Veronica transcends all boundaries with her passion for wellness through her unique brand of *Social Media Medicine*. Through her artfully blended unique and controversial perspectives, Dr. Veronica shares her belief that wellness encompasses everything from mind, body and spirit to happiness, personal growth and sex and relationships.

Currently with a listener base of over 11 million worldwide weekly on BlogTalkRadio and Old Grumpy Radio, her popularity continues to tip the scales. Her weekly talk radio show **Wellness for the REAL World** touches on health, politics and pop culture with edgy viewpoints that engage her guests and listeners equally while often exploring unchartered territory.

A graduate of Princeton University, Dr. Veronica is repeatedly requested to appear on news and commentary programs, including *Nancy Grace* (CNN), *Our World with Neil Cavuto* (Fox News Channel) plus *Live with Adam Carolla* and her fans clamor to get more of Dr. Veronica's straightforward, pull-no-punches philosophy on Facebook, Twitter, LinkedIn and more. Adding to her accolades is the adventure travel web-video series **Medicine Woman Modern World** that she created, hosts and produces. Fans can get more of her on her popular, edgy blog on DrVeronica.com. She also host popular video webinars through AskDrVeronica.com and Facebook.

Having practiced at Robert Wood Johnson Hospital and on staff at Philadelphia's Wills Eye Hospital, this American Board of Ophthalmology diplomat and fellow of the American Academy of Ophthalmology chose to shift gears and realize her dream, emerging as a technology-savvy, smart, outspoken, sagacious voice for healthy living in today's world. Dr. Veronica left practice as an Eye Surgeon to bring to the world wellness through *Social Media Medicine*.

CHAPTER 3

TAKING CALCULATED RISKS

BY GRACE DALY

Taking calculated risks has ultimately propelled me to a life of fulfillment. There is a sense of peace in living with no regret – whether the decisions made were proven beneficial or not. It helps to take action and move forward. Many folks are too obsessed over analyzing; because of their fears, they are frozen in making a decision. Learning to take calculated risks has pushed me to test, retest, pilot and launch many ideas. This immediate action to implement always gave me the upper hand over any other competing person or factor. I learned to take calculated risks at a young age, which in due course sparked my lifelong career in retail. This repeated action also banished most of my reservations for taking calculated risks going forward. The fear of the unknown, fear of failure or fear of success no longer held me hostage with inaction. Whichever doubts may have crept up at various times throughout my life – I fondly reflect on this one original calculated risk I had taken at the age of 19.

In the winter of 1985, I was a freshman at the School of Visual Arts. This was a private art college in New York City that required a portfolio review and an art test for admission to the school. I had graduated from the High School of Art & Design, so it was a natural for me to follow in the footsteps of my art education, specifically in Advertising Design and

Media Communications. I did very well in my first semester and was looking forward to the following spring semester. With financial aid and my part time job at a retail, wholesale and importing company, I was able to avoid taking out a student loan, keeping me clear and very mindful of debt at a young age. In the retail division of the company, I started as a stock person, was promoted to cashiering and then eventually became a buyer. It was a small company which allowed me to learn the many facets of the business. The owners were looking for a general manager to run the entire retail division and offered me the role with a lucrative starting annual salary of 42K and a profit sharing option.

My college friends thought I was crazy to leave after only one semester, especially since I loved it so much. Some thought I was in some sort of trouble and some made comments that I was selling out my art passion for the money. I always felt school would be there for me and that this was a fleeting opportunity worth considering. From a profitability standpoint, it sounded too good to be true; a no brainer. However, I conscientiously performed my due diligence in exploring all the risks and benefits that taking this role would bring. The risk was that I was leaving my passion for art, and having studied it for many years in school – I might never be able to get back into the field. Future risks were not finishing college if I got so busy working full time. This was a small business – how financially sound were they? What if I failed in this larger role of general manager? What if I hated the new role? I knew I loved my art. After further exploring, the benefits started to outweigh the risks that questioned my decision. It would be my first real full time job role with a title and salary.

I could learn a whole new trade and continue to build on my management skills, I loved Tribeca – the neighborhood of the business. It would be a healthy lifestyle for me being around all the natural and organic foods. Then it hit me. The primary attraction of taking this role would involve a first duty of hiring a new employee. The open position was a packer. This person packed all the organic and non-sulphur-treated dry fruits and nuts from large 25-50 lb cases to small 8 oz packages that we would sell through the store. This was a role that required a self starter, an independent worker since it was behind the scenes from the retail floor. I knew exactly who I wanted to hire for this; it was the perfect role for my Mom.

I am the second youngest of six children in my family. My parents came to the United States in the mid sixties. I am the first born here in America. We grew up in very modest conditions in New York City's Chinatown – in an old red brick five-story 'walk up' on Grand & Mott Streets. We lived in two adjacent one bedroom apartments on the third floor with my parents and my grandmother, so there were nine of us in total. When we were kids in grade school, my mother worked part time at the elementary school as a lunch aid for a short period of time. This contributed to the household financially, while my dad worked long, late hours as a bartender and waiter. I never saw much of my Dad growing up; we had completely opposite schedules. My siblings and I would wake up and get ready for school while my Dad slept. When we came home from school he would've just left for work. On occasion during the stillness of the night, half-asleep, I would hear my dad get home. He'd set into his lonely midnight routine: heating up his dinner and eating while he read the Chinese newspaper. Sometimes I woke up from the familiar cigarette smoke that would waft throughout the small apartment and then I knew my dad was home and had finished his dinner. So with my Mom working, even part time, that contributed greatly to the family. When the school cafeteria work was no longer available, she found work through her friends who were seamstresses in the garment industry.

In the Chinatown factories, a seamstress took big bundles of pre-cut pieces of fabric and sewed them into dresses, skirts or jumpsuits while the Chinese radio station blared in competition with the operating noise of the machinery. This was in the 70s, long before the majority of these types of jobs were outsourced to other countries. This was before there were stringent labor laws to protect employees from the grueling unhealthy conditions they worked in; conditions that coined the phrase "sweat shops". The working conditions were so harsh – you'd work in your winter coat during the cold seasons and the skin on your fingertips would crack and bleed when you tried to maneuver rough unforgiving materials such as denim. During the summer months, the windows were left wide open allowing in the heavy city traffic noise below and any hot breezes to blow in. Industrial fans on makeshift stands would stir the garment fibers, creating an invisible dust storm throughout the factory. Many of the seasoned seamstresses wore their own gauze-like masks over their nose and mouth. The freight elevator shaft was a dark deep pit that was exposed with open doors on each floor. It was only during the winter season they would close the elevator doors to reduce cold drafts. Most of the factories supplied an electric rice cooker and the employees chipped in for and took turns making the rice. They would bring in their own meats or garnishes for their lunch and were lucky if they had an old fridge to store them in. Those that did not have refrigerators would store them on the fire escape outside their windows during the winter season. Lunchtime meant they usually ate at their sewing machine tables, while the novice or slower seamstresses continued working in an attempt to catch up with the required daily quota. The seamstresses would receive an average of 47 cents for each completed garment they sewed. There were no building codes or even safety codes. This was just the way it was back then.

This became the main factor for me to take this new role. As the general manager, I would get my mom out of the factories. This requirement was defined to the business owners as part of the deal before I accepted this role. They were very supportive, excited and greatly welcomed my mother. My mother worked there for over 5 years before she retired. She made much better than minimum wage, and during the second year, her duties expanded to setting the organic produce on the retail floor. She interacted with the customers, especially resonating with all the nannies and mothers that came in with their babies in strollers. The customers loved her, and her English vocabulary expanded greatly. As general manager of the business, I held multiple roles: procurement, human resources, and eventually learned the wholesale and importing business. I was making good money, had access to the Battery Park City corporate apartment and first traveled to what became one of many trade shows and conferences. I was not in a rush to complete my college, but eventually got my degree through night school as I worked full time.

All this came from taking one calculated risk, of breaking out of my norm, learning new things and helping someone else in the process. These good "ripples" came from the one stone that I cast in my pond of faith. My career in retail operations was jumpstarted, and I was able to positively impact my mother with a better occupation in a healthy environment. This was a pivotal moment of my life, when I would take on more calculated risks that spurred on my learning and growth in business.

Based on what I've learned and practiced throughout my life, here are seven keys to help you in taking calculated risks:

1. Have a bigger "WHY". This will neutralize any fears of moving forward. You develop an understanding and fight for your cause that far outweighs your concerns. The risk of not proceeding is greater than the risk you're taking.

2. Aside from your own personal gain, will this help someone else? Will this make someone else's life better?

3. Complete due diligence. Be thorough in investigating and calculating all the risks and benefits. Have faith in your findings that inform you to proceed.

4. Imagine the absolute worst case scenario. If you can accept this worst case outcome, if it does not devastate you financially or break you emotionally, then you can proceed without trepidation.

5. Have a well thought out plan B. Should you encounter the absolute worst case scenario, which will not be a dreadful surprise since you've already imagined the worst in #4; this simply becomes an implementation of several additional steps for which you have already planned.

6. You need to ask yourself: Is this a once-in-a-lifetime opportunity? Will this opportunity ever come around again?

7. Understand and accept that everything that crosses your path ultimately has its' own risks. So why not choose to live your life by your own decisions.

ABOUT GRACE

With more than 25 years in the retail industry, Grace Daly, also known as America's Retail Facility Coach™, is an inspirational speaker, coach and bestselling author who helps individuals maximize their full potential by harnessing the power of their innate strengths. Her latest coaching program, "Actualizing Your Full Potential" designs a blueprint to success and fulfillment for the client.

Grace Daly International, Inc. was founded in 2008. In addition to her acclaimed inspirational writing in her published books: *The Seven Success Keys for the Retail Facilities Professional* and *Everyday Inspiration*, her signature keynote: "Rediscover and Share Your Gift Within™" encourages her audiences to seek within for the empowerment and creativity to boldly pursue the life of their dreams. By sharing her life experiences, Grace shows her clients how to work through challenging times in their lives and utilize that same energy to propel themselves to spiritual and career growth. Grace also teaches a writing class, and partners with diverse organizations to coach individuals and groups seeking her advice on business, life balance, and at times, just the necessary "shot of inspiration" when faced with difficulty in various stages of their careers. Grace holds a degree in Advertising & Media Communications from F.I.T. and is a Dale Carnegie HIP & GA certified graduate. She received her coaching certification from Certified Coaches Federation.

Grace's coaching expertise is regularly sought by business colleagues through her column: "The Daly Dish™" – published in leading industry trade magazines: *Retail Facility Business®* and *Restaurant Facility Business®*. Her heartrending keynote speeches of leadership, service and inspiration are sought out by business leaders who want to impact their teams to take positive action. A passionate coach, inspirational speaker and writer, Grace is dedicated to 'paying it forward' to her community and working with those who courageously pursue the life of their dreams. *Get Ready, Get Inspired!*™

To learn more about one of the country's leading authorities, Grace Daly, please visit: www.gracedaly.com or email: grace@gracedaly.com

CHAPTER 4

SWEAT EQUITY

BY DARYN CLARK, MA

The "Big Easy," New Orleans, Louisiana is where 'I cut my entrepreneurial teeth.' The start-up phase for my business was so exciting. The long hours worked paid off with company growth and profitability. This hyper-dynamic start-up time was filled with many meetings with those owning and managing businesses related to my own. Being a service provider who coordinates life-saving services required intense discussions dealing with many other agencies outside my own company.

One person in particular began to emerge from the plethora of meetings as someone that really knew his stuff. He was tough, well spoken, knowledgeable, successful and caring. He had started his business a couple years before me, and there were things to learn from watching, interacting and listening to him. Female leaders typically dominate our industry which provides services to people with developmental disabilities, so it was enjoyable seeing another man make it in such an exemplary way.

I headed out one muggy, hot, New Orleans morning to another meeting with the regional group that gathered consistently. My mind was on my business and what had to be accomplished that day. Things changed however when I arrived at the location for the meeting. I got my coffee and then started making small talk. Halfway through the coffee, I learned that Lane, my unofficial mentor, had died the night before. He had gone to sleep on his couch, a much-needed break from work, and he simply never woke up. A heart attack took him very, very, early.

Your health is the greatest asset you have. Lose your health to a disease, accident or other illness and that is all you will want back – your health. The mindset you have about yourself is critical. You are talented at giving time to your business, your work and your family, but have you developed the mindset of focusing on your best health as a part of the normal assessment of your business? You are one of the greatest, if not THE greatest asset your business has. You must recognize this consciously, and not allow the hectic pace of business and life to take your eye off the greatest asset you have…. *YOUR HEALTH*. A terrible case of the flu will soon bring to light the benefit of feeling great, but far too often people lose sight of that epiphany when they start feeling good again.

Look at the basic fact that exercise stimulates your metabolism, which affects your productivity in extremely positive ways. If you add the time you gain due to sharper mental focus and increased productivity, this will more than make up for the small amount of time you invested in your health. Exercise is the remedy physicians most commonly recommend when fighting diabetes, weight problems, high blood pressure and so on. Getting your heart healthy and metabolism going also shows long-term benefits in fighting early-onset Alzheimer's and bone and joint diseases.

More and more men, women and children are ill now, or getting ill because of weight challenges. In 2010, the U.S. Army initiated real and serious changes to the diets and exercises programs they have in place due to the weight issues of the soldiers. These are soldiers that have most of their days and meals set out, and yet they need help too. Obesity and morbid obesity are labels no one wants to claim. Most people know if they fall into these categories. If your weight is a challenge for you, taking it on and fighting for better health is more important than any other business task you have today, next month or five years from now. Remember, you are considering a life change and not a fad "quick fix". You and I know there are NO "quick fixes" if your health is compromised. The market for American consumers is almost always "the quick fix."

Business has financial reports that identify the health of the company. Your body has measures that identify your basic health position too. Health has real identifiers. Your body mass index, cholesterol levels, triglycerides, kidney and liver function – these are all numbers you should ensure are in great shape. When they are not in great shape, you and your doctor can formulate a "business plan" for your body. Then you can get to work to improve the numbers.

Just like you need to focus on a project or division within your company when a period of 'running in the red' exists, there are aspects that you must pay attention to that relate to your body and its chemistry. Just like the accountant or legal counsel you meet with for advice, a primary care physician that you have a good relationship with is at the top of the list when ensuring you surround yourself with a great team. Even the youngest entrepreneur needs a physician they can trust and see annually. Insurance companies frequently have annual health visits scheduled within health benefits. Use this health visit to get your blood work done, and use it as a time to communicate things like your approaches to better health. This is the time to ask your doctor questions about your health. I recommend you write brief notes on any questions you have, so that when you leave, you know you've covered everything.

I've developed a 7-Point plan to help entrepreneurs take as good or better care of themselves than they do their business. How can you put a value on adding productive years to your life? We can calculate returns on investments, costs of goods sold, and many other business mathematical calculations, yet many business owners and managers fail to look at the investment they can put into their own health, and the real returns that come with that investment over the long haul.

Here they are:

STEP 1:
SET THE AMOUNT OF TIME YOU WILL INVEST IN HEALTH/SWEAT EQUITY

The simple math: if you sleep 8 hours a night and are awake 16 hours per day you are awake 112 hours per week. If you did NOT exercise 97% of your waking time, you would have 3.25 hours per week to exercise, meditate or take some lessons. That's over an hour three times a week ... perfect! You get to do whatever you want 97 percent of the time and exercise just 3 percent.

Be selfish with this "health" time – You have to strive for balance in your life. There are real priorities that cannot be ignored. One of these priorities must be making and taking time to improve your own health.

STEP 2:
NOW THAT YOU'VE FOUND THE TIME, SCHEDULE YOUR WORKOUTS.

Identify what you want to do with your 3% time investment. A real challenge to some is deciding what they want to do to get their metabolism going. The activity should be convenient, effective, and something you look forward to eventually. *Write it down – when/where/what.* Set date specific goals and treat it as though on that day you have a fight, a REAL fight with someone that wants to cave your head in. Your training will take on a real sense of urgency if you'll follow that simple suggestion. I've never trained a fighter that did not keep their eye on that upcoming fight date and focused their training around that.

Even though you may not be a fighter when it comes to getting motivated, you are fighting for your best health and maybe your life. That should get you moving. From martial arts, fencing and yoga to dance lessons – there are many, many choices that not only exercise the body but also stimulate the mind. I find having the mental workout of focusing on new skills or the perfection of existing skills is the perfect balance to high intensity workouts to prevent boredom.

STEP 3:
GET ADDICTED TO THE POSITIVE.

Stick with your schedule for a few weeks and get addicted. Do something 21 days in a row and it will become a habit – as shown in many studies including that of Dr. Maxwell Maltz. Continue that habit and you'll find that when you don't cater to the positive habit you won't feel right. Get addicted to the positive feeling that comes from the work you are doing to improve your health. William Glasser's theory of Positive

Addiction shows that to get rid of negative habits, one must replace them with positive habits if the change is to be a long-term one.

STEP 4:
GET THE SUPPORT TO PUSH YOU WHEN NEEDED.

Communicate to others what you're doing so that it becomes a part of normal conversation. They can then help you find balance in your pursuit of better health and fitness. This can come from a friend with common interests, your spouse, child, family, personal trainer, coach or instructor. More and more busy professionals find support online too. Online support groups tend to gather a community of like-minded people looking for similar results, …in this case, fitness and health.

STEP 5:
DO I KNOW HOW TO BREATHE?

Learn to breathe – breath is the fuel that feeds the furnace of life. If you learn to focus on your breathing, you can unlock stress relief and stored energy depending on what part of the breath you concentrate on. Have you ever paid attention to the part of your body that expands when you breathe? Learning to listen to your own breath and heartbeat takes just a little practice in a quiet setting. The result of gaining this ability and awareness can reduce immediate stress that exists. Do you breathe from your upper chest? Your lower abdominal area? The difference is vital. To take breath in and allow the abdomen to expand means a more relaxed body. Some call it a cleansing breath. Next time you find yourself really in a pinch, breathe with your stomach and feel the calmness it brings, …if only for a few moments. After very consistent practice, you can summon the relaxing breath at will.

The sound of breath going into the body makes a very different sound than breath leaving the body. In times of quiet reflection, pay attention to these different sounds. Focusing on the inhalation can increase energy, while concentrating on the exhalation can help release stress in muscles and the mind. In both cases, ensure your abdomen is expanding as you breathe.

STEP 6:
YOU ARE WHAT YOU EAT.

Pay close attention to what you put in your body. There are many free websites such as myfitnesspal.com where you can create a daily diary of what you put in your mouth. It also measures calories burned through activity and exercise in a general way. The 10 minutes a day for four or five days used to check your intake is 50 minutes in a week very well spent. You'll find the information you learn amazing and potentially life-changing. It is a fantastic return on the investment of your time. You may even choose to continue to invest your time to track your diet or to simply learn more about nutritional science.

STEP 7:
GET REST

The amount of sleep we get per night has decreased consistently over the last few decades. The great news is that if you have trouble falling asleep at all, as you start your fitness lifestyle, you'll find sleep comes easier as long as you don't workout late at night. The body will require more rest the more it engages in physical fitness. Sleep is the ultimate recovery tool for your mind and body. Remember that sleep is not like your bank account. You can't "catch it up" by sleeping more one night of the week while short-changing all other nights. Strive for consistent sleep patterns.

CONCLUSION:

Your health investment is the part of your day/week that gets you away from your business while adding intrinsic and real value to your long-term health. Follow the steps and you will find progress in bettering your health week-over-week and year-over-year. Pass on the lessons you learn to those working with you, and see the gains your company makes in productivity and decreased down-time due to illness. Make this a lifestyle choice for the decades, and not for the moment. Then you will build a finely-tuned body and mind that are more capable of running the businesses you have – to their fullest potential.

ABOUT DARYN

Anyone who starts a company for a hundred and fifty bucks total out-of-pocket expense, and then proceeds to collect $42 Million in revenues understands the work and rewards that Daryn Clark has put into and gotten from Southern Ingenuity, Inc. This company was born of a calling to help others, and being able to do so in such an exemplary fashion, he attracted consumers of their services quickly and constantly. Once they find Clark's service business they remain for an average of 13 years. Reaching 145 employees in 2010, Clark's initial company, Southern Ingenuity, Inc., remains a leader in services to the aging and the developmentally disabled in Louisiana, and Daryn stands ready to help you.

Daryn Clark brings the same principles and spirit to his venture *What's YOUR fight?*. Clark's Masters Degree, martial arts black belts and Mixed Martial Arts Conditioning Coach Certification bring health, life, conditioning information and workouts via: whatsyourfight.com to the web. Clark understands the importance of forming strategic alliances and has done so with some great fighters and writers that travel the world and feed his site unique and exclusive stories.

What's YOUR Fight? is a division of Daryn Clark, Inc., which is also the hub of his consulting business. Daryn offers consulting to businesses and life coaching to individuals via his website DarynClark.com. If you never ask the question you may never know the answer and this site is a great place to ask your questions.

A marriage and family counselor by education, Clark finds that helping others is not only great for the community and the country, but is a great career and business. When one does what they love and they do it with all their being, people see it, like it and come on board as long-term customers and friends. The fact that one can provide fantastic services that help people while sustaining a healthy business, lets Clark enjoy a career that is a win/win situation for all.

Daryn will tell you reaching 25 years of marriage and raising three children is the greatest education he's received to date, and this family man has never let the companies he owns run his life. "I work to live...I don't live to work" is a motto that keeps him grounded in family.

Find out more:
www.darynclark.com
www.southerningenuityinc.com
www.whatsyourfight.com

CHAPTER 5

YOU CANNOT HIT A HIDDEN TARGET! BECOME A MASTER OF TARGETED THINKING

BY MIKE DENISON

I have been coaching leaders and managers in business since 1997 and there are a number of common areas where people are ineffective - for example: leading and managing, building relationships, communication, making presentations, clarity of desired outcomes, maintaining focus or effective investment of time. Whilst I help business leaders in all these areas, the area that many have the most difficulty with, by far, is comprehensive clarity of desired outcomes.

Take a moment to vividly picture a successful archer faced with a target. Watch him as he adjusts his stance – he draws up the bow and lines up his sight and takes aim, the arrow positioned carefully, so he can focus on and see the target very clearly. He closes his eyes and pictures the arrow flying through the air to hit the target dead centre. He knows in his mind's eye why he wants to hit the centre: he is passionate about his skill and the recognition of his practice and success at the sport. He is determined, committed, focused and relaxed in preparing his mind. He can feel inside what it will be like to hit dead centre. He invests his time carefully by pulling back on the bowstring with two fingers, all his efforts and thoughts are on the perfect action, the value of carefully tensioning the bow string, and taking his time to adjust his aim. He has the arrow now ready for flight, focusing in on the target, feeling the light breeze, making a final adjustment. He takes a deep breath, exhaling to relax and remove all tension, and then.........calmly releases the bowstring to let the arrow fly through the air and hit the target dead centre.

There is a lot to be learned from this metaphor - targeted thinking, i.e., investing time and leveraging only those high value actions and thoughts that are aimed on hitting the target, plus an unwavering focus on what is wanted and why. These principles apply in any field, any area of life and any business or organisation where accelerating achievement and continuous progression is all important.

Let me make a significant and obvious point here. If your target is surrounded by fog, if you cannot see your target clearly, if you fail to work on your most valuable activities, if you allow distractions to interfere with your aim you will never hit your target, no matter how much you say you want it. Does this sound like someone you know?

Most business people see targets as goals, figures or results. My Targeted Thinking system is about being aware of everything necessary to bring your attention for hitting the centre into clarity or focus. Your target includes what you want, your outcome, by when, why you want it, your passion, drive and motivation, how you will feel once you have succeeded, as well as what you will give up to hit it. Without this level of clarity, the distractions life presents will quickly pull your focus away.

Targeted thinking encompasses five focal points: they are the 5 "P"s:—

> Passion
> Purpose
> Product
> Process and
> Performance

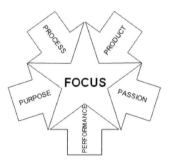

Your *Passion* is why you do what you do and your heightened desire to hit that target, your *Purpose* is your reason for wanting it. It is both your passion and purpose that will motivate you to maintain focus, not the result. Your *Product* is your outcome, what you will achieve and the results from hitting your target. Your *Process* is your routine activity and thinking that will ensure you hit the target, which includes a vividly clear picture in your mind of what it looks and feels like when you have achieved it. Finally, your *Performance* is the interference you will choose to remove, in order to commit your focus and realise your potential. Without this level of clarity, you will be like a rudderless boat tossed about at the mercy of whichever way the wind blows.

Many entrepreneurs I've worked with lack clarity of purpose, firm direction, and are unclear what success and the outcome really means for them. They overlook the immense value of single-minded focus, engaging their passion in their work, and the need for the personal organization necessary to be truly successful in hitting their targets in life or business. Having lots of ideas and great solutions for the world's problems is only part of the formula for success.

The most successful people I have worked with are those who love what they do, know clearly why they are doing it. There is an inner passion for what they do, it is part of their life and they have learned how to focus their attention and leverage their time onto a few high-value activities for the greatest impact. They are Target Focused.

In my time with Toyota, whilst setting up a new facility, I came to realise the power of targeted thinking. Being in charge of an area, I was mentored to continually ask "What is your target condition?"… "What are you aiming for?"… and… "What can you do now to take a step forward?" This approach encouraged members to constantly focus on adding value and how to invest their time on activities to achieve the end result, and what the outcomes of their next steps were. This solution-focused attitude, keeping the end in mind, is what builds great companies.

Studies show that more than 93% of people are unaware of their potential, of their ability to create more choice and be more influential in their lives, especially in how they think, how they feel, and what they focus on… that success, achievement and happiness is completely in their own hands. Much of this is because they have not understood the impact of targeted thinking.

Spend some time getting really clear on your targets. Take a large sheet of paper or a flipchart if you have one and draw the following diagram:

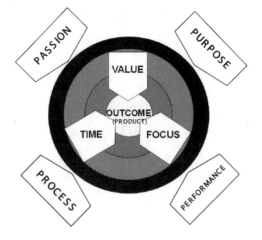

Now surround your target with information about your passion, your purpose, what you will stop doing, how you will focus and how much time you will spend on those high value activities that will steady your aim to hit the target. This level of clarity is important, because this is who you are and must be aligned with what you want.

Targeted thinking is not new; in fact we all do it every day, but unconsciously. Many of the choices and decisions we make are to satisfy short-term pleasures or avoid perceived pain, because the longer term benefits are unconscious. The power of targeted thinking is in making your target a more conscious action.

Do you know that people are naturally goal-seeking beings? Humans are designed to have targets and goals to aim for, everything we do is based on having some direction or other, to achieve something or get somewhere.

Everything you do starts with a thought or feeling and is stimulated by an outcome, you may not be aware of it, but your subconscious is. It's the targets that we unconsciously set that get us up in the morning, eat when we want to, shop, watch TV or visit the movies to gain some pleasure or comfort in our lives. Our biology is designed to transform thought-energy into reality and create things or make things happen.

Take a car journey you made recently: you had a clear destination in your mind and you had a reason or purpose for going there. There was a clear context for going, you planned a route, filled your car with fuel and set off on the journey; you may have been held up by traffic or diverted by road works, but you found an alternative route because you had a clear destination and purpose or passion to keep moving in the direction you set yourself. You also kept your eyes on the road ahead; otherwise you would have veered off into a field or hedge. Life Targets or Business Targets are just the same: a clear destination in context of a purpose or passion, planned, aimed at, continually focused on and driven towards.

Few people really know how to get their targets meaningful and clear to use as their context for decision-making in life or business. My clients find Targeted Thinking helpful to construct the clarity they need to aim and maintain focus; many have pictures of targets in their diaries or offices to maintain their aim.

Meaningful target setting is a skill necessary to create context for decision making in life or business and you should have Yearly, Quarterly, Monthly, Weekly and Daily Targets to measure against and keep you on track. Whilst you may not go through the 5 "P"s exercise for your daily and weekly targets, in essence they are the activities that support your bigger targets which have more comprehensive clarity.

But what if I don't hit my target that day? Sometimes stuff happens outside of my control. Not achieving a target in the time you set isn't a problem as long as you always ask "Why?" to understand the root cause of your miss, just like the archer who is continually improving his aim. Put in an immediate personal improvement to ensure you are learning and developing your aim for the future, identify those distractions and commit yourself to improve tomorrow with a focused mind and attitude. Be honest with yourself - "What was it that interfered with your aim?" Making small but continuous improvements every day to keep on target, to improve your aim, is a technique I learned working with Toyota. Known as Kaizen, it's the relentless focus on continuous personal improvement.

There are 168 hours in a week, but distractions and interruptions will consume that time if you don't organize it to maintain your focus on your target. Time is an essential resource for achieving your targets, unfortunately taken for granted. "I haven't got enough time" is the dilemma facing many people in business today. Time is never really the problem; the issue is always what you invest your time on. Time is far more valuable than money, you can never create more time, once consumed its gone forever, never to be available again. Invest it in your highest value activities and you will be focused on the things that keep you on target.

The reality is, to be successful at anything, you have to give up stuff to maintain your focus. When you are focusing on one thing you cannot then focus on something else – it's obvious! You have to prioritize some of the things you don't like doing over those you love to do, and you have to stop doing some things you like doing, avoiding distractions or interferences that move you in the wrong direction, or slow you down. It's this thought of giving things up and letting things go that many people find difficult. Whether you are an individual who wants a happier life or a CEO, letting some things drop to pay attention to other things is a difficult choice, but with a clear passion and purpose for your outcome, using a process to increase your focus, you will be pulled excitedly towards your target.

When you were small, did you do that experiment to focus the sun's rays through a magnifying glass onto a piece of paper – causing it to combust, channelling all that energy to create transformation? That is some power. If focus really is energy power, then why don't we focus more to achieve more? There are more choices, options and experiences available to people today than ever before. This has promoted interest, excitement and desire to try as many experiences as possible while we can, which in turn has led to greater levels of distraction, frustration, dissatisfaction and annoyance that we can't do it all or have it all right now! For those people who are easily influenced emotionally towards new fads, "toys" or experiences and the lure of instant pleasures and successes, distraction and a lack of focus means a lack of progress towards achieving their deeper desires or dreams.

Focus is really easy, once you understand what it is that encourages you to get distracted. It requires attention, concentration of thought energy, and a high interest in the subject to be focused on. Focus is a mind skill, one of our mental muscles that include willpower, logical reasoning, imagination and perception, all of which need routine practice and repetition to master the skill of focus. Like our physical muscles, mental muscles need exercising regularly to get the most out of them, then we can consistently apply them to help us get what we want. Maintaining daily, even hourly focus on your target, to the exclusion of other less important, less valuable or unrelated activities, must become a habit if you are to hit your target.

Anyone can learn and develop focus through consistent repetition and routine. Watch a cat as it stalks its prey, eyes focused, ears turned forward. It may flick its tail or ears, aware of possible distractions, but not breaking that concentration. Step-by-careful-step a cat advances towards its prey not allowing anything to interfere with its intent. We have this innate ability and we can develop this skill. We may have forgotten it or possibly believe that we don't have it, but changing beliefs is a technique for another time.

Imagine being in a crisis situation: you have to escape from a tall burning building by a rope. You have to concentrate all your thoughts and energy on holding onto the rope, distracting yourself from feeling afraid and just concentrating on moving slowly across the rope, hand over hand, not swinging on the rope, keeping steady, not looking down, or around. You are just looking forward to your target escape route, thinking and believing you will get there; you force yourself to concentrate, to focus on what is most important at the time.

Why wait for a crisis? Start developing that skill now of creating attention and focus on your clearly defined targets. Practice aiming and focus every day, until you can focus at will.

Earl Nightingale is quoted as saying "Success is the progressive realisation of a worthy ideal." If your worthy ideal is unclear, if you cannot see your target, if you don't focus your time and energy consistently on the most important things that move you progressively towards your target, then both progress and realisation will continue to be out of reach.

Success and winning is not easy, it takes clear vision, personal effort, a persistence and resilience to keep going and stay focused when times are tough. It also takes a way of thinking that keeps you on target.

TARGETED THINKING

PRODUCT

HIGH VALUE
ACTIVITIES

PROCESS

TIME MASTERY

LASER FOCUS

PERFORMANCE

PASSION   PURPOSE

For more on Targeted Thinking, Developing Focus and Creating Personal Success, or to know the key questions and techniques to get you really focused on your targets, contact Mike Denison at Lean Mentor International and Cleareality Coaching Ltd

www.lean-mentor.co.uk

www.cleareality.co.uk

ABOUT MIKE

Mike Denison is a human performance expert, working with individuals and organisations to help them achieve greater levels of performance, productivity and personal effectiveness. Mike founded his companies of Cleareality Ltd and Lean Mentor International Consulting in 2005 with the aim of changing the thinking that limits people and holds organisations back from greatness. Mike specialises in success coaching, executive support and business performance improvement.

Mike's High Performing Leaders Programs have helped clients better understand and clarify targets, increase personal value, amplify focus, leverage time and effectively influence their resources to improve their bottom line results. Through the identification and elimination of low value, wasteful and unproductive activities and by challenging others for quantifiable increases in quality, service and people performance, his clients develop greater clarity and transparency of their business, leading to a healthy performance-focused culture that continually reduces costs, and increases customer value.

Mike works with clients to structure their targets and goals – to learn how to play a bigger game and expand their awareness to change how they think and act. He encourages and leads those he works with to routinely think outside the box, expanding their possibilities. His emphasis is on highlighting; that you cannot achieve significant breakthroughs in life or business until you challenge your own current way of thinking and acting.

By cutting through the fog of his client's thinking and their business complexity, Mike helps them simplify what they need to do to make breakthroughs, and realize results they never thought possible. By eliminating interfering thoughts, habits and routines, Mike offers an energizing insight on personal and organisational growth possibilities, resulting in measurable performance improvement.

Mike's clients are executives, professionals, business owners and entrepreneurs, who all want to know how to develop the successful habits practiced by high-performing individuals.

Mike is fortunate to have worked and consulted with some of the world's largest and most successful organisations such as Toyota, British American Tobacco, Ford, Jaguar Cars, Bombardier, Mercedes Benz, Tyco, and Westinghouse Electric Company among others, and has clients in many different sectors including healthcare, automotive, transportation, aerospace and nuclear industries.

The *ethos* in which Mike works, and what is most important to him, is value, openness, honesty and trust, enthusiasm, fun, challenge and creativity. He loves nothing better than solving problems – and most of all working with people, to help them understand how they can add more value to achieve results beyond their expectations.

Mike's insight and expertise is regularly sought out by organisations embarking on changes and transformational programs. He regularly contributes articles for business leadership, sector journals and lifestyle magazines. Mike is an engaging and inspirational speaker, delivering presentations for universities, institutions of higher education, business clubs, social enterprises, as well as charities.

The best way to learn about anything is to imagine and think about it, study it, and then experience it.

To learn more about Mike Denison, and how you can get access to his programs, receive free special reports and other valuable personal breakthrough techniques from one of the UK's leading human performance experts, visit www.cleareality.co.uk or www.lean-mentor.co.uk

Mike's motto: *Develop the habits of a high performing individual, increase your influence, augment your performance, expand your impact and boost your results.*

CHAPTER 6

BRAIN TRAIN

BY SUMMER KNIGHT, MD, MBA

I have two stories to share with you.

The first story is about a baby. This was a little girl born to teenaged parents in an environment of chaos – poverty, drugs, and hunger. This little girl's mother was jailed when she was only months old. As this child grew, life was tough. Her parents divorced. The child was raised in dangerous environments early on. She was onsite as drug deals were consummated; she was abused and even shot at. She became lost in the shuffle. She began to run away.

Stress has a way of erupting. This girl developed a debilitating disorder at a young age. The medications that were supposed to cure her only made her more ill, weak and unable to bear weight on her legs. She was hospitalized.

Over the next few years this girl began to stand up to her abuser. As the abuse eased, she began to feel better physically. As a teenager, she moved from her house and in with a friend. She was growing up and had to get more serious about her future. She worked several jobs barely making rent. Just as her situation seemed to be turning around, tragedy struck – her mother died.

That girl was heartbroken. She was broke; she was alone and hopeless. She was in danger of losing her job due to her grief. How would she make it? What did her future look like? She was approached to supplement her rent by selling drugs. She was in trouble.

That's really glum... but I promised you another story.

This is the story of a beautiful child! She was lovable and innately curious about her surroundings. As she grew, she was a sponge for information. She wanted to explore; she wanted to learn.

This girl grew and explored her surroundings. She would lie deep in the long grass of a farmer's field watching the wisps of clouds scuttle along the blue sky – talking to God, the animals and birds, the trees and grasses. She tried lots of things – she enjoyed sports even though she was average; she wrote little poems and songs and strummed guitars imagining herself as a country singer; she tinkered on mechanical items figuring out how they worked. She had a particularly curious mind. She noticed that she got attention for good grades from her teachers. She liked that attention so she worked harder. This girl showed promise.

One day, this girl saw a burning building. She watched as firefighters went in to save someone trapped in the building. She saw the building collapse. Later, she learned the firefighters had cleared the building and survived. They were heroes! She was filled with pride and decided she would help people too.

She worked hard and became a firefighter / paramedic. She loved the thrill. She fought fires – sometimes in the dead of winter until her hands were frostbitten. She worked in the ambulance saving lives on the side of the highway. She even learned underwater search-and-rescue techniques.

But this gal was curious and she knew there was more to learn and many more people to help. She was determined to become a doctor. She went to medical school and loved taking care of patients. She opened a medical practice and an urgent care center. She later followed her passion and became the Director of Emergency Rooms.

She was passionate and she wanted to help more people. So, she became a Chief Doctor for an entire state. She helped millions of people. She was satisfied... but she was still curious.

She saw an opportunity to help even more people by ensuring health care dollars were spent appropriately rather than going to fraudulent causes. So, she gave up her prestigious career to start ALL OVER AGAIN. She launched her own company. The company was successful and later sold. Now many states are using her **original ideas** to save hundreds of millions of dollars and to make sure the people who need care, receive it.

For most of her career she has been a leader, an executive, someone at the helm of critical decision-making. And yet, she is still like a kid and she loves everyone who comes in her path.

So, what about the first girl? What do these two little girls have in common?

… They are both the same person. They are both me.

And why did I share this story? To say to each and every person, that – however you define it – we all have the power to grow and be GREAT!

But how can you do this? It's simple and anyone can do it. Despite a difficult start in life, I remapped my brain thought patterns to structure my story and experiences as springboards for excelling in life. Later, upon becoming a physician, I learned that I was actively reTraining my brain on the cellular level. I was changing the firing of the cells inside my head, and I was restructuring my thoughts and thus the direction of my life. And if a small child can learn to do it, so can you. It is simple to learn to reTrain your brain to WIN (and live GREAT).

"So, Doctor, what do you mean I can reTrain my brain?" you may ask. **It means retiring the neural pathways that do not serve you well and developing new neural pathways that do. To do this efficiently, you map what you want in your conscious mind, then systematically imprint that to your sub-conscious mind. This is done by lowering the threshold of your nerves to "fire" in thought patterns that better meet your needs. That means you are working within your brain and actively using a greater percentage of your brain to get you what you want – to WIN in life.**

Let me explain how the brain works…

Think of the brain as a network of tracks. The original tracks were laid before you were born during fetal development. As your brain developed as a child, you began having experiences. These experiences caused changes within your brain – equivalent to the building of "Tracks" where your "Trains of Thought" would routinely ride. As the Trains (of Thought) ran their routine routes, the "Conductors" became experienced, and pretty soon the route became automatic without much thought required. More scientifically: you receive a stimulus, and your thoughts move through your brain along neuronal pathways automatically offering the same response.

Our brains are made of cells called neurons. Until recently, scientists considered our brain cells to be unique from other cells within our body in many different ways. For instance, unlike most other cells in our bodies, scientists thought once neurons were formed, that was it… they couldn't grow, they couldn't change, and they couldn't multiply or regenerate like other cells. It was thought that the brain cells we were born with were the only ones we would have for the rest of our lives.

Science has a way of correcting itself. Over the past several years, through studies and new high-imaging techniques, we learned that neurons were not only changing throughout our infancy, but they are in a constant dynamic state. Through experiments and imaging, we learned that not only are the brain neurons themselves capable of growing, dividing, dying, and replenishing like other cells within our bodies, but the very essence of these cells, including their interaction patterns, can change as well. This is called neuroplasticity – which means the brain is able to change.

There are two different phases of our brains – the conscious and the *under-conscious* (I made this term up because all the other terms seem confusing!) parts of our brains. Conscious is the thinking that you direct. *Under-conscious* is all the remainder - breathing and digesting, emotions, immediate reactions; it's when you get somewhere and realize that you don't remember driving there because you were thinking of something else.

The greatest percentage of our brain function occurs at the level of our *under-conscious*, which moves at a faster rate than our conscious. For example, before you have had time to think about how you should react in an emergency, you have already done so because your *under-conscious* moves more swiftly than your conscious thought. When we interact with our environment, many of our interactions are on autopilot performed by our *under-conscious* "Conductor" rather than the conscious "Conductor".

When you want to change something about yourself, such as focusing on a new goal, you begin "stimulating" parts of the brain that you have not traditionally used. You do this by having your conscious brain "alert" the *under-conscious* to stimulate those areas of the brain. But habits of thought are difficult to change because your "Trains of Thought" are running on the old tracks. Therefore, you have to consciously work on the new "Trains of Thought" repetitively over time (I usually suggest 60 days). The new "Trains of Thought" must be repeated to develop new tracks and the old Train tracks become disused because they are less stimulated. It is like bramble and weeds growing up in old, unused tracks.

Thus managing the most misunderstood part of your body, the brain, is within your ability, and in fact you are already doing it. Most of the time, our thoughts occur automatically; thought habits – they are Trains running automatically on their tracks. But as you can see, by melding conscious thoughts into your *under-conscious*, you can have influence over your thoughts and actions. That is how you "ReTrain your Brain!"

RESTRUCTURING THE FOUNDATION OF THE TRACKS

This step is designed to "re-organize" the material we initially took in and allocated as children, based on our immature view of the world, and to re-organize it using our adult knowledge and experiences. This is useful, indeed necessary, because the foundation of our Thought Trains were developed at a young age, and material was being organized as parts of our brain were still dominated with a child's perception of reality rather than our adult perceptions.

Now as an adult, most people's brains continue to run on the same tracks when they encounter similar stimuli. In other words, when our needs transition from immature to mature situations, we don't hire new Conductors for our Trains. We keep the same ones, thus have the same responses to stimuli that we had as children – as the tracks of our thoughts have not been re-engineered or updated with new adult content. Therefore, the brain automatically runs the child-like system, because that is what it is used to doing. While we go through developmental stages as humans, these are incremental, rather than a complete overhaul of our thoughts. Without understanding how to "re-engineer" and lay down new Tracks of Thought that benefit us, oftentimes our immediate thoughts and reactions to situations can inhibit us from living up to our true potential.

There is a tremendous amount of brain activity that is going on behind the "conscious scenes" of which you are not fully aware. In addition, our genetic wiring is so strong, that even when a little piece of our brain is screaming, "But I really want to do something different!" the habitual process of the brain – the genetically programmed or human habit, the "Thought Train" in the brain that are most used – override your drive to do things differently. That's how we are programmed!

But there's hope! We actually have the tools already in our heads to reTrain the brain. We do this by building new paths or making new connections, laying down new track, moving from dilapidated, archaic, dangerous routes, to brighter, more direct, and efficient routes that get you where you want to go.

The brain doesn't understand the difference between what you want and what you don't want. What the brain understands is what you are focused on. The Reticular Activating System (RAS) is the part of the brain that brings things into our awareness. It is part of our *under-conscious* system. It makes us notice things in our environment. It also filters what we bring into our awareness – including what we ignore. Its part of the system that wakes us up in the morning, notices that the paper is at the end of the driveway, and notices a child needing comfort. The RAS is pre-programmed and from birth it knows genetically how to perform. It works without us telling it what to do.

Because it is part of the *under-conscious*, people do not have control over the RAS or understand how to use it. But we have learned that in fact our conscious mind can leverage our RAS to get what we want in life. **If you learn to use it, you can change your life – you can WIN.**

Oftentimes, people are baffled that the very thing they do not want is what they get. Why is this? It is because what we focus on is what we bring into our lives. Let's take the example of a woman who is overweight and wants to shed the pounds. On New Years day, she decides this is the year. Everyday she focuses on her weight, and after a couple of weeks, she is filled with despair, not only because she has not dropped the pounds, but she has actually gained weight. It is a familiar story. So, what's the problem? The problem is that the woman was focusing on her weight – she was focusing on what she doesn't want. However, the brain doesn't understand the difference between what you want and what you don't want. What the brain understands is what you are focused on. Therefore, if you are focused on weight, weight is what you will get from your RAS.

Now, this same woman learns to use some of the tools to reTrain her brain. Instead of thinking about losing weight, she becomes clear about her image of a healthy body. She focuses on how she looks when she is healthy, how she exercises, where she will go when healthy, the clothes she wears, and the types of healthy foods. Not only does she imagine these things, she begins to do and be these things. She doesn't think about what she cannot eat, she thinks about the healthy foods and portions she will eat and is eating in her healthy image of herself. Before she realizes it, people are commenting that she looks better, healthier - maybe even before she sheds a pound. She has switched the image from focusing on her weight to focusing on her health. Therefore, she has alerted her RAS to focus on those items. Rather than reaffirming the weight – she is reaffirming healthiness.

Be very clear on what you focus on because your conscious mind informs your *under-conscious* what to look for. When your conscious informs your *under-conscious* that it is focused on "healthy" rather than "weight", your RAS, part of your *under-conscious*, notices "healthy". By focusing on "healthy", you will create a new habit of thought, which is essentially laying down new tracks in your brain. The more you focus on "healthy", the more that "Healthy Track" will be used by your new "Thought Train" and your brain will automatically choose healthy situations for you. During those same periods, old tracks (habits) of "weight" will go into disuse and become dilapidated. After a period of time, the old "weight tracks" will no longer be accessible, and the trains of thought will only run on the "Healthy Tracks"… and healthy is what you will get.

By purposely reTraining our brains, we are laying a foundation where "Thought Trains" run in our brain that help us, rather than hinder. By retracking your own brain, you have the ability to stop such habits of "Thought Trains" that are not helpful in your life. Instead, build new tracks with "Thought Trains" that help you WIN. ReTrain your brain.

ABOUT SUMMER

Dr. Summer Knight is a physician and health care expert with significant expertise in the clinical, governmental, and private sector health care arenas. As the former Chief Medical Officer of the State of Florida, Dr. Knight worked with the Agency for Health Care Administration influencing Medicaid policy, health care facility regulations and stakeholder interactions. From this experience, Dr. Knight started her first company IntegriCor, LLC, changing the Medicaid marketplace rewarding providers for improving health care quality and increasing stakeholder communication while eliminating fraud. This technology became the leading platform for long-term care integrity in several states and managed care markets.

Dr. Knight has participated in creating scalable entrepreneurial businesses and supported high-growth organizations by joining organizations as CEO or Chief Medical Officer. She has extensive experience and has contributed value to companies in Strategic Planning and Transformation, Problem Solving, CEO and leadership coaching, Capital Acquisition, Business Development, Sales and Marketing, Health Care innovations, and mentoring and consulting CEO's and decision-making executives to focus on rapid growth of scalable businesses.

Dr. Summer Knight is an Entrepreneur-in-Residence and alumna of Springboard Enterprises, a non-profit organization representing women who have led successful high-growth businesses and who have collectively raised $5 billion in equity financing. She is passionate about innovators as well as helping people to find their "inner entrepreneur", hence she founded DSK Companies to support ventures relating to innovations in health, wellness, and sustainability with a focus on helping to develop success through networking, tools, and skillsets to accelerate the organization's rate of success.

In addition to her corporate experience, Dr. Knight founded the State Government Physician Leadership Council and was appointed by the Governor to the Florida Cancer Control and Research Advisory Committee. She also has served on the boards of the Florida Dialogue on Cancer Access Committee, the Pharmacy and Therapeutics Committee at Capital Health Plan, and both the Quality Practice Management Committee and the Governmental Affairs Committee with the Florida Academy of Family Physicians. An author and frequent public speaker, Dr. Knight has been an invited presenter at Medicaid Management Information System and Home and Community Based Services national meetings, the Council of State Government for Disease Management in Washington, DC, the Florida Medical Association, the Florida College of Emergency Physicians, and the Florida Medical Directors Association.

Dr. Knight is also very active in philanthropic and community affairs serving as a college Trustee, a member of a community Leadership organization, founding member

71

of the Oasis Center for Women and Girls, board member of Big Brothers Big Sisters, and the Advisory Committee of Tallahassee Community College's Fostering Achievement Fellowship Program. She has served as Secretary and Sub-Committee Chair for the Gilchrist Elementary School Advisory Committee and received the Outstanding School Volunteer Award from the school's PTA during the 2008 school year. She has also volunteered with organizations such as Cornerstone Learning Center, Refuge House and the Governor's Mentoring Initiative.

Dr. Knight received her M.D. from the University of Illinois at Chicago and her MBA from Warrington College of Business at the University of Florida. She has gained valuable medical experience as a family physician, urgent care and Emergency Room physician, and as a firefighter/ paramedic. Dr. Knight loves to have fun, inspire people to succeed, and facilitate transformation in individuals and organizations.

Summer Knight, MD, MBA

PO Box 671
Narberth, PA 19072
850-545-7480
877-544-3775
sknight@dskcos.com

CHAPTER 7

TRADITIONAL RULES FOR A SUCCESSFUL LIFE

BY PEGGY LUSK

I f you are like me, you were raised with some of these traditional rules for living a successful and abundant life:

- Graduate from college in a field where you have talent and interests
- Find a great company where you can advance and be rewarded for your accomplishments
- Focus on today; Work hard and do the best job that you can, and the company will provide the stability you need to enable you to pay your bills, send your kids to college, and enjoy leisure activities along the way
- Enjoy retirement without money fears by saving everything you can (preferably in a pre-tax investment account) and staying with one company to maximize your retirement income
- Live a balanced life with ample time to spend with family and friends

How have these rules been working for you so far? …And what does the future look like? It's becoming increasingly obvious that they are not working effectively for a lot of people. Many of us have had to run faster and faster just to stay in place. Increasing expenses and high debt levels are weighing us down. Taxes and inflation are taking an increasing large bite out of our ability to save for our future, and for the future of our families. The solution for many of us has been to try to put more activities into our already busy lives, without determining whether these commitments and responsibilities are getting us any closer to living an Abundant life.

Changes in the economy in recent years have now made it more obvious than ever that *true job security* consists of adequately managing your career, which is your most important asset. For some, that has meant creating their own business. If you have chosen to become an entrepreneur, are feeling 'a sense of overwhelm', or are concerned about your financial future, I'm sure that at least part of the reason for that choice is that these "traditional rules" weren't working for you. They weren't working effectively for me either.

I've been involved in the Accounting and Information Technology sectors all of my adult life; where the method of keeping pace with change, and with pay scales that were rising faster than company averages, has been to change the company I work for. This trend seems to be much more common in the workforce in recent years, and for some it has not been by choice. I also suspect that I've always had an entrepreneurial side to my nature, one that just hasn't been satisfied with the constraints of a corporate job. I woke up one day to the realization that I was trading my life for a six-figure salary that continued to demand more of my time each year – which actually equated to a reduction in my hourly pay.

In my case, the small amount of time I was spending at home, between out-of-town work assignments, was devoted to recovering from my last trip out-of-town and preparing for my next one. In terms of spending time on MY most valuable activities, I was not in control. I was also frustrated that after working my way through college and graduate school, I was not using my education and experience effectively; and I certainly didn't feel that I was adequately compensated for it.

THE IMPORTANCE OF TIME AND MONEY

Whether you have your own business or whether you are working for someone else, it's important to your satisfaction with life that your work matches your values. The work you do determines the amount of time and money available for you to spend. If you have chosen to own your own business, you are likely aware of how important money also is to the survival of your business. Not only do you need enough cash flow to support your style of living and allow you to continue to be an entrepreneur, but also you need enough to supply the business with necessary equipment and supplies. What may not be as obvious is the need to have adequate time, either your own time or time purchased from others – to allow your career and your business to grow and prosper. Since most entrepreneurs choose to start their own businesses to increase control of either their time or their money, it's important that their business reflects their values.

SPENDING YOUR TIME

I'm sure you know that your time is precious. It is your most limited asset. None of us gets more than 60 minutes in an hour, or more than 24 hours in a day. There are really only two things you can do with your time: You can spend it, or you can invest it. Time that you waste is gone forever. However, time invested in activities, such as training, personal development or building your own business, creates a lifetime of payoff in increased knowledge and abundance.

Streamlining the way you work can also give you an extraordinary amount of your time back. The reduction in stress level, and the increased control over time - as a result of improved work methods - can be astonishing. For entrepreneurs, it's also important to know when an activity should be outsourced, rather than doing it yourself.

Most of us knew how important it was to grow personally and professionally before we began to work full-time. Some of us even worked our way through college to prepare for a brighter future. But somewhere, that zest for learning and growth gave way to waiting till retirement to live our lives. Is retirement the goal you are really striving for? Or is it living an Abundant Life right now?

SPENDING YOUR MONEY

There is an old saying that if your outflow exceeds your income, then your upkeep will become your downfall. This is true of both your business and your personal life; and each needs to be tracked and monitored separately. There are two ways to change a negative cash flow: increase your income, or decrease your expenses. Determining which area should receive the most focus requires understanding of your unique values, as well as your overall plan for your career/business and your financial goals. A life full of Abundance doesn't have to mean expensive jewelry and pampered travel. It can just as easily mean living a life full of purpose, pleasure, satisfaction and fun.

Many of us spend time and money on things that really aren't important to us. Taking the first step to determining what Abundance really means to you is to look at what excites you and makes you feel good inside. Living in Abundance also means that you eat well and get plenty of regular rest and exercise to maintain your health. Your career and its earning potential are dependent on you remaining healthy and able to work, as does your enjoyment of life. Allowing spending for these things is much more important than spending for items that really don't make you any happier. A comprehensive plan for your money should include changes to both the income and expense sides of the equation, and should be readjusted on a periodic basis.

BUILDING A FINANCIAL FOUNDATION

Do you know how to build a sound Financial Foundation? Before you can safely invest a portion of your income, even if it's for a business of your own, you need to have ample savings and insurance coverage that won't be affected by a job change. You also need to have a full understanding of all the options available to you as an investor, and what your personal comfort level is for different types of investments. Without this information and the creation of a flexible plan for your earnings and spending, you may find yourself under constant stress as you handle changes in the world around you. Many people have become much more interested in taking control of their financial life after changes in the past couple of years made them realize they were taking too much risk with their assets.

THEORIES ABOUT TIME AND MONEY

Did you know that there is a strong correlation between time and money? Spending time ineffectively can cause health problems, relationship problems, or increased costs for delays in completion of necessary or important activities. Spending money ineffectively can result in increased time to complete an activity or increased work requirements – sometimes to the point where there is a delay in the date when you are able to live without working (also known as Financial Freedom Day). If you don't spend the effort to determine whether your time and money are being spent on things that are important to your system of values, you will find that you are living a life that matches the values of the people around you, or the values your parents have taught you. These values may not match the values that are important to you, which can create increased stress as you try to find balance in your life. Here are three competing theories about the relationship between time and money that may help you figure out what your values are:

CHOOSING TIME OVER MONEY

The amount of money you make doesn't mean much to you. You'd much rather have your time to yourself (or at least under your control) than to let someone else control it. Some indicators of this value are:

- Working at a lower-paying job than you are qualified for in order to get more days off or to be able to control your personal time
- Working as a free-lancer, or owning your own business, in order to take time off whenever you need it
- Working from home to spend time with your children in the morning and after school

CHOOSING MONEY OVER TIME

The amount of money you make is important to you: Whether it's for financial security or so you can buy something you really want. You're willing to give up total control of your time (and possibly other people's time) to get it. Some indicators of this value are:

- The stress of taking on major responsibility is worth it to you, because you make more money when you take on the added responsibility
- You'd rather take a job that pays a higher salary, but it

increases commute time to an office by an hour or more a day
- You'd rather work through weekends, or work overtime hours, in order to earn some serious additional income. Your decision to work additional hours is unaffected by plans to spend a date-night with your spouse or to attend your child's soccer game.

TIME IS MONEY

Your time is only as important as the amount of money you can make with your time. You focus on a specific task for a specific amount of time and are rewarded with a specific amount of money for your trouble. That money (or its equivalent) and nothing else, shows you the value of your time. Some indicators of this value are:

- Feeling that your personal value depends on your salary or your personal contribution to your business's performance, or how much you can make in an hour. For some people this is only true during the workday, not for personal time. For others, this is a ruling principle of life that guides all their decisions about how they spend their time.
- You tend to use a strict formula (such as the one below) for determining whether to hire outside assistance for household activities, such as cleaning, cooking, or yard work; or for assistance with your business – without consideration for whether you enjoy those activities.

$$V = \{W (100\text{-}t) / 100\}$$
where: V = Value of an Hour
W = Your Hourly Wage
t = Your Tax Rate

DETERMINING YOUR VALUES

Most of us subscribe to all of these theories to varying degrees and at different times in our lives. Sometimes money is more important (as long as there is ample time for vacation), sometimes family time is more important (as long as there is sufficient money to cover living expenses). What matters most is determining which would normally take priority. Here are some questions that may increase your understanding of yourself:

- If you had the option to make extra money by working over the weekend or late at night, would you do it? What if your child had an important event during that time, or you had purchased tickets for an upcoming date or evening with your spouse? Would that change your decision?
- Do you have a tendency not to take time off for vacation, or when you are ill? How many days of vacation have you taken in the past several years? Do you take a vacation every year? Have you used any time off for illness? Have you ever gone to work instead of taking time off because your absence would reduce the amount of money you make?
- How do you feel about your compensation? Do you feel as though you are not paid enough, or are you earning plenty to meet your needs? Do you feel as though you trade your time for money? If so, is it a fair trade? If not, would you prefer more money, or more free time?

CONCLUSION

The traditional rules for living a successful and abundant life are clearly not working for many of us. We're overextended and overstressed. Many of us aren't any closer to achieving our goals because we've been squandering our time and our money. We have spent the first portion of our lives learning and growing and building our Life of Abundance. But then, something happens …and we stop investing in ourselves. It is important that we become empowered to spend our time and money in ways that match our core values. Becoming empowered requires a full understanding of the options and trade-offs, as well as the clarity that our decisions are right for achieving our goals. Here's to changing the way we spend our time and money, …to create a Life of Abundance by Design!

ABOUT PEGGY

Peggy A. Lusk, CPA, PMP is a Business Consultant, Financial Coach and Instructor who broke away from Corporate America to create her Life of Abundance. Peggy's 'aha moment' that impelled her to make this break came in 2007. Physically and mentally exhausted from weeks of relentless business travel that left little time for relaxation, joy, or connection with others, she left a high-paying corporate position to create a better life for herself and her family.

In 2010, Peggy bundled up over a decade of corporate and freelance business consulting experience, credentials, and happy client referrals to debut Abundance by Design. She is committed to providing others the knowledge and skills they need to design their own Life of Abundance. Helping clients fill the gaps between their current life and financial circumstances, and guiding them to get where they want to go are always top-of-mind priorities. Men, women, and couples at mid-life, are among her most appreciative and engaged clients.

What sets Peggy apart from other coaches who focus on money and life matters, is that she is truly gifted at customizing workable action plans that clients really can apply to achieve the results they seek – with ease and complete understanding. Peggy has the talent of translating and communicating complex and potentially confusing financial concepts in ways that bring about insight and understanding.

When they come to Peggy's care, many of her clients are struggling with money myths that are holding their dreams at bay. They are worried and concerned about making ends meet, saving enough money to fund college tuition for their children, and still having enough money remaining to retire and enjoy life. No matter where they stand, she expertly guides appreciative clients to make educated choices about how to wisely invest and align their time, money and values – so they can escape feelings of fear and scarcity – and feel happy and fulfilled.

Peggy also believes that money is just one part of a much bigger life equation:–
How you spend your time to live an abundant life is just as important as how much money is left later. It won't matter how wealthy you become if you sacrifice your health and personal life to build financial wealth.

As a CPA, Peggy is bound by the highest standards of ethics and client confidentiality. The ultimate result Peggy seeks for every client is that they feel empowered to make smart financial decisions that fuel a vibrant, rich life with all its blessings – for both today and tomorrow.

To engage with Peggy and begin the process of designing your abundant life, visit: www.abundance-by-design.com. You can also connect by email at: peggy@abundance-by-design.com.

CHAPTER 8

WINNING TRUTHS

BY JOHN E. LEDFORD, CFP®

I started out my life as a musician. From the age of 14, I played the trumpet professionally in any band that would have me, or better yet, would pay me. So when I got a music scholarship to attend the University of North Texas I thought I was all set. My mother, on the other hand, wasn't so sure.

Angela Ledford is a very pragmatic woman, having learned firsthand what can happen to a family with unstable finances, as when my father died during my freshman year in high school. She was at best ambivalent about my desire to pursue something as unstable as music. My parents had been good planners financially, but when my dad died at 40 years old, her world crumbled around her. She was afraid that I was going to graduate from college and be relegated to the role of starving musician playing seedy bars at two o'clock in the morning.

On one of my only trips back home to Central Florida during college, she encouraged me to attend a money management seminar, presumably thinking that if I was not going to earn a decent income, then I could at least learn to manage what I had in a better fashion. Her encouragement changed my life. I sat through the seminar and, to my amazement, realized I completely understood what they were saying.*

Without a doubt, there is a strong connection between mathematics and music. Music is the only art form in which the form and the medium are the same. Mathematics is the only science in which the methods and the subject are the same. Mathematics is the study of mathematics using mathematics. Music is only created and experienced as music. Thus, there is a natural connection between the two.

It was at that moment that I decided playing trumpet wasn't my destiny after all.

Upon discovering this new passion for communicating with people about money, I immediately got a job in a brokerage firm. After college, I was hired by Barnett Bank as a business development officer in their trust department. I excelled but soon realized something was missing. Based on the bank's polices, I was not allowed to work directly with my family and friends, which greatly frustrated me. In addition, I was constantly uprooting my wife and young son to new territories, as my job was to create new money management departments and then move on to the next assignment while the bank sent in a new team to take over. It was certainly a hardship on my young family and it didn't allow me the satisfaction of seeing my hard work grow and flourish. It was at this point that I learned *truth number one* of how to win in your industry or in life…

TRUTH #1
NO AMOUNT OF MONEY CAN MAKE YOU
LOVE YOUR JOB.

I was making great money with the bank. I was one of the best in my field. I was highly successful. But I didn't love my job. An attorney friend and mentor asked me if I was happy, I said "reasonably happy." He asked if I was fulfilled, I said "definitely not." He asked, "If you doubled your income, would it change how you feel about your job? Would you be happier?" I said "No." He replied, "You are young. You need to be in control of your own destiny." I thought about what he said and realized I would not have loved my job any more if I were making a million dollars. So I quit.

I spent the next few years really honing in on what I wanted to do, to reaffirm what my passion was. I spent valuable time with my son and wife using all the money that I had managed to save over the previous four years for our expenses. Then, both my son and my wife were hospitalized with different illnesses during a two week period in which my Cobra insurance coverage had expired and the health insurance from my new job had yet to kick in. I was left with about $30,000 in debt—the same amount I had made *per year* when I first got out of college.

Out of this personal financial disaster came *truth number two…*

TRUTH #2
WHEN YOUR LIFE IMPLODES YOU HAVE TWO CHOICES.

You can encase yourself in the rubble like an insect in amber or you can rise like the mythical Phoenix to begin anew. Sink or swim, you have only one real decision to make; either wallow in your circumstances or take control of what you can. Feeling out of control of one's own destiny is the scariest thing many people will ever face. And I knew that this was a place where I couldn't stay.

I was advised by many people to file for bankruptcy and start over because my debt due to the medical bills was so high. I chose to stick it out and pay off that debt over a three year period. I developed an action plan to be creative in doing well financially. I knew that the only way I could possibly pay this off in a short amount of time was to focus my energy. Everyone has a finite amount of time and energy to expend on earning an income. I decided that the key to my success would be to not be responsible for so many things, which brought me to *truth number three…*

TRUTH #3
REDUCE YOUR LIFE DOWN TO THE LOWEST NUMBER OF VARIABLES YOU CAN CONTROL.

For me, that meant not thinking in terms of "what do I need to earn monthly or annually?" as is the average person's goal. I needed to know "how much do I need to earn TODAY?" It became necessary for me to only concentrate and plan on a per day basis. This extreme focus allowed me to stay on top of whether or not I was moving forward toward my daily goals. I continue to use this type of focus in my business today.

This core belief and a strong work ethic enabled me to pay off my debt. This was also the impetus to the creation of my first million dollars. I went from debtor to millionaire in a very short period of time by reducing my life to the smallest number of variables that I could control. How much do I need to earn today? At one point, I had three jobs to create the income that I needed to generate each day in order to achieve my goal.

When I was completely broke and our debt was at its highest, I had an 'A-ha' moment during a great conversation with God. I said, "God, I am gonna go crazy at an early age if this doesn't change. I know what my safety net is, $45,000, this is the amount I need to feel safe and keep the creditors from harassing me. Please, help me figure out how to create those dollars. You guide me and we will partner and get there together. But God, the success level for me is $75,000. At that income I can breathe a little bit; I can have vacations, I can treat my kids or my wife to something, and I can give a little back." And finally I told God, "I have this third level of success of $125,000 that will allow me to do whatever I want to do. If you release me from the financial bondage I am in today, show me how to get to those levels, then anything beyond that $125,000 I make I will give away."

Those goals, along with God's help, allowed me to achieve and surpass my expectations. It was in that next year that I gave away about $75,000 dollars and was able to begin a foundation that encouraged other small business owners in third world countries. From that 'A-ha' moment came *truth number four…*

TRUTH #4
ENVISION WHAT YOU WANT TO ACHIEVE AND APPOINT SOMEONE TO MAKE YOU ACCOUNTABLE FOR IT.

One side of money management is to control spending. The other side is "visioning" which is what I am most passionate about. Have a vision of what you want to achieve. Have a conversation with God or your spouse or your business partner or a mentor. Be clear about what your goal is. Each person is different; define what you stand for. What creates your drive and what can propel you there?

By this time, my business was moving along at a pretty good clip until the early 2000's, when my business partner had a breakdown and our firm nearly collapsed with him. So in 2002, we parted ways and I started over again managing $9 million in assets (from $100 million) and five employees, all of us working out of my own home. We decided to re-brand ourselves to better serve our clients. Ledford Financial became one of the largest, independent investment advisory firms in Central Florida. How did we do it? We identified a new niche in which to focus our efforts that meshed well with our strengths. Our strength and passion are in production, not maintenance. This is *truth number five…*

TRUTH #5
STAY TRUE TO YOUR PASSION.

I was raised in a sports-minded household, so I liken what we do to a basketball player. A basketball player's passion, his primary focus, is to get the ball in the net – not to play defense. Some firms advise clients to maintain and play safe defense. We believe that you cannot always play defense or you never win Focus on actively seeking that which you are passionate about. Our passion is to grow people's money.

During the economic downturn of recent years, many financial planning firms have had great difficulty. They had too many clients invested that they were trying to maintain (think defense) so when clients called asking questions, they were forced to develop canned responses to their questions. They went into reactive mode, which for most of these financial firms caused their business to decline. At Ledford Financial, on the other hand, we understood that hope is not an investment strategy We've always believed that we do what we can plus a little bit more— not sitting back and waiting for the market to right itself. So we took the approach of making some great tactical decisions based on trends that we saw. *Truth number six* focuses on what we found…

TRUTH #6
IF YOU DO WHAT EVERYONE ELSE DOES YOU WILL GET WHAT EVERYONE ELSE HAS.

Most people in our industry focus on organic referrals— those referrals that come from within your current client base. While we recognized that it was true you could achieve a nominal growth of your business annually based on organic referrals, we also noticed these types of referrals tended to refer down. In other words, people suffer from financial inferiority complex. If you are successful and you invest with me, you will tend to refer to me clients who are not doing better than you financially. Instead of referring your neighbor who is financially superior to you, you may instead refer your cousin who has just been released from incarceration and has a settlement check to invest. While client referrals are sought out and appreciated they can have the adverse effect of moving a growing practice in the wrong direction by creating more clients of lesser net worth which is inevitably less profitable. And this was not what we needed for our business.

At Ledford Financial, our greatest referrals come from like-minded professionals representing entrepreneurs, business owners or entertainers. They tend to refer to us the type of higher-end client that they would want to have referred to them in return. So we changed the focus of our referral business to work with these types of professionals where the growth potential is much higher, which brings us to *truth number seven…*

TRUTH #7
HOW DO YOU SURVIVE AND THRIVE DURING A RECESSION? …YOU ADAPT.

The relationships we created with professionals that we are doing business with have helped us to survive and thrive during this time. It seems while the average firm has not folded, they have also not grown. Many investment advisors have been playing defense not offense. We have adapted our business by changing, even what we offered a few years ago, to continue the growth trend that is our primary goal and focus. In the past, our philosophy was "give us all of it or give us nothing." While we still value our clients' complete trust, we understand that for some clients, creating some action is better than creating no action. What we found and learned in this economy is that some clients only want us to manage a portion of their important and precious assets. Adapting your business while staying true to your goals and beliefs will allow you to survive and thrive.

At Ledford Financial, we practice what we preach. Our tagline "Wall Street solutions, Main Street relationships" is one I truly believe in. I recognize that in my business I am a great front man but that I also need a great team to help keep our clients feeling loved. So, *truth number eight* might be called "you need to know your strengths and guard your weaknesses." Whether you are seeking to succeed in your personal finances or in your business, I think the lessons I have shared with you can get you there. Stay true to your passion, reduce the variables in your life, envision what you need to achieve, adapt when needed, and remember that what is true for others might not be the truth for you.

ABOUT JOHN

John E. Ledford's career in finance began at the age of 19 with a major Wall Street brokerage firm. From there, he quickly advanced to a trust officer with one of the nation's largest trust and investment banks. In 1996, John joined Financial Advisory Service based in Winter Park, Florida. In 1998, he became president and co-principal of Conte-Ledford Financial Group (formally known as Financial Advisory Service). He held this position until July 2002, when he formed Ledford Financial.

In 2008, Ledford Financial was honored by *Orlando Magazine* as one of the "Top Financial Planning Firms" in Central Florida. Also in 2008, *Boomer Market Advisor* named John "Socially Responsible Advisor of the Year" for his work providing funds to micro banks throughout Latin American and the Caribbean, which spurred the creation of Change MicroFund. In 2009, John was a top 10 finalist for *Registered Rep's* "Outstanding Advisor of the Year" for which he was again recognized for his work in micro lending in emerging-market countries.

John's registrations include FINRA Series 6, 7, 24, 63, and 65. He is a Registered Securities Principal and Investment Adviser Representative with Commonwealth Financial Network, and a CERTIFIED FINANCIAL PLANNER™ practitioner. John is a member of the Financial Planning Association (FPA) and a former member of the Gulf Coast and Space Coast Estate Planning Councils.

John attended North Texas State University and is also a graduate of the University of Central Florida and the College for Financial Planning.

He currently lives in Winter Springs, FL with his wife, Valerie, and four children. Away from the office, he enjoys diving, music, coaching, flying, and just about every sport. Additionally, he spends much of his free time supporting a variety of local charities, including Change MicroFund, of which he is a founder.

John's firm, Ledford Financial Group, is located at 605 East Robinson Street, Suite 640, Orlando, FL 32801. He can be reached at john@ledfordfinancial.com or (407) 999-8998.

CHAPTER 9

GREED AND THE GOLDEN EGGS

BY JIM STACEY

Most of us remember the children's story from Aesop's Fables about the couple whose seemingly ordinary goose suddenly began to lay gold eggs. After harvesting an egg of gold every day for a while, they became greedy and unwilling to wait for what seemed to be an indefinite amount of gold to be had over time. So they killed the goose to get all the gold in one day, but found none inside. The foolish pair, thus hoping to become rich all at once, deprived themselves of the gain of which they were assured day by day.

In many ways, this story is the modern-day picture of corporations and businesses of all sizes. Greed has pushed customer service aside. The people who provide the "gold" by buying products and services have become unimportant. Business has become, in far too many cases, "The Money Machine" that has but one objective. That objective is to realize a profit that doesn't just pay the bills, but allows corporate executives and business owners to heap wealth upon themselves at the expense of the source of their revenue – people.

That money machine doesn't care about the needs of the people who feed it. This concept is seen dramatically in the financial meltdown of the last few years. Those who were gambling with the assets of many people were looking for a financial "golden egg" at the expense of those who lost their homes and the value of their investments. At that point, all they wanted was a bailout to save their assets. They threw a party while many people threw in the towel.

These problems are also seen in the way many lawyers charge for their services. They often work on class-action lawsuits and gain millions of dollars from them. But what is the percentage charged? In many cases the lawyers get more money than all the people they were supposed to be helping. They buy another home, sports car, or boat, while those harmed get the 'crumbs from the table.'

In the business world today, the value of people is often minimized for the sake of making a profit. People are surely worth more than just being customers who pay for goods and services. But in far too many cases, this is all forgotten and/or minimized for the sake of the profit. Corporate law defines corporations as "persons", yet they forget that those who send them money are also "persons". Anyone in business who wants to keep the "golden eggs" coming, must see people for who they are--real people that send money. Later I'll list some principles of customer service that will ensure the flow of "golden eggs".

One of the most frustrating experiences that customers have these days is the navigation of the phone systems of almost every business. "Press #1 if you want... press #2 if you need... press #6 if..." and on and on it goes. Many times there is not an option to speak with a real person. We all know that these phone systems were put in place so that companies can save money and eliminate paying real people. That is the only reason. If none of the telephone answering options are what you want, then just go to www.com and you'll find even more non-personal services. If customers were truly valued, companies would gladly spend the money to gain the confidence and goodwill of their customers – who'd feel much better sending their checks – having received respectful and helpful communication.

When we experience soaring credit rates on our credit cards, we know "something is rotten in the state of Denmark." When banks insert hidden fees, surcharges, taxes, interest, and a host of tricky names for adding to the bottom line, we are all frustrated, but can do nothing about it. If we change credit cards, we'll be dealing with another greedy bank. Corporations have become so powerful that they can get away with almost anything in the short term. Even with lawsuits that eventually make them pay back their illegal gains, the consumer gets little or nothing.

Most trucking companies added a "fuel surcharge" and increased freight costs for all of us when the cost of diesel fuel soared a few years ago. But when the cost of fuel came down, most of them didn't remove the surcharge. It was too convenient to keep adding it for the sake of profit. To put a value on people only as a source of revenue, and forget that they too are human, is irresponsible at best. The worst part is the destructive energy that harms the very source of the revenue needed. How many billionaires really give any thought to the people that have made them rich? They'd rather give all the credit to themselves and laugh their way to the beach house on some exotic island. Welcome to predatory capitalism.

I realize that I write from the perspective of small business. And, we all know that small business is the backbone of the economy; or at least it used to be. I mostly retired from my business two years ago. And, while I had no previous experience in business, I built a successful one by doing it "the old fashioned way." I earned it. I did have "people experience" in my background and what I learned from that helped me become the "go-to" person in my area of expertise. The principles I'll share here are the same for businesses anywhere, because **people always have been and always will be what we need to succeed.** It is a "no brainer" to figure out **what people need** and then provide it for them. We'll always get paid for that. Indeed, that is the driving force behind all inventions, new products, and all services.

Seven Principles to Keep Your Golden Eggs Coming – These are all built upon respect for people as real humans, and valuing them as more than just a source of revenue.

1. **GET PAID FOR SERVING PEOPLE'S NEEDS AND ENJOYING THAT PROCESS** – Ask yourself what your own needs are. Make a list of them and keep adding to that list indefinitely. What you need – respect, integrity, self-worth, connection, inclusion, appreciation, empathy, trust, presence, harmony, choice, and so many more, is exactly what your customers also need. What you give to others is what you will gain for yourself. The value of people is not only to be found

in their wallets. Truly gaining a satisfied customer yields far more than inner satisfaction. It will bring you more business, more money, and more opportunities to grow your business. Customers can always provide me with insights that will improve my products and services. In return, I give them more of what they value. This will only happen if I truly listen to them and follow the principles that follow.

Example: One of my earliest customers was a woman who had a chair to be fixed. I looked at it, gave her a price and took it to my shop. When I delivered it back to her, she was very happy with the quality of the repairs and gladly paid me. Then, she showed me three other pieces and I repaired them with the same result. After that came the restoration of her kitchen. Little did I realize that this woman worked for a major university in the department that was responsible for furniture, wood repair and restoration. She gave me a referral and I enjoyed almost 30 years of income from that valuable source. It all began with one chair and a customer who appreciated the quality work, respect and honesty I gave her and the restored value of her furniture.

2. **RECIPROCITY IS THE "GOLDEN RULE"** – Few corporations ask their customers how they would appreciate being served. Where is the CEO that says, "let's learn how to serve one another" to those who buy the goods and services that his company provides, and then chooses to practice that? We've all seen the commercials on television that seem to promise recognition of the customer, but then falls far short of actually doing what they say or what they want people to think is true. Everyone needs to be heard! Everyone! **Asking** our customers what they need and then really **listening** to them is the beginning. Of course not everyone knows what they need, so I learned to hear the needs behind the words and work to meet them. It took some experience, but the more I asked and actually listened, the more I gained their confidence and their future business. And, of course, some people never know what they want or need, so in those times, I learned to keep it simple and just do quality repairs. A wise person will make it

clear to customers what his/her part of the agreement is and have a clear understanding with the other person so that they know their part too. Here's where we can get creative for the benefit of all.

Example: One day a customer who had asked me to restore her dining room table and china cabinet wasn't sure what she wanted it to look like. All she could say is that she wanted it to "match everything else" in the room. As I looked around, I could see many colors, textures, designs and a variety of possibilities for a "match." I knew I didn't dare advise her at this point. So, I began to ask a lot of questions and listened. In one respect, she didn't really know what she wanted herself, but I knew that when she saw the bigger picture, she would know. It took an extra hour or so to figure it all out. When she finally realized that what she wanted, it was for her furniture to "match" the color in her drapes and carpet, and I knew how to do that. Upon delivery she paid me an extra $200 for helping her get what she really wanted. All I did was to help her understand her needs. When she moved to another home about 15 years later, guess who she called to work with her on a new project?

3. **COMMUNICATION IS THE KEY TO RESPECT** – I made it a policy to always keep my word and not keep anyone waiting and wondering when I might arrive. I had heard the frustration in many voices related to service people not showing up when scheduled or maybe not at all. I decided I wouldn't be one of those who contributed to my customers' negative feelings, I would be punctual. I vowed to myself that if at any time I realized that I was going to be more than five minutes late, I would call and let the person know. Even in the days before cell phones, I would find a phone booth and call – even in rain or snow. That practice paid off many times. "You are the only person that ever comes on time." I heard this many, many times over the years. People know when they are honored and when they just don't matter. We all need to "matter." This kind of communication will always increase business, whatever your product or service might be.

Example: A customer I'd worked for in the past called me to look at another piece. I arrived on time as usual to see what the need was. He just happened to have a visitor there, and introduced me to the other person as "the only one who is always on time." That person got my number, and in a couple of months, called me for some work.

4. **KNOWING THE PRICES AND SERVICES OF YOUR COMPETITION IS PARAMOUNT** – I knew that I couldn't do everything better than everyone else. That is sheer folly. But when I didn't know what to charge for a particular repair or service, I simply called my competition, posing as a potential customer, and asked the questions for which I needed answers. I knew which questions were pertinent to the job at hand. When I gained the information needed, I gave my customer a better price and guaranteed both the price and the work in writing. If I could quote a price, then beat that price, and bill them for less, I would do it without hesitation. None of my customers ever had that experience from anyone else. In doing that, I "knocked out" the competition many times and my business flourished.

Example: On one occasion, a customer asked me to make a restoration that I knew I wasn't very good at doing. I also knew that my competition was very good at that process. So, I referred her to them and asked her to tell them that I did. She was very surprised that I would refer her to one of my competitors. I told her that I wanted her to have a quality job done on her table and I didn't want to deliver something that wasn't as good as she could get elsewhere. I also knew that I was better than them in other areas. She not only gave me all her remaining work, but the competitor later referred someone to me. From that day on, we helped each other and it paid off for both of us.

5. **EXTEND YOUR GUARANTEE BEYOND THAT OF THE COMPETITION** – We all know of the 30/30 guarantee! That is where the work is guaranteed for either 30 seconds or until the repairman is 30 feet away - whichever occurs first! I made it a common practice to tell my customers that I guarantee my

work indefinitely. If it was damaged again, I'd have to charge for that. But if my work didn't last, **I would come back and take care of it, even if it was a year later.** I knew that would never happen, but I also meant it. Once or twice I had to go back a month or two later to make sure the customer was happy, but never a year. I absolutely would have if needed, but I knew my work and the quality of it.

6. **EXTRA EFFORT IS ALWAYS REWARDED WITH MORE BUSINESS** – There were times that an extra effort was needed. In my early days, it was difficult to do this especially when I had two young children at home to feed and clothe. But I knew it would pay off, so I did what I could. Sometimes an extra stop at a home, an extra ten or twenty minutes touching up something other than what I was paid to do, or a few minutes "going beyond the call of duty," seemed to be more trouble than it was worth at the time. Yet my experience was that it always paid off in other referrals, more work, and my inner self-esteem.

7. **IN THE CASE OF A DISPUTE, MAKE IT NO DISPUTE IF POSSIBLE** – This isn't always possible, but anytime that I can serve a customer (even the grouchy ones) by eliminating a dispute, it will best serve everyone's interests.

Example: Only once in thirty years did a customer change their mind and blame me for a problem. I could have walked off, but I chose not to. By this time in my business I could afford "the extra mile" so I took the piece and completely reworked it – at no charge. As far as I know that never got me any more work, but I know I maintained my integrity, which was my reward.

Remember that above all else, it is the volume of business that still wins the day. Instead of charging less customers more money, I charged more customers less money and I retired with dignity and money in the bank. It all began with one chair to be glued. Later on, several five-figure jobs proved to me the value of my customer service.

Jim Stacey – All Rights Reserved

ABOUT JIM

Years ago, Jim Stacey looked at his skills and his desire to be successful. He accurately envisaged what people would need in the realm of furniture repair and antique restoration. He later expanded that to complete wood exterior and interior restorations. He started as The Furniture Doctor and became The Wood Doctor.

Jim took his hobby to a business level. He later took his skills to television, where he made over 100 local shows in the Detroit area and later became The 21st Century Wood Doctor on public television. He succeeded in business by using the principles listed in the chapter.

Jim Stacey worked for major corporations, major universities, and countless homeowners all around Lower Michigan. But his success was no accident. The seven principles that he shared were used to gain that success. You too can use these principles to get to the top of your field of expertise, and stay there.

Even in tough times, Jim was never without work. And now, in retirement, he still has people calling him after more than ten years since he last worked for them. If he can, he still works for those that he enjoyed working for the most.

CHAPTER 10

HOW TO PROFIT FROM THE INFORMATION REVOLUTION

BY DAVID SCHWAB, PH.D.

T he Battle of New Orleans, a bloody conflict fought on January 8, 1815, was the last major battle of the War of 1812. General Andrew Jackson led his troops to an improbable but decisive victory, which later helped propel Jackson to the White House. American and British forces have not faced each other as enemies in a war since that time.

The Battle of New Orleans is also a remarkable historical event for another reason: soldiers on both sides who were destined to die that day were unaware that their sacrifice would be in vain – regardless of the outcome – because the peace treaty that ended the war had been signed more than two weeks earlier. Communications between Europe and the United States were so slow that news of peace reached New Orleans long after hundreds of combatants had been killed on the battlefield.

Today, we wince at this ironic turn of events, but we no longer worry about information traveling too slowly. Now we are at risk of being swept away by a never-ending flood of instantaneously generated information. The postman brings stacks of stuff, some that cannot be ignored, such as bills, but also business journal articles that should be read, other important correspondence, and much direct mail that could contain interesting offers if only one had the time to sift, sort, and consider them all before the next imposing pile of paper arrives. In addition to our overflowing inboxes, there is also the incessant barrage of electrons: e-mails, online newsletters, tweets, text messages, alerts from social networking sites, electronic faxes, voicemails, online video clips and photos, and websites replete with an inexhaustible supply of links to more links. As Hamlet said, "It is as though increase of appetite had grown by what it fed on."

Although the speed and quantity of information are now daunting, it is better to embrace the information revolution rather than wish for a bygone era when the pace of life was slower. To be successful in business in the twenty-first century, you need to have a strategy for working with the information revolution, rather than fighting against it or passively being carried along by it.

Here are seven strategies to help you profit in the information age.

1. **Select and Apply**: *National Geographic* photographers take thousands of photographs for each assignment. The editors then select just a handful of photos for each article. The reason that *National Geographic* is so stunning is that only the most visually compelling photographs are chosen. The others simply do not make the cut, either because they are not exceptional or because they do not illustrate the point of the story.

   The first rule in dealing with information is to separate valuable nuggets from fool's gold. I cull bits of information and place only the most interesting into three major categories: interesting quotations, factoids, and concepts. I then apply that information in my business to better serve my clients. Here are some examples.

   • Quotation: "Whether you think you can, or you think you can't--you're right"—Henry Ford. Thanks, Henry. You have succinctly captured an important lesson. If your customers think "it can't be done" due to the economy, competition, or other obstacles, they are right. However, this attitude creates a great business opportunity, because you can show them that with your help *it can be done* ...

and Henry Ford says you are right!

- Factoid: Southwest Airlines can board an airplane faster than most of their competitors. If they increased their boarding time by just five minutes per flight, their costs would go up by hundreds of millions of dollars per year, because they would have to buy more airplanes (and hire more crews, pay more for fuel, landing fees, etc.) to service the same number of routes and passengers. Talk about a lesson in efficiency! If, for example, you are in business-to-business marketing, how long does it take your clients to deal with a new customer on the phone or complete a transaction? You are valuable because you point out that shaving just a few minutes from each customer interaction really adds up at the end of the year.

- Concept. Michael Gerber says that most business owners spend too much time working *in* their business and not enough time working *on* their business. When I do seminars, I say to the audience: "Congratulations! Today you have stepped out of the salt mine. You are no longer grinding away in the business. Instead, you have come here to work *on* your business and I am going to help you." It's not enough to share advice from world famous gurus. You have to apply it to the specific needs of your customers. That's what makes you the guru in your field.

2. **Create Content:** Everyone knows that "content is king," so get busy creating it. I have found that one of the best organizational principles when creating content is to make lists. In my seminars I have a list of "The Five Biggest Marketing Mistakes" and "25 Things You Can and Should Do to Market Your Business." There are also "Five Bonus Items" at the end of the list of 25. Lists make it easier for people to follow your flow of ideas, and clients are always impressed that I am providing them with a specific and impressive number of ideas. One periodontist asked me for a list of the "10 Things Referring Doctors Hate the Most." Great idea. I created the list for him based on my years of experience and then incorporated it into my next seminar. The response was very positive.

I also write articles for business journals. Most publications welcome cogent articles. If you expect to get paid for your articles, then you are in the business of writing. However, if you provide articles to publications free of charge, then you are probably a business person, consultant, speaker, or all three. Your articles increase your reach and credibility. You can also keep the content flowing by writing a blog on your website, updating your social media sites, or writing a book. You have the knowledge. By publishing what you know, you solidify your brand and become the "go-to" person in your field.

There are also opportunities now for you to create audio files or podcasts that accompany your articles that appear on websites. In our visual age, videos are also becoming very valuable. I was asked by the publisher of a very well respected online publication to create a short video to accompany one of my articles. The deadline was very short, and at first I thought I needed more equipment and also some help from my assistant, who was not in the office that day. I decided to try it on my own. With good lighting, a camera and tripod, and a corporate-looking bookshelf in the background at my office, I created a five-minute video. I was a one-man band, in charge of camera, sound, lighting, art direction, editing—and of course I was the on-air talent. The entire project took me about thirty minutes, start to finish. I e-mailed the video file to the publisher and he liked it so much that he promptly posted it on the magazine's website. There is a lot to be said for a "talking head" when you are the one who is talking and selling your products or services.

3. **Give it Away:** There is what you sell, and there is what you give away. When I present seminars, I always give the attendees a detailed handout filled with good information they can take back to the office and use immediately. This practice sets me apart from some other presenters who tease the audience with partial information and then launch into a sales pitch: "if you are interested in learning all the secrets, then sign up now." After a seminar, I send attendees a handout addendum that contains even more free information. I also post regular tidbits on my

blog, I provide a detailed bibliography of recent business books that I have read and found helpful, and I have a "free report" available for the asking on a topic that I know my potential clients will want to read. Some free audio and video clips round out my giveaways.

You are probably wondering why I am giving away so much information, rather than selling it. *Actually, I do both, because the giveaways lead to sales.* My first goal is to lower the fence, as it were, by taking away the main obstacle to getting information out – price. "Free" is the most powerful word in marketing, and it generates qualified leads. Also, once people get information from me and appreciate its value, they naturally want more. At that point, they can choose from a variety of saleable items. In fact, the free items, while definitely complete and worthwhile, all come with information on how to order additional resource materials for a price.

Finally, as a consultant, I need to establish both expertise and trust. The free items are very helpful in this regard. Also, if a potential customer has attended a seminar or purchased a CD, I am in a better position to say, "it's time to fully implement what you have learned." I then offer to help the client through my personalized consulting services, which that person is more likely to purchase. So, the free information creates demand for the paid materials, which in turn create demand for consulting services.

4. **Sell it:** In order to sell information, you have to package it, and this means you have to use different media. I am a visual learner. I would much prefer to quickly read an article, book, or other document and pull out the relevant parts. There are many people, however, who prefer to take in information by listening to a CD or audio file. I am grateful to these auditory learners, because they buy my CDs. "Kinesthetic learners" are those who prefer to learn by doing rather than watching or listening.

You should make your materials available in different formats to suit these different learning styles. A recent search on amazon.com for books on "diet, health, nutrition" yielded

14,000 hits. There are also innumerable audio series, videos, and group meetings sponsored by different organizations on this topic. I can summarize all the advice contained in these sources in just four words: "Eat healthy and exercise." The problem is that for this message to really sink in, some people need just the right book. Others need motivational lectures. Still others need to experience group dynamics in a social setting.

You do not want to run the risk of boring your customers or potential customers. Some people lose interest if their learning style is not addressed. Offer written materials (with accompanying visuals such as diagrams or illustrations), audio presentations, and the opportunity for interactive sessions at your seminars or workshops. Your message needs to be in the manual, the CD and the seminar – to reach all potential audiences and fit in with their preferred styles of learning.

By using information as a resource and a saleable commodity, you leverage your brand identity. Because your clients are so busy with their own businesses and personal lives, they need you to gather, interpret, and package information for them in formats they can use. You become the expert, the one who has the answers or who knows where to find the answers.

It is precisely because there is an Information Revolution that you need to be the Andrew Jackson of your industry – this time armed with all the information – leading the charge, inspiring confidence, and positioning yourself for even greater accomplishments in the days ahead.

ABOUT DAVID

David Schwab, Ph.D., is a professional speaker, author, and consultant who helps dentists grow their practices, educate their patients, and train their teams so that the practices will be more profitable.

An internationally-known seminar speaker, Dr. Schwab presents practical, user-friendly practice management and marketing seminars for the entire dental team. Fast-paced, filled with humor, and overflowing with "pearls," Dr. Schwab's seminars are as popular as they are useful. His lecture topics include developing brand identity, effectively using social media, revving up internal marketing, improving verbal skills, providing team leadership, and increasing case acceptance. Using a combination of lecture and interactive sessions, he keeps the audience engaged – while they are learning.

Dr. Schwab also works extensively with referral-based practices to help dental specialists develop and maintain strong referral relationships. He works with specialists and small groups of general dentists to systematize referrals, develop outreach programs to attract more referral sources, and emphasize the importance of interdisciplinary treatment.

Prior to starting his own company, Dr. Schwab served as Director of Marketing for the American Dental Association and as Executive Director of the American College of Prosthodontists. He has also worked with numerous dental schools, major corporations, and private dental practices.

At the present time he runs a marketing consulting firm, David Schwab & Associates, Inc. The company provides in-office seminars, online training and consulting, and other practice management services for fee-for-service dentists.

Recognized as a prolific and insightful author, Dr. Schwab's practice management and marketing articles have appeared in numerous publications, including the Journal of the American Dental Association, Dental Economics, the Seattle Study Club Journal, and the Journal of the Canadian Dental Association. His website: www.davidschwab.com, features blogs, articles, videos, and much other useful information.

Dr. Schwab holds a Ph.D. in English from Northwestern University.

A native of New Orleans, he currently lives in the Orlando, Florida area with his wife and two children.

CHAPTER 11

WIN WITH WISDOM

BY DR. EMMA JEAN THOMPSON

My friend, have you ever *really* wanted something? I mean have you ever *deeply* desired something?

As you read the following story, I believe that you will see some clear solutions to some "life situations." At the end of this story, you will be given some "tips" that are sure to help you "win with wisdom" whatever it is that you want in your life.

Well, I really wanted and deeply desired to have a baby. After twelve years of marriage and believing God, the big "win" that I wanted was on the way – I was finally pregnant.

Our family, friends, and various ones around the country and abroad who knew that my husband and I were 'believing' to have a baby – were excited for us. When we gave the announcement at our church, the people jumped up out of their seats, grabbed one another with hugs and exuberant joy as they praised God for our prayer – and their prayer for us – being answered. My heart was filled with gratefulness to God and thankfulness for the wonderful people who had stood in faith with me.

Then, just a few weeks later, my joy was being shattered. Late at night in October, when I was about eleven weeks pregnant, I began bleeding. The bleeding was steady and so profuse. The sight of it all scared me. As my husband and I were rushing to drive to the hospital, I called our Prayer Support, who would alert designated ones to also pray for us.

"You have to have a 'D and C' right now," the emergency room doctor told me, coldly. He did not examine me nor did he ask questions of me or of the nurse. He only knew that I was bleeding profusely.

"D and C?" I quickly asked. "What is that?"

"It's a procedure to scrape out your womb," he answered.

"But what will that do to my baby?" I asked with great concern.

"Baby?" he responded.

"Well, you know that I'm pregnant, don't you?" I answered.

"You passed tissue," he answered roughly.

"Passed 'tissue'?" I asked. I did not understand.

"You passed tissue. You lost the baby and your life will be in jeopardy if I don't do a 'D and C' procedure immediately. "

As I hesitated, I could see him getting angrier and more impatient.

"You have to do this now," he said.

"But," I shared, "Myra…the nurse said that my cervix is still closed."

"So," he retorted, "We'll just go in and open it."

"But isn't there something I can do to save my baby's life?" I pleaded with the doctor. "Isn't there some test…or…or something I can take to show me whether my baby is still alive?" I asked.

He was leaning over me. The veins stood out on his neck as his face was filled with annoyance, impatience and anger. As he leaned over, his name badge hovered in front of me like a huge billboard displaying his name, which consisted of two "first names", that I will always remember. He had burst into the room without introduction. So now I put a name to this doctor who was seemingly forcing me to make this decision without giving my baby a chance.

"No! There is no test you can take. It's too early in your pregnancy. You have to do this *now* – otherwise you could walk out into that hallway and drop dead."

My husband and I had been married for twelve years, and were waiting to have a child. In my ministry, I had prayed for many women who had been told that they could not conceive. I'd seen miracle after miracle occur as they got pregnant and gave birth. It had not yet happened for me. But the Lord had told me that I too would conceive and have a child one day, and I trusted in His message and had looked forward to it for all these years. When we discovered that I was finally pregnant, we were overjoyed.

"Doctor, we've been married twelve years and really wanting to have this baby," I said, hoping for some understanding and compassion.

The doctor did not want to hear my story. He abruptly answered, "You'll just have to start all over again." In frustration, he stalked out of the room.

My husband and I held hands and prayed. He immediately said "This is a decision that you have to make. It's your body…and it's your life that's on the line, Sweetheart."

I was drawing on what I learned as a little girl that has always helped me to "win" regardless of how difficult or painful the situation. When I heard and read in the Bible that Solomon made God's heart happy when he asked God for wisdom, I wanted to make God's heart happy and began praying every day for God to give me wisdom to bless and lead people.

On an Easter Sunday morning long ago, when I was but ten years old, my father abandoned our family. That day, I had a revelation - and wisdom - from the Lord that although my earthly father had left me, my Heavenly Father, God, would never leave nor forsake me. Since then, my whole life, I have trusted in the wisdom and guidance of the Lord.

For years I had been used by God prophetically to minister to others and to give them messages from the Lord. And I also helped them to know how to hear God for themselves. Now, as I always did, I listened for the voice of the Lord to lead me in making my decision.

I clearly heard, sensed and understood God saying to me, "Do not let that doctor touch you."

The doctor returned in a huff saying "Let's get you ready for the procedure," as if I had no "say so" in the matter.

"I understand what you're advising, but I'm going to wait and see another doctor and see if there is any possibility to get some kind of test. I want to at least give my baby any possibility to live."

He went into a flurry of anger at the thought that I would question what he told me to do – as if I was his "property."

Before I knew it, he had a clipboard in his hand and shoved it at me saying, "You have to sign this document that I warned you that you are putting your life in jeopardy by your refusal to have this procedure."

Skimming over it quickly, the words "own life in jeopardy" seemed to stand out big on the paper. Yet, without hesitation or doubt, I signed it and he virtually snatched it from me.

"You can *leave now!*" he said, and stormed out of the room.

My husband went to pull our car up to the hospital entrance, and since I was weak and still bleeding heavily, the nurse, Myra – may God forever bless Myra – helped me get dressed and gave me hope.

"You go home and rest," she said, kindly. "Doctors are not God," she whispered in my ear so that the doctor who had returned could not hear.

The doctor made sure I got no help at all as I walked out of the room. As I walked down that long corridor by myself, I felt the warmth of the heavily oozing blood and remembering what the doctor said, "you could walk out into that hallway and drop dead."

Yet I chose to dwell on the fact that I knew that I had heard God speak to me, and I was giving my baby the chance to "live" – to "win" and for me to "win," and not to "lose" this precious gift.

It was a long, long drive home from the hospital that night. As my husband and I drove along the dark winding, lonely streets of Prince George's County, my body feeling the effects of the amount of blood I had loss yet we held hands declaring the faithfulness of God. I held back the hot, stinging tears that welled up and demanded to be released.

My mind began to race with thoughts of the words that doctor, the "expert" had spewed out of his mouth, "You are putting your life in jeopardy if you walk out of here without this procedure!" I felt my husband;s hand grasp mine even tighter and again decreed, "God is faithful. God is worthy to be praised." I washed the words that had been spoken by that doctor out of my heart with God's word. I reflected on the Friday Night Praise Service we attended the night before. I thought about the tithe and the offering I had given during the Service. "I gave my tithe, Lord," I said, "I gave an offering to you, Jesus." It was my custom to give my tithes and offerings at our Sunday Worship Services. At our Services during the week, I would give an offering however the tithe I presented to my Heavenly Father on Sundays. This Friday service was different. I was impressed to give my tithes that Friday night at church service. Even though I did not understand why, I believed that it was the Holy Spirit leading me – and the Holy Spirit leads and guides in all truth and wisdom – I obeyed that leading.

As I reflected on the paying of my tithe, the many promises about the tithe and the power of the tithe filled my mind and heart --

> *"Bring the whole tithe into the storehouse, that there may be food in my house. Test me in this," says the LORD Almighty, "and see if I will not throw open the floodgates of heaven and pour out so much blessing that there will not be room enough to store it."*

> *~ Malachi 3:10, New International Version, Holy Bible*

So many thoughts were coming to my mind and in order to stay on the "faith track," I had to respond to each negative thought with a faith-filled response.

Early the next morning, I visited the new doctor. "You're still bleeding," he told me after the examination, "but your uterus is thick, which is a good sign. And your cervix is closed which is also a good sign. We'll do a sonogram and lab tests. I have a wedding to attend. You go home and rest, and I'll call you later today with the test results."

When the doctor called back, he said, "I want to tell you that you are carrying a very viable eleven-week old baby. We don't know why you're bleeding, but we can't find anything wrong and the baby is fine."

We thanked the doctor and hung up the phone praising the Lord, and so elated that God had shone His favor upon us. We called our Prayer Support to alert everyone with the good news.

Later in his office, the new doctor asked "Why did you resist having the 'D and C' when the doctor tried to get you to have it?"

"The Lord spoke to me and told me not to have it," I answered.

Shaking his head in amazement, he said, "It's a good thing you did not have that procedure - otherwise you would have been scraping out a living baby."

Throughout my pregnancy, there were other difficult "episodes," yet there was caring, loving encouragement from my husband, our relatives, our Prayer Support, our church family, and our loved ones in America and abroad. Most importantly, I am grateful for the wisdom of the Lord through His Holy Spirit and His Holy Word and for those who believed with me.

At last, after two and half hours of labor, our precious baby was being born. Oh! The magnificent joy of holding this beautiful bundle of blessings in my arms. How wonderful to see her, to hold her, to kiss her, to lay my cheek against her little cheek.

She was not just our "child"; she was a "representation" of God's faithfulness. Even if she had not lived, I would have still praised God. But what a blessing that she was alive and that God had caused me/us to "win with wisdom" – my faith and His wonderful wisdom.

That "baby" that the "expert" doctor at the emergency examining room did his best to get me to "give up on" is now, as of this writing, our 24 year old beautiful daughter, Sherah Danielle Thompson, who was born in perfect health on May 1st, 1986 – and she is our only natural child. Her names are from the Holy Bible. Sherah means "Builder for God," and Danielle (named after Daniel of the Holy Bible), who was "beloved of God" and who had "wisdom of God". Sherah is known as the young lady who encourages people and builds them up with inspiration, and who asks them "Has anyone reminded you today that Jesus loves you?"

After graduating from Howard University's John H. Johnson School of Communications -- Annenberg Honors Program, with a degree in Film, Radio and TV, Sherah Danielle is presently a graduate student at Regent University obtaining a MFA in Film Directing. Already her writing, directing and production projects have won awards – two of her projects were selected and shown to over 30 million households.

My friend, you may have a dream, a goal – something precious - that you are carrying in the "womb" of your heart. If you don't have such a goal at this time, more than likely you will in the future.

Would you like to know how to "win with wisdom?"

From my many personal experiences and my numerous experiences helping others to "Win with Wisdom", here are:

SEVEN TIPS ON HOW YOU CAN WIN WITH WISDOM

1. **Know that wisdom is "the principle and supreme thing" that you should have to protect, bless and enrich you and your loved ones.**

    The beginning of Wisdom is: get Wisdom (skillful and godly Wisdom)! [For skillful and godly Wisdom is the principal thing.] And with all you have gotten, get understanding (discernment, comprehension, and interpretation). Proverbs 4:7 AMP Holy Bible

2. **Know that wisdom is available to you.**

    ⁵ If any of you lacks wisdom, you should ask God, who gives generously to all without finding fault, and it will be given to you. ⁶ But when you ask, you must believe and not doubt, because the one who doubts is like a wave of the sea, blown and tossed by the wind. ⁷ That person should not expect to receive anything from the Lord. ⁸ Such a person is double-minded and unstable in all they do. James 1:5-8 NIV Holy Bible

3. **Recognize the difference between faith (and belief) over presumption and foolishness.**

    And without faith it is impossible to please God, because anyone who comes to him must believe that he exists and that he rewards those who earnestly seek him. Hebrews 11:6 NIV

4. **Be prepared to handle risks, obstacles and criticism of your decisions.**

    Consider it pure joy, my brothers and sisters, whenever you face trials of many kinds, ³ because you know that the testing of your faith produces perseverance. ⁴ Let perseverance finish its work so that you may be mature and complete, not lacking anything. James 1:2-4 NIV

5. **You can receive heavenly guidance and direction so that you make decisions that cause you to "win with wisdom."**

    So shall you find favor, good understanding, and high esteem in the sight [or judgment] of God and man. ⁵ Lean on, trust in, and be confident in the Lord with all your heart and mind and do not rely on your own insight or understanding. ⁶ In all your ways know, recognize, and acknowledge Him, and He will direct and make straight and plain your paths. Proverbs 3:4-6

6. **Make Room for Jesus in your everyday life so that it is easier for you to make all kinds and sizes of decisions.**

   But seek (aim at and strive after) first of all His kingdom and His righteousness (His way of doing and being right), and then all these things taken together will be given you besides. Matthew 6:33 AMP

7. **Prayer and a prayer covering are important to help you to know how to reap the benefits for you, your loved ones, your situations and your future.**

   I do not cease to give thanks for you, making mention of you in my prayers, Ephesians 1:16 AMP

   Now to Him Who, by (in consequence of) the [action of His] power that is at work within us, is able to [carry out His purpose and] do superabundantly, far over and above all that we [dare] ask or think [infinitely beyond our highest prayers, desires, thoughts, hopes, or dreams] Ephesians 3:20 AMP

   ⁶ Do not fret or have any anxiety about anything, but in every circumstance and in everything, by prayer and petition (definite requests), with thanksgiving, continue to make your wants known to God. Philippians 4:6 AMP

To learn more about the importance of prayer and a prayer covering, please contact me at info@MakeRoom4Jesus.com for your free CD.

It is my joy to have shared with you one of my many experiences of how these principles and prayer – operate and bless my life and enable me to daily "win with wisdom " over any circumstance and situation I may encounter.

You can receive your FREE video and audio on "God's Wisdom Success Principles" that give you greater and deeper insight on how to use these lessons and principles to "win with wisdom" in your life situations.

Please visit: http://www.MakeRoom4Jesus.com.

ABOUT EMMA JEAN

Dr. Emma Jean Thompson is internationally esteemed as a speaker, #1 Bestselling Author, motion picture producer and trusted advisor serving leaders in Ministry, Business, Education, Entertainment and other arenas.

Passionate about empowering women and men in business and in life, Dr. Thompson's powerful and proprietary **"God's Wisdom Success Principles™"** have guided thousands of people worldwide to achieve business breakthroughs and personal transformation. With audiences praising her work as "miraculous" and "inspirational", media including CNN, CSPAN, Time Magazine, USA Today, Fox TV, Christianity Today Magazine (twice on the front cover), BET, Jet Magazine, Time Magazine, and Miami Herald have already featured Dr. Thompson and her team. Other TV and media appearances include "The Brian Tracy Show," "The Michael Gerber Show" and "Success and Hope for You".

As an end-time Prophet and Apostle of God and Jesus Christ, Dr. Emma Jean will help **you** to profit and prosper. Building on timeless biblical principles, Dr. Thompson uses documented success stories and case studies to create step-by-step blueprints for her audience on how to more than double their income and their free time at the same time, enjoy rock-solid, meaningful relationships, and thrive in complete health (III John 2 Bible). Guiding men and women to joyfully discover and fulfill their God-given purpose, all while keeping "Make Room for Jesus™" in their everyday life their priority and foundation, is the compelling message that Dr. Emma Jean Thompson feeds her hungry crowds, leaving them filled with valuable insights, yet always eager for more.

Her husband, Dr. James J. Thompson Jr., along with the leadership and congregation of Integrity Church International, which is headquartered in Landover, Maryland, joyfully acknowledge Apostle Dr. Emma Jean Thompson as the lead Pastor and International Overseer of their churches, missions and outreaches which include Ghana, West Africa, India and Jamaica.

Their daughter, Sherah Danielle, who at the time of this writing is a Masters of Fine Arts Graduate Film Directing Student at Regent University and also received her Bachelor of Fine Arts at Howard University. Sherah is also a #1 Bestselling Author.

Dr. Emma Jean Thompson is the Founder and CEO of **"MakeRoom4Jesus.com"** of which the December 2009 Dedication Celebration was sponsored and hosted by dear family friends **Dr. Nido R. and Mariana Qubein** at **High Point University in High Point, North Carolina.**

For the past 18 of her 33 years of ministry, Dr. Emma Jean has been in a time of intense prayer, preparation and research documenting that individuals, churches, businesses, schools, and any organization that are experiencing significant success are using **"God's Wisdom Success Principles™"**- even if they are not aware.

Her "Purpose Passion" is to *"cause young people and adults to be blessed in every way in this earthly life AND to be ready for the coming of Jesus Christ and Judgment Day.*

You may contact Dr. Emma Jean at Info@DrEmmaJean.com or DrEmmaJean@MakeRoom4Jesus.com.

CHAPTER 12

SUCCESSFUL FAMILIES

"SECRETS TO RAISING SUCCESSFUL AND MOTIVATED CHILDREN"

BY MASTER GARY A. SCHILL

As children we all have aspirations and dreams of being something grand: a super hero, a princess, a millionaire. Our dreams are filled with hope, promise and an unbridled power with the belief that nothing will stand in our way. Today many children are over indulged, and have developed a distorted sense of entitlement.

As a military brat, I traveled to many different countries at a very early age. Unfortunately, my sister was diagnosed with a very rare heart defect. My mother and sister immediately went back to the States for treatment. My family was separated, and when we were reunited it seemed as though everything had changed. I didn't understand as a child that much of the family focus centered on my sister because of her illness. Because I was angry and in a great deal of pain, I missed many opportunities as both a youngster and as an adult.

Everything We Have Learned About Parenting
Came From Our Parents: The Good and the Bad

When I had children, my parents did not give me a "Golden Rule" book. You know that book that answers all of your questions and fears about raising children. It describes every cry, what to do when they

115

fall down and all the other concerns you have about raising children. It puts to rest all the fears you have as a parent. It provides us with everything we need to teach them to be successful in every facet of their lives.

My parents taught me some great lessons Honesty, Perseverance, Good Communication, the value of Hard Work are just a few. There were some lessons they could not pass along to me. It wasn't because they were stupid people Had my mom been raised differently, she could have been the CEO of a Fortune 100 company. These untaught lessons have prevented some real successes for me as an adult.

In my first year of college, I accepted an opportunity with Red Mc-Combs and his wife Charlene. This was a major shift in reality for me. I am from a very blue collar, middle class military family. Mr. McCombs was very much like me as a child As an adult he has overcome great adversity and is now a self-made billionaire. The lessons he instilled in his children, grandchildren, and key business associates are greatly different. "You are the average sum of the five people you associate with most" is a well known saying. Mr. McCombs hung out with other successful millionaires and billionaires The mind set and lessons they were passing on to their families were very different. They wanted to ensure that their children had the Success Secrets that cost them a great deal of time and money to learn on their way to the top.

BREAKING THE CYCLE, PROVIDING THE SUCCESS SECRETS YOUR CHILDREN AND YOU MUST LEARN

FOUR IMPORTANT LESSONS PARENTS MUST TEACH THEIR CHILDREN TO ENSURE SUCCESS

Our children face challenges that were not present even five short years ago. We have to provide them with proven success skills to ensure they are properly prepared for adulthood To break the cycle your parents passed on to you, teach your children and yourself the Four Success Skills I have outlined below.

1. Begin with the End in Mind (Vision): Have you ever created a vision of what you want your child to look like as an adult? What life skills do you want your child to possess as an adult? How many times have you had an idea for a product or invention, then a year or two later you see your idea on the internet or television making millions of dollars changing people lives? *The most important difference between success and failure is taking action to turn your vision into reality.* Many have great ideas, but most never take action.

This is an amazingly simple but effective technique to help you "Begin with the End in Mind." A Vision Board is great tool for taking your vision ("The Have") and adding the success steps to bring a successful outcome. This process can be used for many different projects with either short or long term goals. This process teaches them about focus, responsibility, hard work and the rewards achieved by fulfilling your dreams and aspirations.

Below is a sample Vision Board separated into three sections. Staring with the "Have" Section, have your child come to you and say 'I want XXXX. This statement typically starts with an "I" List the item or goal they want in the Have section and add a reasonable date for reaching their goal. Now make up some ways they can earn the "Have" item. These chores, tasks, and jobs are listed in the "Do" section. Fill out the "Be" section with personal conduct and character traits, and then start the process.

Be	Do	Have
Responsible	Mow Lawns	iTouch
On Time and	Clean Out Garage	"Reasonable Date"
Prepared	Do Weekly Chores to	"Print Out a Picture of the
Committed to my	Earn Allowance	Desired Item or Outcome
Goal	Make a goal and	and Place it on Your
Be honest	progress chart	Vision Board"

Put the completed Vision Board up on the wall where your child can see it every day. Put together a savings chart to chart their progress so they can see their success. It provides positive, visual reinforcement that will keep them on task and motivated. The results will amaze you. The great thing about this tool is it will work for you, and will set an example for your children to follow.

2. Goal Setting: Once you have finished your Vision Board, it is time to define your goals and time-lines. Refine your goals using the SMART method.

S = Specific: What is the "Have" on your Vision Board?
M = Measurable: Use a "Success Chart" to track your success.
A = Achievable: Is your "Have" achievable?
R = Realistic: Make the goal within reach. Do not set yourself up for failure.
T = Time Frame: Set an end date. This allows your brain to know when this must be completed.

ONLY 3% OF THE POPULATION SETS CLEAR-CUT DEFINED GOALS.

IT IS THAT IMPORTANT!

Using a Vision Board and SMART Goal Setting builds habits that ensure your children turn assignments in on time, teaches them the value of money, to manage time, behave responsibly, focus their energies, and most importantly SUCCESS!

3. Preventing the Quitting Habit: I often hear people complain that they "Shoulda" / "Coulda" / "Woulda". In reality they didn't finish what they started. Many probably didn't realize they had formed the Quitting Habit early in their lives. The Quitting Habit is an easy habit to form, a hard habit to break and the consequences can be devastating to future successes.

Quitting Habits are often developed during childhood. Maybe parents are embarrassed by their child's behavior during a team sport. Maybe practices interfere with a parental activity. Maybe it just becomes too time consuming and the child is allowed, or even encouraged, to quit. Once established, the Quitting Habit makes it easier to quit again and again. Thomas Edison tried over a 1000 times before successfully designing a working light bulb. When he was asked if he was discouraged by so many failures, Mr. Edison's response was "I didn't fail, but I can tell you 999 ways on how <u>not</u> to make a light bulb." *Winners never quit and quitters never win, period!*

4 Major Fears that Fuel the Quitting Habit

The Quitting Habit is primarily motivated by "4 Major Fears".

- ➤ Fear of Rejection
- ➤ Fear of Failure
- ➤ Fear of Acceptance
- ➤ Fear of Success

The Fear of Rejection and Fear of Failure begin when our children take their first steps. When they fall down, the first thing they do is look to us. Overreacting and hovering over them increases their Fears of Failure and Rejection. By playing it cool, often they are encouraged to get up and keep on going believing the fall was no big deal.

Fear of Success and Acceptance are equally powerful and paralyzing. Can you remember your first visit to a full service restaurant or hotel? You may not have known what fork to start with or how much to tip the porter for taking your bags to your room. Once you have experienced many situations like this, you begin feeling uncomfortable because you do not have any experience at this level of success.

Our children face this fear in everyday in social situations. Everyone wants to be accepted and unfortunately many will compromise their integrity in an effort to be accepted by their peers.

Most of our fears are the same as our parents. Often we unintentionally pass these fears along to our own children. When I started my first company, my mother sat me down at the kitchen table and said, "Honey, you need to forget this idea of starting a business. Businesses fail. You need to get a job and stay with the same company until you retire". That was my mom's reality. Her fear of failure was given to her by my grandfather and it kept her from achieving her full potential. Had I not broken this cycle, it would be affecting me the same way. I would now risk passing this same fear on to my children.

4. Communication and Public Speaking Skills: Did you realize that 7 out of 10 adults HATE public speaking? With the advent of texting and social networking sites, verbal communication skills are declining quickly. In many schools reading aloud in class is no longer mandatory. No matter how uncomfortable it may be, this required public reading is a child's first introduction to public speaking.

We understand the importance and necessity of public speaking and communication skills. Why do our schools not make this a mandatory skill set? Social Networking and texting allow our children to communicate without ever saying a word. It provides a false sense of security, and they will say things they would never say in person.

It is CRITICALLY IMPORTANT that we build the "Communication" skill set in our children. This improves their social confidence and provides them with skills many of their peers will not possess. This increases their future marketability and chances for success.

There are 72 known traits that leaders possess. Not all leaders possess all 72, but there are 12 success traits that the most successful people in the world have in common. With the 4 I have outlined here, you can make a significant difference in the lives of your children.

I have worked with thousands of families just like yours, and I have seen parents and children improve the quality of their relationships. Children are better prepared for the challenges they will face in life. They develop Success Skills that greatly improve their focus, confidence, self-esteem, perseverance, integrity, communication skills, self-discipline and self-motivation. They possess an indomitable spirit that is impervious to bullying and negative peer pressure. They have become True Peak Performers in every aspect of their lives.

All of these lead to one thing, a greater chance to WIN!!!

ABOUT GARY

Master Gary A. Schill is the owner and chief instructor of Peak Performance Training Center. A Child, Family and Professional Coaching Program that provides Personal development and Success Coaching to children, families and professionals via the Martial Arts.

Gary is married to his beautiful wife Paula, and together they have 5 children ranging in age from 4-30. The 3 oldest boys all have black belts, his daughter will test for black belt in 2012 and his youngest son is working towards black belt sometime in the near future.

With more than 38 years of Martial Arts and Life Coaching experience. Master Schill has developed a revolutionary development program that is proven to develop a child's emotional, mental, physical and social intelligence, that will make them impervious to bullying and negative peer pressure. Understanding that most parents were never taught proper success traits or parenting skills, he developed a revolutionary Parenting Program (Parents as Coaches - "PAC"). The PAC program which is part of Master Schill's SuccessfulFamilies.com Program, provides parents with a new set of Success Secrets that will ensure their children possess life skills found only in the top 3% of the world's population.

Master Schill works with the local school districts teaching anti bullying, anti-negative peer pressure and abduction prevention techniques to more than 25,000 children annually. In addition, he provides parenting classes to local parents and various organizations.

Master Schill is the author of the Parents As Coaches Program, A Success Guide to Parenting that Your Parents Never Taught You. He can be seen on ABC, CBS, NBC and FOX for his parenting and life coach programs. Gary Schill has also been featured in USA Today and on the cover of Tae Kwon Do Times Magazine as well as a contributing editor for local newspapers and magazines.

For more information on these programs please visit SuccessfulFamilies.com or call 512.918.8921

CHAPTER 13

THE POWER OF CHOICE

BY MELINDA HUTCHINGS

Choice is a powerful concept.

In life, we have the freedom to choose who we invite into our world, the career path we'd like to pursue, where we are going to live, along with the simpler decisions such as what we are going to have for breakfast, or whether we choose to enjoy a cappuccino over a hot chocolate.

In business, we also have the freedom to choose:

- Premises
- Staff
- How the business is structured
- Systems and the process of implementation
- How we decide to position and market our products
- How we choose to handle our competitors
- The type of relationships we develop with our employees – whether it is: arms length, mutual respect, gratitude, offering guidance to help them reach their potential or providing opportunities for personal and professional growth
- Short and long-term goals that are in the best interests of the business

This freedom of choice will dictate our ultimate well-being because it influences the decisions we make as entrepreneurs – and thereby directly influences our internal sense of well-being.

My chosen field is helping people, especially women, teens and young adults, face and overcome hardship, and I have developed programs tailored to each market.

With regard to young people, my work encompasses a range of health-related issues – including eating disorders, anxiety and depression – as well as the effects of bullying and cyberbullying, family break-ups and relationship issues, and the negative behaviours that can stem from these issues. These behaviours are underpinned by insecurity and a lack of confidence.

There are enormous pressures on young people today. Peer pressure, societal pressure, parental pressure, the fear of disappointing mom and dad and being branded a failure. Then there's the pressure that young people place on themselves to please others and do the 'right' thing.

The concept that often evades young people is *how powerful choice can be* – and that once we give ourselves permission to let go of the judgments, opinions and beliefs of others, and have the courage to follow our own individual path with conviction, how liberating it is because we begin to open up to what is possible.

Rigidly adhering to the expectations of others can bring dissatisfaction and unhappiness. If a person instead makes an informed choice about how they decide to manage something, it can be an empowering experience.

This principle applies in business – rigid thinking and planning means an inability to adapt to change. Making a decision that is market driven, and having the confidence to change direction quickly, is what can make or break a business.

Freedom of choice is about making decisions that feel right. When this is incorporated into the decision-making process, as entrepreneurs we start to intuit what feels right for our business – which indirectly affects what we choose for ourselves *outside* of our business, because it influences how we 'do' life.

Intuition plays an important role in the decision-making process. Just as in day-to-day life, your inner voice, gut feeling, instinct – whatever you choose to call it – is there to guide you to make the decisions that feel right for you as an individual, in business – your business, the one that you have created from an idea and nurtured as it has evolved – the same principle applies. Whilst you can listen to market reports, monitor trends, conduct feasibility studies and dissect research analysis, once you have all the information, it will be your business aptitude coupled with instinct that will lead you to choose the direction your business will take next as it powers forward.

This is an exciting concept and one which has the potential to elevate the employer / employee relationship to another level. Whereby previously the employee presented their findings and a viable conclusion based on those findings, in this scenario, the employee could present a range of options as possible next steps, so that as the business owner, you get to brainstorm each option and then choose what instinctively feels right for your business. Of course logic will come into play, however, there is also the secret ingredient that cannot be quantified – and that is your intuition which drives the entrepreneurial spirit into action. What evolves from here will be exciting for you as a business owner and entrepreneur, because embracing freedom of choice means shifting a level up from the traditional ways of doing business.

The great thing is that once you 'get' how freedom of choice works, and how empowering it feels, you can adopt it in every area of your business – and it will overflow into your personal life too, because it offers a new way of 'being'.

In my business, I currently devote my time and energy to three major markets – women 25 and up, teenagers and people with eating disorders. The exciting thing is that, because my global message is about overcoming adversity, each market dovetails into the other, which means there is enormous potential to repurpose information and adapt speaking presentations and workshops accordingly.

Originally I intended to focus primarily on teen issues, however, due to the myriad of issues facing teens today, this diluted the effectiveness of my message.

Having worked in the eating disorders community for the past decade, this represents the foundation of my knowledge and expertise. The reason is because I have personal experience. I suffered with anorexia as a teenager and therefore have an intimate knowledge of what it is like to live with an eating disorder – the pain, struggle and the heartache – and what it takes to recover.

Sadly, according to the *Eating Disorders Coalition for Research, Policy, & Action,* eating disorders have the highest mortality rate of any mental illness. About 20 percent of all people with eating disorders will eventually die as the result of their illness. In those who suffer from anorexia, the numbers may be even higher. One-third of all patients will recover after an initial episode, one-third will experience a relapse, and one-third will suffer from chronic deterioration and multiple re-hospitalizations.

My successful recovery from anorexia fuels my passion for helping others recover because I have intimate knowledge of how desperately hard it can be. It is far from a linear process. My recovery was littered with lapses and relapses, and each time I thought I was making progress, I'd suffer a setback. At times I'd feel hopeless and convince myself I was doomed to a lifetime of torment. It was a constant, conscious effort to reframe my thought process and eventually I was able to let go of anorexia and move towards creating a happy and fulfilling life.

I am grateful for this, because not only do I have amazing inner strength, courage and self-love, I have the greatest gift of all – I know how to overcome adversity and therefore I am able to help others find the strength and courage to move forward, and in doing so, I am making a positive contribution to the world.

When it comes to the 'issues' affecting teenagers today, I have limited personal experience. The landscape is vastly different from when I was a teen. And many of these 'issues' revolve around the changes in technology. Teens are speaking a different 'language' in today's society. And although the pressures affecting young people today are not limited to eating disorders (which is why I broadened my work), I know instinctively how to talk to a teenager with an eating disorder, compared to one who is suicidal as a result of cyberbullying, because I have first-hand experience coupled with more than a decade speaking out to raise awareness of the early-warning signs. I also possess years of interviewing medical professionals and industry spokespeople, conducting research and holding in-depth discussions with people of all ages who have suffered and recovered from various forms of eating disorders.

With this in mind, I took a step back to evaluate my business structure. My program of focus is called *The Evolving Door*, a one-on-one transformational coaching program designed to empower teens to evolve to their highest potential, uncover hidden challenges that may be holding them back and/or sabotaging their sense of achievement, with the intention of showing them how to harness their potential so they feel motivated and inspired to soar towards their goals. This program has a spin-off workshop … *Evolutionise*. I also developed a post-treatment mentor program for people in recovery from eating disorders.

Initially, I had decided to drive *The Evolving Door* and *Evolutionise*, because my fourth book *It Will Get Better; Finding Your Way Through Teen Issues* had recently been published by Allen & Unwin.

I then considered my existing network of medical professionals who have known me for several years and are familiar with my work, who deal primarily with eating disorders. My first three books are about eating disorders, with the fourth broadening into other issues affecting teens (including a section dedicated to eating disorders). And I have a solid reputation and a profile in the eating-disorders community. It has taken me years of hard work to achieve credibility in this area – so I decided it made good commercial sense to leverage my profile and focus on promoting my post-treatment mentor program for people in recovery from eating disorders.

FREEDOM TO CHOOSE

The concept of 'freedom to choose' is something I apply to all areas of my life, including how I structure and manage my business.

After I launched my post-treatment mentor program it became obvious the market is very niche – so in the best interests of my business I chose to create a new direction and expand my marketplace. Because I have overcome so much adversity in my life, I decided to develop a 90-day empowerment program for women called *Turnaround* – to help them turn adversity into possibility and opportunity through encouraging self-love and self-belief.

So whilst my previous focus was teen issues and then eating disorders, after evaluating the return from those two markets and recognising how niche they were, it made commercial sense to develop a new program that reached a broader market so I can continue to help people overcome adversity and at the same time ensure my business keeps growing.

Turnaround Coaching is now my primary focus, and this is a brilliant example of why it is important not to be attached to ideas and expectations. Being open to adapting and improvising on a market-driven basis means that it's possible to change direction quickly in the best interests of the business by making affirmative choices.

THE EVOLVING DOOR

My secondary focus is *The Evolving Door*, which as I mentioned, is my transformational coaching program for teens. In the teen market, parents make the purchasing decision –therefore I also offer the opportunity to conduct sessions with parents and caregivers. This can be helpful if a parent requires insight into how to best communicate with their child – in order to support them through whatever challenge they are facing, without breaching confidentiality. In this way, I can support and empower the teen, whilst at the same time help the parent come up with strategies that will benefit their child – which adds a greater degree of value. The *Evolutionise* workshop is designed to compliment this program.

MENTORING PROGRAMS

My third area of focus is my post-treatment mentor program for people in recovery from eating disorders. I set about creating a strategic marketing plan for this program targeting health professionals in my network, and reworked my speaking presentation to adapt to three markets; teens/young adults; parents & caregivers; teachers & school counsellors. I developed two new workshops for teachers & school counsellors – one for the primary school market and the other for the secondary school market. Because the market is so niche, reworking my material to take these sub-markets into account gives me greater range in terms of audience, and therefore, as a speaker and presenter I am more versatile.

Another potential market is young aspiring writers, and in the future I intend to launch a mentor program to help young aspiring writers become bestselling authors. As this area evolves, I aim to become a talent scout and add another component to my business by becoming an agent representing young writers. Because I have four published titles, I have a strong network of contacts in the book publishing industry – so this is an area with the potential to experience significant growth. Through this avenue, I can indirectly continue to spread love and healing for the greater good through helping young writers share their message. Therefore, this component of my business will be in line with my platform.

CHOICE

Freedom of choice is powerful, because as I monitor which areas of my business experience growth, I can decide at any time to change direction or reinvent a program if something isn't working. I am not attached to the decisions I make because I understand that growing a successful business is a process of evolution, and as long as I stay abreast of industry trends, new products and potential exposures, my business will be fluid and responsive to my decisions. I also have the freedom to improvise and be creative about the ways in which I choose to market my products. Again, if something isn't working, I can change direction at any given moment, whether that means repackaging and relaunching a product, adapting a workshop for another market, or altering my marketing strategy.

The freedom to choose can be applied to any area of life. Having this freedom means I can decide how I want to achieve and maintain work/life balance. Instead of struggling to 'find' a balance between work commitments and my personal life, I 'choose' the balance that works best for my individual circumstances.

- Choice removes the rigidity of having a concrete plan which can cause stress if a new trend emerges or the market shifts.
- Choice brings the flexibility to prioritize when creating business plans, timelines and task lists.
- Choice is empowering and enhances well-being.

...And best of all, choice equals freedom.

ABOUT MELINDA

Melinda Hutchings is a media commentator, writer, speaker and mentor who is dedicated to helping people overcome adversity.

Having lost her teenage years to anorexia, Melinda is passionate about promoting positive body image as well as empowering young people to trust the voice that speaks from their heart to create a happy and fulfilling future.

She has written three books about eating disorders, including *Why Can't I Look the Way I Want? Overcoming Eating Issues* (Allen & Unwin 2009) which have helped thousands of people understand the dynamics of eating disorders from early warning signs through to the recovery process.

A high profile role model and mentor, Melinda was a Finalist in Cosmopolitan magazine's 'Fun Fearless Female 2009' awards in the category 'Inspirational Role Model'.

Her fourth book, *It Will Get Better; Finding Your Way Through Teen Issues*, was recently published by Allen & Unwin and aims to help teenagers find their way through the maze of emotions and challenges facing them today as well as providing a deeper level of awareness for parents and carers.

Having devoted several years to interviewing teens and young adults who have suffered through hardship, Melinda is attuned with the struggles young people face and believes that by increasing their knowledge and awareness, they will better be able to develop strategies to face and overcome challenging issues and recognize their enormous potential.

Melinda is an Ambassador for the Butterfly Foundation, the only national foundation for eating disorders in Australia, and the Life Changing Experiences Foundation which runs the SISTER2sister mentor program helping 'at risk' teenage girls around Australia break the cycle of trauma and develop strategies for personal change and growth.

Website: www.melindahutchings.com

CHAPTER 14

IT'S ALL ABOUT FREEDOM!

BY KATHY WENSEL

L et's talk about life! Smile! Always!

We do not know how long we have on this earth – so let's make the best of it.

We were all born free to be what we were supposed to be, so what are we all waiting for?

Who are we and what do we really, really want? What do we really believe? Have the courage to take the first step! The second, third, fourth, etc. steps come easier!

This Taurus was born at 7 months, weighed 2 lbs, 14ozs. and stayed in the hospital for 5 months. Daily, I was told that I was going to die. Only weighed 5 lbs. when I went home. Wanted to live my life! I am still here! Thank you, God!

We all have our trials and tribulations, it's how we handle them that shows people and ourselves what kind of character we have or do not have.

Sick a lot as a child, I adapted to it – homework, reading, TV, friends. My Dad also taught me poker and when I was better I learned to bowl. Still love Poker! Since I had time to think, I wanted to do a lot of different things in my life.

How many of us were bullied in school? Raise your hands! (Bullies turn to Harassers in the Workplace!) Always very thin, I looked like I did not eat. But, I did eat. I was healthier than I looked. Along came high school, Notre Dame High School in Moylan, PA (now the Pennsylvania Institute of Technology). I was so glad the building remained a School – beautiful grounds. Dances at St. James High School. Studies, travel, fun, modeling, ice-skating, dating and living life.

I was a Freshman in High School when Mom had George, and 18 months later Mom had Brian. My parents were so happy. I told my parents my two little brothers were going to do great things. George in Sports TV and Brian in Motion Pictures.

Knowing different opportunities were in the wings. Yes, I am also psychic. Sorry, psychics cannot pick lottery numbers. If I could, I would be living on a big compound by the sea.

I chose to work instead of going straight to college. Worked in the Financial World and The Pennsylvania Railroad. I was there when it changed to Penn Central. Loved working there. On my 21st birthday, my hair went from Honey Blond to Light Blond! A present to myself. People did not recognize me. Who is the new girl? So much fun.

Married in 1969, to the wrong man, but I had the right children. Go, Figure! Divorced in 1998. I did the Happy Dance through the Courthouse.

We all make mistakes. Forgive yourself and others. If I can forgive my ex-husband, you can also forgive people who hurt you. John F. Kennedy said, "Forgive your enemies, but never forget their names."

In 1977, I went back to school at Widener University. Political Science, Sociology and Management. Even made the Dean's List, full time and part-time, I graduated in 1984. Since I was older, I was a Mom to a lot of the students. Loved it!

Twenty-four years ago (1987), I had a health scare. My whole left side from the tip of my head to the tip of my toe went numb, I could not feel anything. I was in the hospital for a week, they did not know whether I had a Heart Attack or a Stroke. Luckily, it was Total Stress. This week gave me time to take a good look at what I was doing to me. Decided, I was not going to make a return trip to the Hospital. So, I decided to close my outside business, fired my partner, ran another business from home, and wrote four yellow legal-sized pages, front and back, of what I was not going to do again. A separate sheet of 1 to 10 that I was going to do for me. If I do not take care of me, I cannot take care of anyone else. This was the best Wake-Up Call I could have had. Thank you, God! Healthy ever since. Laugh Daily!

Keep the Faith, Hope and Love. Just keep going. Laugh Daily! Always loved to help people. I could be the female Larry King! Want to help everyone that I could, still do!

Sometimes, future-ex's needed a wake-up call. Decided to help a friend in Las Vegas, NV. Just a few people knew. Left a note and when my future-ex came home from work, he read the note. "When you are reading this note, we will be landing in Las Vegas" See you when we see you." We were gone 7 months. We still divorced in 1998.

Being psychic connects me with good and bad. In 1995 I did not want my brother, George Wensel, to go on a family reunion vacation at the Outer Banks, NC. I told him that I did not have a good feeling about this vacation. Take the boys to Disney World or anywhere else on the planet. George said he wanted the boys to get to know the cousins. While on vacation George drowned. It was a good thing my daughter was there to be with George's 2 sons (8 and 10). When I got the word, I hit the floor. George was VP of NEPINC in Pittsburgh. George, Technical Manager of the Olympics, Wimbledon, helped put together the Golf Channel, The Academy Awards, Dick Clark Music Shows, NASCAR, NBC, etc. George was inducted into the Sports Broadcasters Hall of Fame in NYC in 2007, and each year The National Academy of Television Arts and Sciences - Sports Emmy Awards instituted The George Wensel Technical Achievemnet Award.

Two weeks before 9/11/01, I called Washington, DC and spoke to Former Congressmen Curt Weldon, to let him know we were going to be hit. I was living in Las Vegas at the time, and knew that the East Coast was going to be hit. DC and NYC. When I flipped on the TV and saw the plane hit the second tower, all the bad feelings were gone and now what I was feeling since August 1, 2001, all the rest of the country was feeling now!! Don't want those feelings, ever again.

Then, very recently, two weeks before the earthquakes started in New

Zealand, went to Japan, Tonga, Burma, Myanmar. I said to my son that the Earth is going to start to Rock and Roll. He looked and said, Earthquakes? I said yes. They will keep coming around the World. My opinion is, *The Man Upstairs* is not happy with us!

Whenever you are in a situation and something does not feel right, it is your gut reaction, intuition, whatever you want to call it. Tell your family. If it really serious, call the police, news media. Works like a charm! Do not be afraid, just do it!

Karma can be good and bad. Stay positive always. I must have very good Karma. The Blessed Mother showed up in the middle of the night in my hallway, a few months after my Mom passed on in 1987. She said that my Mom was fine and happy. I knew but had to know for sure. How cool was that! Also, Padre Pio sat at my kitchen table about six months after Mom passed. He visited twice. How cool was that! My friend Roz was attacked in her apartment six months after my brother George passed. I had sent Roz a photo of George and she had it on her night table. Some guy broke into her apartment, when Roz looked at George's photo and said "help me." Just then, the guy on top of Roz was picked up and thrown against the wall. There was no one else in the room but Roz and the guy. There was a big hole in the wall and Roz was sure he had a few bones broken. Some things cannot be explained. Watch what happens when Karma comes back on people that really hurt other people. The Karma Van makes stops at people's houses all the time. Karma, Free Will and Destiny go hand in hand. I've never seen it fail.

Think about your life. Claim your freedoms! Do it now! Put together what you want to do for yourself. I see so many unhappy people; I see them all the time. There is so much going on in their lives. Life is so complicated for them. Their lives are chaotic. This is not good for their families, their health and their lives. Some people do not want to do what they are doing anymore. Hate their jobs, where they live, want out of their marriages. Life is simple: people make it complicated.

Get all of the clutter out of your life. Clean out your house, garage, and storage places. This helps you to focus on what you want. It's amazing when the clutter is gone – you are more clear-headed. Successful people do not have clutter in their lives.

Inner Peace means living without stress. Sylvia Browne always says, "Let go and let God." Do not complicate your life. Life is not complicated, it is easy. We (humans) are the ones who complicate our lives. Think about it.

Work on your finances. Lots of credit cards, cut them up. Get a debt consolidator to help sort everything out. Watch the show "Till Debt Do U$ Part." Call in and ask for help. Call Suze Orman, too. You will be back on track quickly.

Getting yourself unstuck is important for everyone. Change your environment. Do it early in the game. Let go of the fear. At any age it is never too late. Just do it. Take the first step and the next two, three steps make the next thousand steps easier and easier. Martina McBride sings a song called "Anyway." Nice song, listen to it. If you do not change you will never know what will happen. Here is one of my favorite quotes: "You are only stuck if you want to be."

Keep a positive attitude, work smart, and personal success is on the way. Be an individual, be unique, be different! Step up, stand your ground. Be fearless. Never Give Up! What makes you Unique? Make a list.

Be who you are and always tell the truth. I get in trouble for telling the truth. I tell the truth, anyway. I do not have an agenda and neither does the truth. I have seen so many people get in trouble for lying. When the truth finally comes out so many more people get hurt. What's the point of lying? Mark Twain said, "Always tell the truth; then you don't have anything to remember."

We are all survivors in our own way. Free yourself from what you do not want. Trust yourself and the people around you that have shown their trust to you. Remember, "You can pick your friends; but you cannot pick your relatives."

Another thing about Trusts: You do not have to be wealthy to put your money, house(s), cars, boats, other possessions into a Trust. This safeguards what you have. Check it out.

Get rid of what is not working for you. Do not wait as long as I did (twenty-nine years). Life is too short for anything else. It's just that simple! Think yourself free, soon you will be free. Freedom takes the fear away. People ask me why am I always happy? And I answer, "Because I am free."

Think about all the new things coming to you, new jobs, new locations, marriage or divorce. Make your dreams a reality for you.

Read this list – make your own

1. Who are you?
2. What do you really want?
3. What do you have to do to achieve this?
4. How long will it take?
5. Do you need extra schooling?
6. Apply for a new position?
7. Want to work from home?
8. Can I work at home and outside the home?
9. When to tell your employer?
10. Time to move onto your new life?

Have the Vision to do this for yourself and the ones that you love.

➢ What is your Bucket List?
➢ What do you want to see in the world?
➢ Jump out of a plane?
➢ Meet someone you always wanted to meet?
➢ Go to a Bon Jovi Concert? (Do not miss that one)
➢ What State do you want to see?
➢ Travel Oversees?
➢ Walk on a Beach in Hawaii?
➢ What do you want to learn? Golf, Bowling, Baseball, etc.

See the Olympics, Wimbledon?Think about it. Add to your Bucket List and then go do it. (I have been to 48 States – have Hawaii and Alaska left to visit.)

I am so glad I got the opportunity to share my thoughts and opinions with you. This is just a small part of my life.

My Motto is: "If it is not fun and Legal, I am not doing it."

Remember, "Life is not a Dress Rehearsal; It's the Main Event."

ABOUT KATHY

Kathy Wensel is a professional in travel, real estate(agent), retail and wholesale, marketing sales, commercials, model and teacher.

Now, an Entrepreneur, Radio Show Guest Across America, Author, Writer(Articles) Real Estate Investor, Speaker and TV Host.

Widener University – 1984 Graduate – Pollitical Science – Sociology – Management

Wrote "FREEDOM IS...A Book/Journal with a Twist." October 2008

One of America's PremierExperts®

Contact information:

ALL ABOUT FREEDOM TV SHOW HOST (Wednesday - 3PM EST) – http://www.realcoachingradio.net/content/live-studio-call-vip-show-hot-line-303-872-0503

Website: www.KathyWensel.com
Twitter.com/kathywensel
Facebook.com/kathleenwensel
Linkedin.com/kathleenwensel
kathywensel@blogspot.com

CHAPTER 15

WIN! WIN! WIN! AN ENTIRE BOOK ABOUT WINNING!

BY SUE FERREIRA

Why would all the authors in this book share enough passion about Winning, to take time out of their lives to write a chapter about our need to WIN?

I cannot vouch for the motivations of the other authors, but for me, this time is very ripe for such an important book to be published, so, please relax, settle down, put your feet up, and enjoy my story about why "Winning" is crucial to your future.

To use the words that start many stories, "Let us begin at the beginning…" with a definition of the very simple, three-letter but very powerful word – WIN.

First, there is the "Duh" definition, the obvious one, the achievement of coming first in a competition, …of being victorious, as in: "She won the Olympic Gold Medal" or, "Little Leaguers win again."

But there is also the wider, more comprehensive definition of "Win", which involves the emotive concepts of "Success" and "Struggle", of attaining goals and realizing dreams: "She struggled to overcome her handicap and won."

It is around this wider definition of Win that I wish to build my story.

As humans, we love stories. Perhaps more than "love stories," we *need* stories and particularly stories about "Winning." My younger daughter is a writer; one who has taught her rational scientist mother to appreciate the fundamental role of storytelling in our lives.

Sit back for a moment and cast your mind through all the stories, books, movies, myths, parables and epic poems that we humans have created. What is the dominant theme of the vast majority of these stories? They are about Winning.

They are the stories of the "Hero Journey", the struggle of an individual or group to overcome adversity and achieve success. They are the movie with the "Happy Ending" – where the hero or heroine, accompanied by their family, friends or followers, ride off into the sunset to stirring music, as the credits begin to slide up the screen. We, in the audience, our hearts full of elation and eyes all weepy, blow our noses and hurriedly put away our tissues as the lights go up, for fear that anyone should see our emotion. "Good movie," we say, as we shuffle out of the cinema, with the crowd. Yet, the story stays with us in our brains, and sometimes, we are shocked as we leave the cinema, to see that there is a real World still going on outside, so caught up have we been in the story. These good movie memories and stories can stay with us for many a day.

We need these stories. To be born human, we need to tell and hear stories. But also, remember every one of us is unique; there has never been anyone like us before and there never will be again, so we all have our own stories. To be human is also to have a story, and we need to tell stories about ourselves.

We know we all are on our own unique journey; we are all handed different cards from the genetically-shuffled pack at the beginning of our journey; we all have different advantages and different challenges, as we journey through our lives. We all trundle down the road of Life with varying degrees of focus and ambition; we can all control some events in our lives and have no control over others. Unforeseen events can come at us with no warning and sideswipe our lives, leaving us broken and crushed. We are then left to re-evaluate our lives, to decide whether we will "sink" and let events overwhelm us forever or "swim", and make decisions and take action to climb up and out of our despair, to join the successful winners on the Hero Journey. We have choices.

So why do I think Winning and The Hero Journey is so important at this particular time?

You will all have heard the saying, sometimes quoted as being a Chinese Curse...

"May you live in interesting times."

Most of us would probably agree, we are living in very "interesting" times. Perhaps all times are interesting, but periodically, we humans really mess things up and create big convulsions, causing great upheavals and instability, which bring us fear and angst. We become gripped with fear, as we sense we have lost control over events and our lives.

And I would suggest that many of us seven billion humans, in many countries around this beautiful planet, are currently feeling they have lost control of their lives. But, I will focus and limit this story to the Western World – the so-called "First World".

Over the past couple of years, we have experienced an economic earthquake and the after-shocks are still reverberating around the planet now – and will do so for years to come. All our hopes, dreams, plans and assumptions are now on wobbly quicksand. Good, hard-working citizens have lost their homes, their employment and their savings. We are still more fortunate than most in the "Second" and "Third" World countries, but as the mighty engine of the US economy slows, it slows the economies of all other countries, interlinked as we are these days in the "Global Village". The rapid unraveling of the world financial markets in 2008 brought that message home with a resounding thump.

So what to do?

And now, we return to my scientific upbringing, where all is either/or, or black/white, and we also return to the Hero Journey.

Although we are all affected by political, financial and social events outside our lives, ultimately, we can only be responsible for our own lives, and as choices present themselves to us, we usually have at least two options. Those two options are usually quite simple, either you say "Yes" or "No" to a choice that comes your way. You either move on or stay where you are, for not choosing is a choice.

We can decide to "sink", and like Chicken Little, run around yelling, "The Sky is Falling, The Sky is Falling," give way to panic and fear, then jump into bed, pull the covers over our heads and hope the problem will go away.

Or, …

We can individually each take a big deep breath, resolve to take responsibility for, and control of, our lives, and do whatever it takes to get us back on the rails and moving down the track again. We can make the decision not to change, to stay where we are, or we can choose to embark on our own Hero Journey to become a Success and a Winner.

If we choose to take the Hero Journey, our path will not be easy, and many on the journey will need support and advice. So we will have to come together to build groups and communities, to co-operate and help each of us solve our challenges and move towards our goals. There is always strength in numbers.

At times, this journey will seem too great a struggle and too frightening, making us long for the old comfort zone. But, if we take the risk and move out into new ventures, we will discover a ton of fun and satisfaction, as we experience our success and progress. The World is full of neat and wonderful people waiting to enter our lives, and the new knowledge and skills we acquire will excite, stimulate and enrich our lives.

However, we have a huge roadblock in our path, which must be overcome. Sadly, over the past several decades in Western society, it has become trendy to be dumb – think of the movie "Dumb and Dumber". Education, knowledge and using our brain to expand our minds have not been considered worthy and desirable goals. To be a Nerd and interested in learning is anything but trendy, and to quote Wikipedia – "Nerds are considered to be disproportionately males with very large glasses, braces, severe acne and pants highly lifted up, socially awkward and isolated."

Yet, the less-advantaged nations know that education is the key to their success and future. They are hungry for knowledge and many nations have overtaken the United States and other Western countries in their educational scores. These nations will be the Winners of the future, if we do not decide to pull our pants up high, start using our brains and become Nerds.

At the time of writing, the latest ranking figures for 2009 provided by the Organization of Economic Co-operation and Development of the 33 OECD countries are summarized in the table below, for the four largest English speaking countries of the United States of America, The United Kingdom, Canada and Australia.

Country	Reading Rank	Math Rank	Science Rank
Canada	3	5	5
Australia	6	9	7
United Kingdom	20	22	11
United States	14	25	17

Reference PISA/OECD Dec 2010

All Western countries are falling behind, yet with our wealth and advantages, we should be Top of the Class and #1, in all categories. The United States of America in particular has a very significant challenge, as unless these OECD statistics for the USA are rapidly improved, there is no future for the United States as a Leader or a Winner on the World stage.

EDUCATION IS EVERYTHING

IGNORANCE IS NOT BLISS

Sobering as these figures are, it is preferable to know them, accept them and take action. Burying our heads in the sand and remaining in ignorance will allow our nations to fall even further behind.

Every one of us in the West has a massive task ahead of us, to pull ourselves out of the mighty hole which we have steadily and complacently dug for ourselves, over the past few decades.

Now, not next year or the year after, but now, today, we have the challenge individually and nationally to choose whether we are a "Can Do" or "Can't Do" person or nation, whether we are "Action Takers" or "Couch Potatoes", whether we are Winners or Losers.

Just as "Necessity is the Mother of Invention," and improving our education is mandatory for our survival, we have no choice but to move out of our Comfort Zones and embrace "Nerdism."

To quote the Primo Nerd, Albert Einstein: –

"The definition of Insanity is doing the same thing over and over again and expecting different results."

We are already behind and must catch up and overtake the developing countries, but we have a Catch-22 situation. As the general knowledge base is so low, many are unaware of the degree to which we have fallen behind, so how do we reach out and awaken the unaware? A difficult question, but I think we need to develop a network of concerned citizens, who are willing to evangelize education and raise awareness of our plight.

All right, I know many do not bond with "The Bard of Avon", but for me, "He Da Dude!" His words are timeless and so elegant. These words below were written over four hundred years ago, about an event over two thousand years ago, yet they are apply perfectly to us today —

> There is a tide in the affairs of men,
> Which, taken at the flood, leads on to fortune;
> Omitted, all the voyage of their life
> Is bound in shallows and in miseries.
> On such a full sea are we now afloat,
> And we must take the current when it serves,
> Or lose our ventures.
>
> ~ *From the play Julius Caesar* by William Shakespeare
> (Act 4 Scene 3)

Who would agree "There is a tide in the affairs of men" and that the tide has turned?

Who feels "On such a full sea are we now afloat"?

Who wants to put their head in the sand of denial, and "Omitted, all the voyage of their life Is bound in shallows and in miseries"?

Who is prepared to take the risk and "taken at the flood, leads on to fortune" and know they "must take the current when it serves, Or lose our ventures"?

The choice is yours – will you decide to become a Winner?

Are you willing to take the necessary steps to become a Nerd?

We are all unique. Will you choose to leave your unique mark?

Every one of us, with our freedom, has the choice to take action to craft our own Hero Journey. Will you take the risk to embark on your Hero Journey?

Are you already a Winner?

Will you become a Winner?

Everyone has a story to tell – will yours be worth reading?

ABOUT SUE

Sue has been practicing as a physician for forty years, and is at the time of her life where she firmly believes that inside every older person is a younger one wondering what happened.

Born in 1947, in England, making her a "Leading Edge Boomer", she has been ever conscious of and interested in, the social consequences of being part of this bulging demographic.

Early in her life, she made the decision to make her career in medicine, and accepted that by concentrating her studies on the basic sciences, she would have to let go of her primary love of history and the social sciences. Sue's love of history and its relationship with the social sciences has continued throughout her life.

She completed her medical training at University College Hospital, London, having experienced the tumultuous years of the social activism of the Hippie era in the UK and in the US – again the Boomer Generation. She sub-specialized as an anesthesiologist and in 1976, left strike-bound, pre-Thatcher England for a new life in Canada. The provinces of Alberta and British Columbia have been her home ever since, and she currently resides in Victoria, British Columbia. Sue also knows the United States very well, having spent a significant time south of the 49th. She has visited every state and has a daughter, who lives in New York.

After a divorce at 60 years of age and beginning a new life, a year later in 2008, she was watching the financial meltdown and realized with deep sorrow, how many folk, especially in the United States, were facing and suffering financial ruin – through foreclosure of their homes, loss of employment and seeing their savings vaporize in front of their eyes.

Always interested in the fortunes of the Boomer demographic, Sue realized many years ago, the challenges that would face our society, when such a large cohort began to retire. The financial collapse of 2008 has accentuated these difficulties, not only for Boomers, who have no time left to re-build their losses, but also for their children and grand-children, who will inevitably be affected both by their elders' difficulties as well as their own.

Having always been in a caring profession and wishing to make a difference in her later years, Sue has built the community of Boomer-Bucks to offer support and advice for Boomers (and anyone else), who are realizing their retirement plans are on hold, and who need to clarify their life and financial priorities and to transition or re-direct to new ventures.

www.Boomer-Bucks.com

CHAPTER 16

STICKY NOTE TO-DO SYSTEM

UTILIZE STICKY NOTES AND STOP WASTING YOUR TIME RE-WRITING YOUR TO-DO LISTS.

BY NANCY KRUSCHKE, CPO®

"HELP, how do I keep track of all of my to-do's?" This is by far one of the top questions I hear daily. "Should I use my computer? …a PDA? …to-do list on paper? …What is the 'BEST' system?" What I tell you is that there is no "best" system, no right or wrong system only one that works for you. An electronic medium works great for some people, but many of us are tactile, we need or want to touch and feel our to-do list; me included.

Over twenty years ago, when I started working in the financial planning industry, I would write my "to-do" list on a sheet of paper. As I completed a task, I would put a squiggly line through the item. After a couple of days, it was hard to see what still needed to be done and would then spend time re-writing the list. And since I had everything on one sheet of paper, those items that didn't need to be done today or this week were re-written many times. It always seemed like a waste of time to re-write and re-write.

I can remember how excited I was to get a computer at my desk. I didn't have to sign up for a time slot, I didn't need to share, and I could work on it anytime I wanted. Hallelujah! And it also meant that I could STOP re-writing my to-do list over and over and over. The word processing program wasn't very user friendly, but at least I could easily update my 'to-do's' and group like items together.

It was easy at first to type up my to-do list. I would print it out, cross items off, and write new items on the printed page. Every couple of days I would update the computer version. This printed computer list was a bit neater and tidier than the handwritten sheet, but I was still re-writing and still cumbersome.

Over the years, I have tried many times to remove the scraps of papers and sticky notes from my desk and computer monitor by putting everything into a computer program (Word, Excel, Outlook task list, Palm task list, the list goes on), but all that accomplished was to clear all the papers off my desk and monitor, and put my 'to-do's' in a black hole, the computer, that I never looked at again. At first it felt really good to get everything in one place, but I soon had a new set of lists and post-its all over my desk, office, calendar, house, car, etc.

After ten years in the financial planning industry, assisting financial advisors in being more efficient and organized, it was time to move on to assist other business owners with office organization, productivity, and efficiency. As a Certified Professional Organizer®, I am always searching for solutions to help my clients and myself be more organized, more productive, and save time. So finally several years ago, I decided to stop fighting the sticky notes and paper lists all over my desk and start using them as an organizing and productivity tool to my advantage.

Using sticky notes for to-do lists is a bit controversial in the organizing and productivity industry. Many systems encourage you to get rid of the sticky notes, put everything in one location, the computer. But since 2001, I personally have used the sticky note 'to-do' system with success and I have shared it with my clients, friends, family, and class attendees with overwhelming success.

SET UP YOUR STICKY NOTE 'TO-DO' SYSTEM TODAY:

SUPPLY LIST:

1. Small 1½"x2" sticky notes
2. Square 3"x3" sticky notes
3. Paper 8½x11 or 5½x8½plain paper or card stock / white or colored paper
   (I personally use 5½x8½ size paper)
4. Pen, pencil, or marker

Once you have collected the supplies, you can begin setting up your personalized sticky note 'to-do' system.

1. Start with a piece of paper to put the sticky notes on.
2. Stick the small 11/2"x2" sticky notes on the page, 10 fit nicely. Only place sticky notes on one side, you don't want to flip the page over.
3. Write your 'to-do's' on the sticky notes. Each sticky note ONLY gets one to-do item.
4. There are four areas on each sticky note: (see picture)
   a. Date – the date you write the to-do
   b. Deadline – when does this items need to be completed
   c. To-do – what it is that needs to be done
   d. Category / Grouping – call, e-mail, project name
5. As you complete each to-do, remove it from the page and toss it (other options listed below).

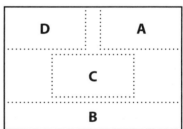

PAPER TO PUT STICKY NOTES ON:

Choosing what size and colored paper to stick the sticky notes to is a personal choice. As I mentioned above, I personally use 5½x8½ size paper, typically I just fold a piece of junk paper in half. It helps to not blend in with other papers on my desk.

Use a heavy card stock to give your list more sturdiness.

Also, using different colored pages for different projects or types of activities will help them stand out. Example: I use green paper for all of the items that I need to update on my website. It makes it easy to locate when I need to add a website update task.

It is OK to have multiple pages with sticky note to-do's. Broken down by project or similar to-do actions such as calls, notes, e-mails, web updates, staff meeting, etc.

Some of my clients have found that using a manila or colored folder and placing the sticky notes on the inside reduces the chance of them being torn off and lost. Example: Purple folder for the Annual Banquet Project. The inside top left holds sticky notes regarding the location. The inside bottom left holds sticky notes containing to-do's about the food. The inside top right silent auction to-do's and bottom right speaker to-do's.

By using folders, this also give you a place to put other papers pertaining to that project and keep all of your items together; meeting notes, quotes, samples, etc.

When breaking down projects into small pieces or individual action items, use one sticky note per action and one page or folder per project.

STICKY NOTES:

The 1½"x2" sticky notes fit will allow you to put 10 to-do's per page on the 5½x8½ paper. Sometimes, you might find that an 8 ½ x 11 page is needed and then you might want to use the 3"x3" sticky note. The 3"x3" sticky notes allow more space to describe the task that needs to be done.

ONE TO-DO PER STICKY NOTE:

It is important that you ONLY put one 'to-do' per sticky note. If you put more than one it's just like having the full page 'to-do' list that you cross stuff off. You will have to re-write those items that you didn't get done.

The only exception to this is when you use the sticky note 'to-do' list for your errands. If you have multiple things to pick up at a store, write them all on ONE sticky note.

AREAS ON THE STICKY NOTES:

1. Date – the date you write the 'to-do'
   a. Write the date in the top right hand corner
   b. Very important, put month-date-year (01-01-11)
   c. When you review your list, you will easily be able to see the age of your action items

2. Deadline – when does this items need to be completed
   a. Write the deadlines on the bottom center of the sticky note
   b. It is easy to see
   c. Helps when determining when to schedule tasks

3. **'To-do'** – what it is that needs to be done
   a. Write in the middle of the sticky note
   b. Be as specific as possible with the 'to-do' / action item that needs to be done
   c. The more specific you are the easier it is to remember what you need to do without straining your memory
   d. You may also want to put where additional information is located, if you have any to assist you in completing your 'to-do'

4. Category / Grouping – call, e-mail, project name
   a. Write this in the top left corner
   b. Writing the category or grouping can help you to easily identify like items
   c. When you focus on like items, you are more efficient and can get more to-do's done

USING THE SYSTEM

Now that you have started putting each individual 'to-do' item on an individual sticky note, you are probably wondering, "What's next? How do I manage this system?" Here is how I use the system successfully.

1. Schedule time on your calendar daily to
   a. Review your sticky note to-do's
   b. Block time on your calendar to DO the to-do's; tomorrow,

this week, this month, whatever is appropriate.

2. Arrange your 'to-do's' on the page in the order you will do them

3. If you have project pages
   a. Review those 'to-do's' also
   b. Block time to work on the project

4. During the day as new 'to-do's' / action items come up, write each one on a sticky note and place it on your page. If the 'to-do' is about a particular project, place it on that project page

5. As you complete a 'to-do', toss it
   a. If that 'to-do' is significant to your performance review, put it in that file. When you are working on your quarterly review, you will have your sticky notes to remind you of the tasks you did that meet your quarterly goals.
   b. A few of my clients will designate a spot on their desk to put the done sticky notes so that they can see their accomplishments at the end of the day
   c. You could also stick them on the backside of the page

OTHER WAYS TO USE STICKY NOTES

1. I use the sticky note pages for my errands. On a daily basis I set up one page for the errands or meetings that I have that day. Example:

Store 12-10-10	Meeting 12-10-10
Target Return shoes Buy batteries	8:00 am Smith
Store 12-10-10	Meeting 12-10-10
Post Office Mail Packages	11:00 am Lunch with Sue Discuss seminar

This helps me to stay on task and I then remove the 'done' items and toss them.

2. Manila folder labels – easily label manila folders with 3"x3" sticky notes
   Quick to label
   Easy to remove
   Easy to change if you have the wrong name

3. Hanging folder plastic tabs – quick and easy with 1½"x2" sticky notes
   Labels are important to increasing productivity
   Using sticky notes makes it easy to label hanging files

4. Projects – write each individual task for the project on individual sticky notes
   Group like tasks together
   Schedule time in your calendar to work on the project

KEYS FOR SUCCESS

There are five things that will increase the success of the sticky note 'to-do' system.

1. Scheduling at least 15-30 minutes daily to review your 'to-do's'
2. Only putting one 'to-do' per sticky note
3. Blocking time in your calendar to DO your 'to-do's'
4. Actually doing your 'to-do's' when they are scheduled
5. Stop putting sticky notes in other locations

You might be asking "Won't this be just like other 'to-do' lists I've tried?" This is a valid question and like everything, there is no one system that will work for everyone.

This system has worked for me for more than ten years. I have also shared this with my clients and seminar attendees for over ten years and I continue to hear and receive e-mail success stories on how well this system works when no other system would. Give it a try and see if the sticky note to-do system will work for you.

ABOUT NANCY

Successful Organizing Solutions (S.O.S.) was conceived as a business in 1999. Founder and owner Nancy Kruschke created the company to help individuals and entire businesses increase their effectiveness and efficiency through organizing skills and practices.

After completing her Bachelor of Arts in Business Management from North Central College in Naperville, Illinois, Nancy began her organizing career with ten years of professional experience at American Express Financial Advisors. She earned her Certified Financial Planner Designation and in her first year assisted in doubling the district manager's business and increased the business production of each advisor within the district. Nancy traveled throughout Wisconsin, Northern Illinois, and Upper Michigan training advisors and their staff in Practice Management to help them increase their business through the use of effective systems, client databases, and efficient paper and computer files.

Nancy's passion for organizing led her to start her own business - Successful Organizing Solutions - (S.O.S.) so she could focus exclusively in this area. Nothing puts a bigger smile on her face than customizing the right tools, techniques, tricks, and systems for a client! She offers coaching, consulting, and speaking in the following areas: productivity, time management, paper files, computer files, office layout and organization, e-mail management, and ACT! contact management training.

Certifications include Certified Productivity Coach (CPC) and Certified Professional Organizer® (CPO®). *Nancy is a member of the National Association of Professional Organizers (NAPO), a founding member of the Wisconsin Chapter of NAPO, International Association of Productivity Coaches (IAPC), and several chambers of commerce.*

She is the co-author of "Organizing Your IEPs" and an organizing tip book "Action Organizing Tips for Your Office—Ways to Get and Stay Organized." Nancy appears regularly as the organizing expert on local TV and radio stations in Wisconsin. She has also participated in an episode of A&E Hoarders.

To learn more about Nancy Kruschke and Successful Organizing Solutions (S.O.S.) and to receive organizing and productivity information, visit www.SOS-organize.net or call 1-866-747-5300.

In May 2007, Nancy passed the inaugural Certified Professional Organizer® exam and became one of a small group of organizers to become CPO®'s. Certification is a voluntary, industry-led effort that benefits the members of the organizing profession, as well as the public. It recognizes those professionals who have met specific minimum standards; and they must prove through examination and client interaction that they possess the body of knowledge and experience required for certification.

In February 2010, Nancy participated in a three-day intensive productivity-training workshop. As a result, she is one of a select few who have become Certified Productivity Coaches (CPC) across the USA and Internationally. This certification requires continued commitment to ongoing education and practice of the productivity principles.

CHAPTER 17

TO WIN YOU MUST FOLLOW YOUR PATH

BY HOLLIS COLQUHOUN

W hen I was about 40 years old, life took a few very drastic but fateful turns. My husband and I were partners at a Wall Street brokerage firm, working on a trading desk that was chaotic, exciting, rewarding and all men except for me. We had an extremely successful professional partnership, raised three lovely girls, and enjoyed renovating historic homes. However, one day, while at my desk, I bent down to take paperwork out of my briefcase and as I tried to straighten up, excruciating pain shot through my lower back - a disc had exploded. My life wasn't a bed of roses anymore, it was a bed of nails. Ultimately I had to have two back surgeries over two years to get it fixed.

After the surgeries and therapy, I was waiting in a doctor's office, flipping through a magazine, and found an article about the therapeutic value of practicing Karate. It explained that Karate movements are circular and graceful; therefore all parts of your body get stretched and strengthened with little stress. As it turned out, the author of the article had gone through the same surgery I did. He became a student of Karate, eventually earned his black belt, and believed that the Karate training had totally transformed his physical and spiritual being. Shortly thereafter, I was at a kindergarten graduation party for my daughter where I met a friend whose son was also graduating. His mother informed me that he was having some behavioral problems, but Karate was transforming him into a stronger, more respectful and confident boy.

I must admit, martial arts always fascinated me as a teenager, so I took those two events as a sign. I did further research on Karate and a few days later walked into a *dojo* ("the school"), met *Sensei* Steve ("the teacher") and experienced my first Karate class. I was given a white *gi* ("uniform") with a white belt to tie around my waist as a representation of purity and innocence – an empty slate. I found my 40 year-old self once again surrounded by all males, but this time they were under the age of 18 and wearing a variety of different colored belts: yellow, green, blue, red, brown and black. Each color represented a different level of achievement with black being the highest. That day I felt like a five-legged polar bear thrust in a sea of puffins.

There's a saying in Karate: " On your journey, the first step is the hardest." Well, my first steps definitely felt foreign and clumsy, but I persevered; *Sensei* Steve was a talented and patient teacher. After one month of classes I was hooked, and six years later earned my black belt.

Over the next few years, many obstacles got in the way of pursuing Karate. I had several more surgeries, a knee repair, a neck fusion and I broke my ulna in half blocking a kick while sparring (the *Sensei*) during class. I had several changes in instructors and schools; I even had to change martial arts disciplines when the *Sensei* moved away and the *dojos* were shut down. At one point I switched from Karate to Tae Kwon Do to work with a great teacher. Tae Kwon Do has very similar *katas* but the moves are much more linear, not circular like in Karate. I was excited to join the discipline but realized I would have to relearn the basics, shut down my muscle memory and retrain my arms and legs. Like the first day at *Sensei* Steve's *dojo*, I felt awkward in the new *dojang* (Korean for "*dojo*") surrounded by many high-ranked teenage boys and men. Regardless of the obstacles, I found that my martial arts training kept me sane, patient and focused on restoring my body.

Around the same time, my husband and I filed for divorce. I had retired from Wall Street and he was having a difficult time mentally and professionally - a mid-life crisis. He became infatuated with a friend of mine who was helping me run our church youth group, while her three sons were good friends with my three daughters. It was a traumatic time for everyone, including the congregation.

On top of that, my girls were teenagers, developing very active social lives - meaning BOYS times THREE - which kept me on my toes and often sleep-deprived. It was Tae Kwon Do that gave me the strength and ability to persevere. I must confess, a few times I dreamt of throwing a round kick or ridge-hand strike at one of my daughter's boyfriends or into my Ex's midsection, but of course, in reality, I knew that wasn't the true martial arts philosophy.

As the shock of the divorce started to wind down, I moved into a self-defense mode. Using the teachings of martial arts on maintaining a healthy mind, body and spirit, I was able to stay strong for my daughters. It was also a great comfort to know I could protect them physically if need be, since their father was no longer living with us. With a clearer mind, I gathered together all of my marital financial information, and began to think about how I could structure a settlement agreement that would allow me to rebuild my life. Luckily, my husband and I were able to come to a financial agreement that enabled me and my girls to move forward.

Once I became independent, I decided to re-enter the workforce as a credit counselor for a nonprofit counseling agency. Over the next several years, I spoke to thousands of people who were in serious financial trouble. There was a pattern; the majority of people I spoke to were women, and usually, divorce or death of a spouse left them totally unprepared to deal with their financial situation. I was amazed and saddened to find out that, in most cases, the woman had no real financial education and someone else controlled her financial life.

A co-counselor at the agency named Antoinette became a close friend. We both had survived painful divorces, and spent a lot of time thinking about how we could help our female clients. After much consideration, we decided to write a book that would serve the overwhelming number of women who needed financial help. We designed the book to be a simple guide teaching women how to manage their personal finances, understand their worth, and financially prepare for the divorce process. The book, titled ***Women Empowering Themselves: A Financial Survival Guide,*** took us a year and a half to put together. It generated excellent reviews from professionals in the finance and divorce industries, and the women who read the book felt more confident and financially aware.

From that point on, I was convinced my mission in life was to help women become financially educated and empowered. Knowing the devastation of divorce firsthand, I felt a need to help women become aware, rebuild and take control of their lives, *before* they signed on the divorce agreement dotted line.

I have created a one-on-one counseling program to help women put their finances in order, and I broadcast a weekly web-cast radio show called Wednesday Afternoon F.E.S.T., which stands for Financial Education and Survival Training. My goal is to increase consciousness and financial awareness, and teach a few basic self-defense moves to help women become more physically empowered, too.

I feel passionately about my new career, my hobbies, and helping others. The positive forces in my life are my daughters, financial empowerment, and martial arts. I have found that remaining positive and empowering others has really empowered me, and I deeply believe that maintaining a strong connection between mind, body, spirit and money will lead to success.

So what exactly are the steps that I've taken to design and rebuild my life, and how can you follow a similar path to your own empowerment?

Your pathway to success will consist of four main stages: understanding your worth, finding your purpose, moving toward your goals, and building a successful life. As you progress along your path there may be hardships, and the road may not always be smooth, but if you persevere and believe in your mission, you will become a more passionate, thoughtful, and purposeful entrepreneur.

So, the two big initial questions are: What are your interests and abilities? What do you have to offer your clients? Your business efforts should help people or provide something they want and you must be comfortable and confident with yourself, if your business is going to grow.

Create some long-term and short-term personal as well as career goals. The best way to begin is to identify your long-term wants and dreams. Then anticipate your long and short-term needs. With long-term goals that reflect your wants and needs, you can create short-term goals. These short-term goals will act as stepping-stones on the path to your future success.

One of the basic tenets of Karate is to "be prepared" (I think the Boy Scouts snatched this). Starting your new endeavor with a plan will give you the route to accomplish your goals, and the means to deal with whatever adversity comes your way. For some people PLAN is just a four-letter word. In reality it's an important component of success and forms the foundation for your business and overall life. To maintain the quality of life you desire and achieve your goals, a plan is absolutely necessary.

Consider the following questions. Your answers should help define and develop your business strategy as well as your life plan:

1. *What are your strengths, interests and skills?* Consider your talents and strengths and figure out what really makes you happy. Make an actual list. Think about what you've done in the past that has given you the biggest sense of pride and satisfaction. Even if you didn't have a paying job but volunteered or managed a household, what were you good at and what were you able to accomplish?

2. *What makes you unique?* No two people are the same. Years of experiences have shaped you in a particular way, and that makes you special. Having survived through adversity whether it was emotional, physical, mental, or financial, you have a powerful voice to guide others going through the same experience. If you've succeeded at something - a quest, a project, an invention, a product – you can show others how they can achieve similar success.

3. *What career will showcase your talents and be well received?* How can you package yourself and use your talents to create a thriving business? What exactly could you teach, offer or sell? Putting the answers to the first two questions together,

how could a company, organization or group of people learn and benefit from your teachings and experience? Do some research, understand your market, and identify a need that isn't being addressed. How could you fill that gap or put a different spin - your own unique spin - on an existing product or program? Perhaps you could develop a signature program, create a special product or write a book that would enrich other people's lives.

4. *How can you successfully follow that career path?* What would it take to start your business and financially sustain it? Most people who have the entrepreneurial spirit get very excited about the product or outcome and don't focus on the process - the business planning and financial considerations. It's a ton of work to create and maintain a company on your own, and many businesses fail in the first year because practical planning hasn't occurred. At the counseling agency I spoke to many new entrepreneurs who had enthusiasm but no business plan and relied on their credit cards for initial expenses, hoping that business would boom within a short time. Most of the time it didn't and they were left with a mountain of debt. This isn't a good plan. You need to give a tremendous amount of thought and preparation (there's the "be prepared" mandate again) in order to build a solid business model.

5. *What are your financial resources?* It may seem like an odd question, but you can't begin a new business or restructure an existing one unless you know what all of your financial resources are and what your needs will be. Is your business plan realistic, and how much financing, if any, will you need? Is your product or service strong enough to generate the necessary revenue to handle the monthly expenses? For most small business loans, lenders require a personal guarantee, and as I mentioned in Step 4, you might be personally on the hook if the business can't support the loan payments. Therefore, it's important to know your assets and liabilities, (your net worth), and understand what you can personally support or afford to gamble financially, before implementing a plan that you believe will lead to success.

With the answers to these five steps, you can more clearly see and understand your pathway to success. Having a purpose and a plan will empower you to do great things. Everyone has weaknesses and hurdles to jump over, but as an entrepreneur armed with a good plan, you will have the knowledge and ability to help others and to build a successful business. Using your talents and uniqueness, you can provide something to the world that no one else can. As Bruce Lee said, *"The function and duty of a quality human being is the sincere and honest development of one's potential."*

ABOUT HOLLIS

Hollis worked on Wall Street for 20 years and was one of the first female institutional bond traders. She later became an Accredited Financial Counselor for a nonprofit credit counseling agency and counseled thousands of clients around the country, most of whom were women in financial trouble after divorce or death of a spouse, because they had no clue how to manage their finances. Hollis wanted to rectify this situation, so she and a co-counselor wrote the Amazon Bestseller: **Women Empowering Themselves: A Financial Survival Guide** to give women a basic understanding of net worth, budgeting, saving, credit reports, goal-setting and resources.

Currently, Hollis is working on a special program for women who are just coming out of a marriage; one that will empower them to think more clearly and get financially educated and aware, before meeting with their lawyer and financial adviser. Hollis is passionate about personally and financially empowering women; she writes articles for blogs and magazines such as such as More, WE and Self magazines. Hollis is also a martial artist - she holds black belts in both Karate and Tae Kwon Do.

CHAPTER 18

I <u>TEACH</u> HEALTH … I DO NOT <u>TREAT</u> DISEASE

BY DR. PHIL SELINSKY

Le Chatelier's Principle of Chemical Physics:

"If a change is imposed on a system at equilibrium, the position of the equilibrium will shift in a direction that tends to reduce that change."

In English, this means that the Universe is always in balance. If we place Nature out of balance, Nature will return itself to balance (sometimes with a vengeance and possibly to our personal detriment).

IT'S NOT WISE TO "MESS" WITH MOTHER NATURE!

I am presently in my seventies and am experiencing none of the physical difficulties that many of those in my age group are suffering from at this point in time. This was not always the case.

I attribute my present state of health to the fact that earlier in my life, I changed my "conditioned" behavior (the way that I was taught), to one that would *support* the laws of physics with respect to how my body works, from a lifestyle of the *violation* of the laws of physics, which had resulted in a state of dis-ease for most of my early life.

In addition to going through all the usual childhood diseases, I had a couple of "extras" that I would like to share with you here that might help you to think about your own life and health issues and that of your children.

I'm the eldest of seven children. We grew up at the end of a dirt road on the outskirts of northwest Detroit that at that time was called Southfield Township. Zip codes were not invented yet. Our mailing address was Detroit 19, Michigan. Our "party-line" phone number was "Southfield 3244".

I mention these details just to give a little flavor to the fact that we lived meagerly without a lot of frills. My parents did all that they knew how to do at the time to see that all of us kids had what we needed to make it to adulthood.

As I mentioned, with seven hungry growing kids to feed, there weren't too many choices for good wholesome food. We ate a lot of filler-type foods like macaroni, white bread, spaghetti, and hamburger, and Kool-Aid ... with lots of sugar.

We all learned how to bake cakes and cookies ... with a lot of sugar ... and food coloring (chemical dyes). We ate fairly well in the summer with food from the garden, and in the winter we ate what we canned in the fall. The canning process, of course ... uses a lot of sugar, ...and it's all cooked.

The bottom line here is that we ate a lot of what today I would call absolute junk. Consequently, at age nine, I developed an infection in my appendix and had to have surgery.

At age 13, just as I was getting ready to start high school, I experienced a rather severe flu that led to an ear infection that progressed to become mastoiditis – the entire mastoid bone behind my left ear had turned to mush and had to be removed. During the surgery to remove the infected mastoid bone, the surgeon accidentally severed my trigeminal nerve. This was before antibiotics were used for every malady imaginable as they are today. When I woke up after the surgery, I couldn't move or feel my face on the left side at all. They went back in to repair the nerve by splicing a piece of nerve from my neck into the damaged area.

It took a little over two years before I could eat or drink anything without having to hold my lips together with my fingers. I had to lie on my left side so that the pillow would hold my eye shut so that I could go to sleep at night. On a lighter note, I told the girls that I had to kiss them twice because I could only give half a kiss at a time.

I know that other people have much more severe situations to endure in their life, but at the time, for me, this was an emotionally devastating experience. I was about 17 before I could feel anything on the left side of my face at all. It was totally numb for quite a while. Now, sixty years after the surgery, I have about 95% sensation back and maybe 60% muscle control.

I had severe acne all over my body. Huge pustules would erupt on my face and back and chest. Many times the pustules would break open and soak through my shirt. That was rather embarrassing. This lasted until I was about 26 (when my life changed).

I had blinding migraine headaches almost every day. I had chronic low backaches. I frequently felt nauseous in the morning until I got going. I needed 10 to 12 hours of sleep every night. I had horrible body odor. My breath stank. My feet stank. I couldn't take off my shoes in a room without everyone running for the windows.

And of course, almost every tooth in my head was filled with mercury laden "silver amalgam" fillings …that probably explains my bizarre behavior now, as well as throughout my whole adult life. Mercury is a toxic heavy metal that does in fact short-circuit brain cells.

The good part is that all those experiences got me to where I am today, along with the knowledge and insight into my own as well as other people's behaviors and reactions.

Now when I hear people tell me "I can't do this or that because …(you fill in the blanks)." I can say that I've been there and done that, and I know that you can do it because I've done it.

I know most of the feelings and cravings that people experience in life, because I have experienced the same feelings and cravings myself and have found out how to beat it all.

Over the years I have found myself repeating the same stories and lessons that I have learned over and over again – until I could relate them in my sleep. So in the interest of preserving my vocal chords and taking advantage of the opportunity to reach many more people with the same or similar problems, I have written a book. As a matter of fact, I have written a three-book series.

Volumes I, **II** and **III** of this "**THE HUMAN MACHINE … A Trouble Shooter's Manual**" series explains some of my discoveries over the years – that shed some light on the reasons that this Human Machine behaves the way it does.

Volume I explains some of the structural and conditioning influences that shape our view of life and consequently our behavior in society, which usually creates conflicts, which creates stress, which results in **dis – ease** of some sort.

Volume II describes how blood chemistry drives our behavior within our structural capacity, of course. It also shows how and why we develop conditions of **dis – ease** because of distortions of our blood chemistry. We can then easily see how getting back into balance takes the pain away.

Volume III focuses on the physical sources of the digesting disturbances that begins with the "hiatal hernia phenomenon", which leads to all of the **dis – ease** profiles that cause most of all the aches and pains in our lives, including cancer, heart disease and diabetes.

With this book series, I attempt to show that this **"Human Machine"** that we drive around for a time here on this planet is designed to "run" relatively trouble free. It's designed to adjust itself to its environment and to fix itself if it gets damaged along the way …if we don't sabotage it first, that is.

I have to emphasize here that the body is _designed_ to do all these maneuvers. However, if some parts become distorted or damaged along the way, or if the fuel supply is inadequate or tainted, this Human Machine will be thrown out of tolerance range, or "ease of function," and a state of "**dis – ease**" will ensue.

Volume III of this series will talk more about the structural distortions in the mechanism itself that can result in malfunction symptoms, rather than the actual chemistry of the fuel supply.

I deal with our fuel supply in **Volume II**.

In **Volume I** of the series, I discuss pre-birth and post-birth programming and conditioning, which conflicts with genetic structure, which in turn results in caustic stress, and which typically ends up as symptoms of "dis-ease".

I spent most of my 20's and 30's as a mechanical engineer, designing machines and tools. I think that that experience gave me a fairly decent grasp of how machines work and how chemistry operates on this planet. I have since integrated this engineering knowledge with my Naturopathic training that I acquired in 1980.

Using this knowledge, I have "back-engineered" my past life experiences and can now easily explain the mechanics and the physics behind all the health difficulties that took place in my growing years. I have since come to the realization that my job in this physical space and time, is that of a translator...**I translate pain and discomfort into English**.

Pain is really our best friend. It tells us when we are "in dangerous territory". Pain is not necessary, but it is inevitable. If we do not pay attention to subtle signals from the body that we are "veering off track," "the message" gets louder and more emphatic.

If we continue to disregard the "communication" from the body, organs and organ systems become dysfunctional or shut down altogether. If crucial organ systems shut down, we die. The body must function with "ease" and balance. This is called homeostasis. If the body experiences a "lack of ease" or "dis-ease" for whatever reason, something must be done to re-establish homeostasis.

The body is programmed to automatically adjust itself to return to "normal" balanced behavior. If this machine (the body) has been "pushed" past its design capacity so that it cannot return to balance by itself, sometimes a little "outside'" help may be necessary to get it "back on track."

This "outside help" may consist of concentrated foods, herbs, touch therapies, including massage and acupressure/acupuncture, homeopathic remedies, or in cases of severe imbalance, drugs may be necessary to force the body back into the range of homeostasis.

Western Medicine has given this lack of homeostasis or unbalanced condition a name. They call it "disease". As a matter of fact, they have coined an infinite number of names for the lack of balance or homeostasis as this unbalanced condition manifests itself in different parts of the body. It's really all the same, folks ...a lack of homeostasis or equilibrium (See my opening statement).

Medical doctors claim that they can cure disease. Plastics and ham can be cured. The human body cannot be "cured." It has been designed and programmed to "heal" (repair) itself when it is damaged or disturbed by attack, abuse, or misuse, or when it has been placed in a position of dis-ease (lack of homeostasis).

Health Practitioners cannot "heal" anyone. There is no such thing as a "healer." They can direct and/or instruct behavior or techniques that when applied properly, can assist or encourage the body to "heal itself."

Note that the word "doctor" means "teacher".

I TEACH HEALTH, I DO NOT TREAT DISEASE!

I have discovered that:

The human body is a multidimensional (more than one "octave" of consciousness) electrochemical machine which is designed by its Maker to be self-building, self-maintaining and self-repairing, and to "run" trouble free for a lifetime (120 to 150 years).

By definition, this is a dynamic process. In other words, things are being added (to the body) and things are being discarded (from the body) all the time – to maintain balance or equilibrium.

When the "machine" (our body) gets out of balance, it is programmed by higher realms of Nature to perform corrective maneuvers to re-establish balance.

There are two fundamental methods by which this "machine" gets thrown out of balance resulting in a state of "dis-ease" or lack of ease:

1. Something from outside the body such as chemicals, bacteria, worms, or viruses touches or gets into the body to "poison" or damage the body.

2. Something is missing from the body's mechanism or structure or fuel supply to prevent the body from fixing itself when it is damaged or wears out. (See Vol. I for "subtle energy" disturbances.)

The human body was designed to fix itself when it breaks. The missing component can be from the physical body, the emotional body, the electromagnetic body, the spiritual body, or some combination thereof.

If some substance, which is vital to the maintenance of the body's immune system, is missing from the daily intake of "nutrients", the body will attempt to scavenge or rob 'other stores' of those critical substances from other parts of the body or energy field in order to maintain the integrity of the body's defenses. The body can maintain this "deficit spending" program for just so long.

Every body's storage capacity is different. If these vital substances are missing from these "other places" for a period of time, the body's activities and functions, which were dependant on these substances for integrity, start to fail. We see this depreciation process as symptoms of **"degenerative dis-ease"**.

If some substance or foreign organism attacks the body, the defense system is called into play to somehow disable and/or destroy the invader or irritant. Every body's war-making capacity is different. We see the process of this war between the invader and the body's defense mechanism as symptoms of **"infectious dis-ease"**.

"Dis-ease" then is either the result of an outside invader, which has attacked the body's perimeter and caused dysfunction, or a missing component, which leads to eventual dysfunction.

This missing component can be either structurally missing (a genetic defect from birth) or functionally missing (lack of proper nutrients). Allergies are a reaction to a "foreign" protein in the blood. This is explained in Volume II.

We must keep in mind that, by definition, a chronic degenerative condition can and usually does, lead to an infectious condition. All Life must maintain a strong defense against "invaders". Constant deterioration and erosion of the walls around the "city" will eventually allow "the enemy" to break in.

All Life Forms in this physical dimension <u>must</u> defend their perimeter or some other Life Form will move in and take over their space. If you cannot defend your territory because of deterioration and/or misuse or abuse, or neglect or structural defect, some other entity will move into your space and you must vacate the premises (i.e., you die). This concept applies equally to castles and nations as well as to human bodies.

Sometimes surgical intervention can correct or assist a structural defect. In other words, if there are broken or damaged parts, or possibly defects in the structure at birth, surgery may help to fix the body so that it can work. A functional defect, however, which relates to how the parts work, must be approached from a nutritional perspective by definition. (See the section on Digestion in Volume II.)

If your car runs out of gas, removing the spare tire or welding the transmission parts together will not help your engine to start. You must put more gas in the tank to be able to start your engine and continue your journey.

Surgery cannot correct a functional defect.

In other words, surgically removing parts or fusing parts will not solve a nutritional deficit or a toxic overload. More aptly stated, if your body worked at one time and now does not function correctly, we must strongly suspect that you either put something into, or kept something from your body, to cause it to become damaged or dysfunctional.

Please note that some or all of the above can result in pain of some sort and intensity.

As I stated earlier…

I TRANSLATE PAIN INTO ENGLISH.

I TEACH HEALTH … I DO NOT TREAT DISEASE!!!

ABOUT PHIL

After almost 20 years in mechanical engineering designing automated machines and tools for GM, Ford, and Chrysler in Michigan, and McDonnell Douglas, Convair and Proctor & Gamble in California, Phil Selinsky decided to apply his engineering skills to more complex machines (human bodies).

He completed training as a Hypnotherapist from the Hypnosis Motivation Institute in 1974.

He graduated from the Los Angeles College of Massage and Physical Therapy's Instructor Training Course in 1976.

With the very creative help of Karen Halcyon, Phil founded the INSTITUTE FOR HOLISTIC STUDIES in Santa Barbara in 1976.

Phil obtained the California Office of Private and Post Secondary Education approval for:

The first 1000-hour Holistic Health Practitioner Program in the State of California

The first massage instruction video program in California

The first "approved" school of hypnosis in California.

He created the first "Chair Massage" program, instruction book, and video program in California.

He also founded the Central Coast Chapter of the American Massage Therapy Association (AMTA) and served as the Public Relations Director for the American Massage Therapy Association (California Chapter).

He received his certification in Advanced Modern and Traditional Acupuncture from the Occidental Institute for Chinese Studies in 1979.

Phil Selinsky, N.D. graduated from the Anglo-American Institute for Naturopathic Studies in 1980.

Phil has also maintained a private Naturopathic practice in Santa Barbara, Thousand Oaks, Ojai, Glendora, and San Diego, in addition to his teaching commitments, over the past 20 years.

He has taught a 528-hour NATURAL HEALTH AND MASSAGE THERAPY class at Citrus College in Glendora, and 100 hour workshops at PACIFIC BEACH YOGA AND HEALING ARTS in Pacific Beach and S.B. BODY THERAPY INSTITUTE in Santa Barbara.

Phil Selinsky, N.D. is the author of the soon to be published three-volume series book, "THE HUMAN MACHINE … A Trouble Shooter's Manual".

What is the design purpose of this machine (our bodies)?

Volume I: STRUCTURE GOVERNS FUNCTION … the shape of something determines its potential function.

How does the structural purpose of this "machine" conflict with the present environment to create stress, which results in symptoms of disease?

How do personal and business relationships generate stress, which results in symptoms of disease?

Volume II: BLOOD CHEMISTRY DRIVES BEHAVIOR … within the structural capacity, that is.

How does blood chemistry alter and affect behavior, which results in aches and pains and symptoms of disease?

How can you read the "dashboard gages" on this machine to avoid a major organ breakdown years in advance?

Volume III: HIATAL HERNIA SYNDROME … the hidden weakness that is frequently misdiagnosed, leading to most chronic aches and pains and degenerative disease conditions.

How does this genetic weakness result in symptoms of serious disease profiles like heart disease, diabetes, and cancer, as well as common ailments like arthritis, fibromyalgia, and sciatica?

Phil Selinsky, N.D.

ihss@earthlink.net

www.thehumanmachine.com

CHAPTER 19

CREATE YOUR OWN REALITY

BY LORETTA WASHBURN
PHOTOGRAPHER, ARTIST, AUTHOR, ENTREPRENEUR AND REALTOR®

R eality is merely an illusion so whatever you can imagine your reality to be, so it shall be. You simply have to believe in what you want and own it. Reality is simply an illusion, create the illusion that you desire and your imagination will take you everywhere! Logic will only take you from point A to point B...there is no limit to the imagination. The concepts I will be talking about here may be new to you and hard to grasp but, give it a shot and see how there are no limits to prosperity and a life that you choose to live.

There are many techniques to creating the life that you want to experience. Change your belief system and you change your life. Do you believe that there is not enough money for you? Do you believe in lack? Most people do and whatever it is that you give your energy to is what you create and what you will draw to yourself. If you believe you cannot afford to take a trip, or to purchase something that you really want or simply there isn't enough money to pay your bills. What you are doing is giving power to lack because you believe in it. Stop believing in lack and see what happens, your life will be transformed into the life most of us desire and more.

You aren't afraid of failure, you're afraid of success. Have you ever made great headway and then fallen on your face or everything that was taking you forward came to a stop? More than likely you sabotaged yourself. No, don't think that it wasn't meant to be, we are all put here to live a prosperous life. I would imagine that your thoughts stopped the success. There is energy to thought, energy to the spoken word and energy to the written word and the more you think or speak of something you are giving that thought power therefore, manifesting it. Such as, I don't know if I can pay my mortgage this month...you are telling the Universe that you don't trust the Universe (God) to support you. If you don't believe you will have what you are needing in life, you won't have it. Your mind is a powerful tool and can aid you in having all the deliciousness that the Universe has to offer. Do you ever say, I never win, I am so unlucky, I never get this, I never get that, no one loves me, I'm fat, I'm stupid...and so on. Remember, whatever you believe you are, you become.

Most people worry about money. When you worry about money you will have plenty to worry about with your finances. If you believe there is no end to Universal abundance, you should have all you want and more. We don't have to suffer, abundance of the good things in life are there waiting for you and there is no limit to prosperity.

Through our fears, thoughts and desires, we create our life experiences. Your life is like a movie script and for every thought; you are creating how your life will unfold. Again, if you believe in lack, lack is exactly what you will have. Remove the belief in lack and watch the prosperity come to you. Let's change your belief system. Remove what is negative. I stay away from negative people. I don't watch the news; don't read the newspaper unless someone tells me about someone or something interesting that's in it. I do read the real estate section. In my reality, life is always delicious! There is always plenty of what I am choosing to have. Many people tell me that I have the life that I have because of my attitude. Granted, attitude plays a big roll but it takes more than attitude. Make the people around you smile; make them feel good, it will make you feel good.

What do you want? There are many ways to create the life that you want to experience. Use your imagination, you can be or do whatever it is you choose. Know that you are worthy of greatness, abundance and prosperity. There is plenty of everything that you want and you deserve it. Believe that. Put it writing. You have to be ready to accept what you want in life and cast off any belief of limitations. How would a child deal with this? When you were little you never said you want to be a stressed out bookkeeper, you said you wanted to be a race car driver. Children have wonderful imaginations and that is what I want you to have. Use your imagination!

Reality is simply an illusion, create the illusion that you desire and your imagination will take you everywhere!

Here are the steps I have taken to create the prosperous life that I have chosen. These concepts may be new to you and maybe hard to grasp, but I promise you if you take the steps and stick to them, the world will open up and the possibilities are endless.

I follow the Four Spiritual Laws of Prosperity.

Tithe – You read it right! 10% of any money that you receive should be tithed. You give 10% of all income to acknowledge that God is your higher source. We don't tithe to need, we tithe to abundance. Where do you tithe? We've all heard about tithing to your church. We don't all attend church. Tithe to where you receive spiritual food. Who is it in your life that feeds you spiritually? Who inspires you and reminds you of who you are? Who gives you inspiration and makes you feel enlightened, who brings you up and makes you feel that life is full of joy? You must tithe to abundance to receive abundance in your life. Giving to a charity is not a tithe. Giving to your mother because she can't pay he bills is not a tithe. That is a good thing to do after you tithe. You can tithe to more than one person, you can break it up. Tithe to someone that is needy will make you needy. I tithe too many people. I tithed to another REALTOR® one day simply because she moved me so spiritually and reminded who I was on a spiritual level and she didn't even know that she said anything that made a difference in my life. I have tithed to an author because of what she writes moves me and keeps my on my spiritual path and reminds me of the power that I have within. I have tithed to religious organizations as well. Tithing can be very difficult, don't spend too much time thinking about it or worrying about giving up money...just do it! The first time I tithed... I had a little bit of resistance but I did it. I hadn't even put the check in the mail yet and I started reaping from it. I was also doing the other steps that came with it. Don't be afraid to give and then give some more to those you love. We've all heard the quote from the bible..... ask, and ye shall receive. I promise you, give and you shall receive, give more and you shall receive even more. I tithe and I have people from all over the world tithing to me which I tithe on. I love giving and as I give I receive. Prosperity is mine! Tithing isn't the only step to prosperity and with the four steps together, with an open heart and an open mind; your life will change forever.

Set Goals – Get ready to receive what you really want in life. Goal setting is a very important roll in the laws of prosperity. Write out your goals. Write out ten goals of things that you want in your life. Set a date that you want to meet your goal. Don't be afraid to want and don't be afraid to ask for what you want. Don't worry about how the things you want will come to you, just use your imagination and be very specific. My first time of writing my goals, I wrote that I would learn to play the piano. I don't have a piano and had no intention of buying one. I sold a house and when we went and did the walk through; the seller had moved out and left his piano. The buyer said he didn't want that hunk of junk and I told him I would take it off his hands. I paid $100.00 to have it moved to my home. I did some research and found that it is worth between $11-$15 thousand dollars and I am now playing the piano. As my goals come to fruition, I write them off and add more. The more you want, the more you will receive. I give thanks to God daily for my wonderful life and all I receive. Keep your goals to yourself and be as specific as possible. Don't be afraid to ask for anything big and don't worry about how it will get to you. The Universe will provide! Use your imagination. With the choice of receiving your goals, let go of old beliefs. You must believe that what you want is yours...think about it as though it is on its way. It belongs to you, so own it! No thought of maybe this will work, know that it will. I have a friend that said that maybe this worked for me but it may not for him. If he believes it won't work for him, it won't. It can work for everyone. Be positive, act as though you have received it and change your belief system of lack by believing that lack does not exist in your life. Feel it, know that you can manifest your own reality. Its okay to want a lot...there is no limit to prosperity and it is not being greedy. Being greedy is when you don't want anyone else to have the good stuff of life. We want everyone to taste life in a new and better way without limits. Read your goals several times a day, everyday!

Forgiveness – There is either flow or congestion in life. When we hold onto things throughout our life, it effects our present and future. Your health, relationships, finances and the list goes on that gets affected by this congestion. Think back about everyone that has made you feel bad, embarrassed you, abandoned you and simply hurt you is some way. I want you to forgive that person, write it down say it daily over and over again. Go back to your earliest memory of someone hurting you or making you feels bad and forgive them. Forgive them daily. It may take some time to truly forgive someone for something they have done but repeating it over and over will break resistance to forgiving them and you will feel it when you have let it go. The big thing here is to also…forgive yourself for anything that you have done that hurt someone. If you are forgiving your parents, forgive them for everything, also forgive yourself for not being a better son or daughter to them. At the end of the day, I lay in bed and forgive others for hurting me and I forgive myself for things I have done wrong and if I have hurt anyone or made anyone feel bad that day, I forgive myself. I would never intentionally hurt anyone. Don't blame anyone for anything…let things go. Forgive in the deepest way that one can possibly forgive. When you have forgiven everyone in your life that has hurt you, just think about the room you will have in your heart to receive all that is good.

Divine purpose – Make a commitment in life. Do something that I s going to help heal the planet. Think about this long and hard and choose what feels right. Maybe you want to help feed the hungry. If you don't know what to do, trust your intuition, your higher self will let you know what you want to do. Ask the Universe for guidance and it will come to you.

Make the commitment of tithing, set your goals, forgive and forgive some more and find a divine purpose and commit to these things. Speak the truth, always do the right thing and love your self. Your mind is a very powerful tool and using all of these techniques together, you will be amazed at how there truly are no limits to prosperity.

I have always been able to manifest that of what I was choosing. I haven't always used the techniques described here but would make wonderful strides in life with great successes and then sabotage .myself because I believed in lack. I think that when you grow up poor and weren't allowed to have wants, it can make it hard to not believe in lack when that is all you have known. I did a lot of visualizations, meditations and everything that I could learn about manifesting. I finally got it but it took years. If only I knew then what I know today. How many times have you said that one?

Back in the 80's I was in college studying art. I had an interest in photography and knew nothing about it. However, I was really drawn to it. I received a 35 mm camera as a gift from my dear Jacob and knew I must put it to use. I had no idea of what I would take a picture of and didn't want to take pictures just for the sake of doing it. Before I went to bed one night, I told the Universe that I wanted to receive an image in my sleep that would make a fabulous piece of art. I woke up the next morning and remembered my dream and in this dream was an image. I knew nothing about my camera. I took it into the camera store, told the clerk I would be taking an out door picture and wanted black and white film. I went out into the country, took a picture of one of my daughters running in a plowed orchard holding a piece of white chiffon over her head. The chiffon looked as though it were dancing. I took only one photo and called it a day. I knew I had the picture. I had access to a darkroom, went in with books because I didn't know what I was doing and developed my film and printed a perfect 16X20 black and white print on my first try. It was gorgeous, spiritual and it moved everyone that saw it. A month later it was hanging in a museum. I had found myself and enrolled in a private photography school. I had been exhibiting my work and wanted to be affiliated with a famous photographer. I had been invited to have lunch with a friend of mine from the museum of Modern Art in San Francisco, yes to have lunch with him, Ansel Adams and Adams wife. I got to take portraits of Ansel Adams. This was quite a highlight in my life but exactly what I had asked for. Then I decided that Ansel Adams, as great as he is, is looked at a photographer. I wanted to do this again with an artist. My agent called me and said Andy Warhol wanted me to take a photograph of a model for *Interview Magazine*. Since then I have had five exhibits in New York City alone, San Francisco, Chicago, Japan, Los Angeles and the list goes on.

Why am I telling you this? I created this because this is what I was expecting to receive. I believed it would happen, I owned that these things would happen to me. I had my moments where there was no action and it was because of my belief in lack. However, I had no resistance in getting up and running. You can call this what you want, I believe it was divine intervention... I asked and expected these things to materialize. I had to work for it but made it happen. If I can do these things, you can create what you are choosing.

I decided to write a book, I had a minor in English and loved to write. I had a great book idea and you should write about what you know. I love metaphysics and I am a bit of a metaphysician. I had always been told it was hard to get published. I took my book idea, hadn't written any of it, just a query and a few photos and approached a publishing company...it was rejected. Went to the next publisher and they grabbed it right up. MIND TRAVELERS - *Portrait of Famous Psychics and Healers of Today.* Two years later my publisher asked me to write a book on weight loss. I wrote, LOSING IT NATURALLY, A COMPLETE HOLISTIC WEIGHT LOSS PROGRAM. I have always been very interested in holistic medicine and did a lot of research on the subject throughout the years and I decided to go to the School Of Natural Healing.

I had an intention, an intention to write books and I will write many before I pass to the other side of life. With having intention, I am saying that I expect the things that I want to have happen, and they do. It is so easy, you just have to believe that whatever it is that you want is already yours. I have another book almost complete, THE LADY'S FROM THE PLEIADES, another metaphysical book.

Albert Einstein said: *"Imagination is everything. It is the preview of life's coming attraction."*

The life that you are living is the exact record of your thought.

Selling real estate is what I do now and I have become very successful and of course I use these Four Spiritual Laws of Prosperity to create the life that I choose, the business that I choose and have great intentions! Whatever Loretta touches turns to **SOLD!**

ABOUT LORETTA

Loretta is from northern California and now lives in Chesapeake, Virginia. She has three daughters, Shelly, Heidi and Gerda and four grand children, Mark, Seth, Caelan and Bret. Loretta is a REALTOR® in the Hampton Roads area and has been selling real estate for the last thirteen years. Being an artist is an advantage for her because she has that creative side to be able to think outside the box for new ideas in marketing and getting properties sold.

Loretta Washburn has been featured as a guest on "America's Premier Experts", on NBC, CBS, ABC and FOX affiliates, Live At 10, Look Who's Talking, and The Sally Jesse Raphael Show. She has been interviewed on numerous radio shows, magazines and other publications.

If you would like more information about Loretta Washburn, and how you can purchase any of her books, would like to learn more about CREATING YOUR OWN REALITY, her art or would like to speak to Loretta about buying or selling real estate and would like more information from one of America's Premier experts, visit her at www.LorettaWashburn.com or call her at: 757-288-2247.

CHAPTER 20

DELAY DOES NOT MEAN DENIAL

BY DENISE Y. MOSE, PH.D

Ok, your dream is finally here. The stationary, envelopes and business cards have all been ordered. Your cool website is up and running. That first networking event is in two weeks. Money is in the bank in case you go broke. That old, boring desk job you quit seems like a memory. You told your boss to take that job and shove… well, we can fill in the rest. Sleeping in is now *your* choice. Firing up the laptop is easy because you are on your own schedule. You are going to change the world with your business. Barnes and Nobles knows you by name due to all of the self-help books you bought. You are a star! You are flying! You are the ultimate!

Then, a few months pass. The phone is not ringing as much. That old, boring, desk job is starting to look pretty good. Bills are being paid, but income is a red flag. You've brought no money in, but you sure have given tons of products and services away…for free. …Because, when no one knows who you are, that's what you have to do to get exposure. Advertising is a must, but so is having a hot shower! It's been eight months and your bills now arrive in different colors due to how late you are paying them. You take out the fax line in your house and keep the cell phone. Asking for extensions on all of your obligations is now the norm. You shop at places where you must bring your own bags for groceries, because the fancy places are too expensive (...*Although, weren't they always?*). Secretly, you pawn precious items because hey, you have to eat! Your zest for this 'new venture' seems skewed and completely unrealistic, but you're in it now! Your big dream got you one thing: broke.

So...what happened?

Whenever I consult with people who want to venture out into the world of entrepreneurship, I tell them a few things. One, being an entrepreneur is mental *first*. There has to be a feeling of total confidence that you can do this thing. Let's face it; it takes guts to leave your job. But it takes serious drive to leave a *really good job*! After all, we are in a recession. People are being let go from their jobs every day. So, does it really make sense to quit a job where you are not in danger of being fired? Well, that's the choice of the individual.

Second, I tell them that the results will take awhile to see. Just because what you've worked for has been delayed, does not mean you've been denied. Take High School, for instance. A traditional diploma will take you approximately four years. Guess what? You must pass each grade to completely finish high school. Delay does not mean denial. Haven't we all worked for something only to realize that the result would take some time? Of course, we have! I'll go one step further. When you go to your nearest supermarket, you have to wait in line. You are hungry, the kids are going crazy, traffic will be bumper-to-bumper, but you have to wait. No matter what you do or where you go, waiting will be a part of the equation. My advice is to get busy for the future. Stockbrokers know all about predicting the future. They watch and watch for stocks to go up or down. When they finally see a break they go for it. If they don't, they lose out.

Third, don't forget why you jumped out there to begin with. It's easy to get frustrated when results are slow. There might even be a few friends who drop by and say the signature "I told you so!" to your face. With friends like that, you should be upset! Trust me, we've all been there. When you look back at all you've risked, the ends should justify the means. You can be sure that when they don't, depression, failure and loss of drive arrive on your doorstep! So, take a step back and analyze your dream. If it is your desire to make change, be a beacon of light and leave your mark in a profound way....you cannot lose focus!

So what's the answer? How do you **still** keep it together when you aren't making any money and your will to win is gone? Who is supposed to get you over the hump? To top it off, your confidence has taken an extended vacation without telling you. To prevent backsliding, I advise the following:

- **Secure your swagger**
- **Maximize your mentor**
- **Forge new friendships**
- **Paralyze the past**

Secure your swagger - Reassess your game plan. Go out and buy large sheets of paper that presenters use in seminars. Get the kind that has the adhesive on the back. Invest in some colorful markers and a bag of popcorn. Did you know that popcorn is a scientifically proven snack that produces endorphins in the brain that allows the creative side to function at a higher level? No? …well, you just learned something. Once you have your large sheets, markers and popcorn, get out that old journal you kept before you left your job. Look at all the energy you had in those words. Relive them! Get your 'swagger' back! Take this new venture and remind yourself that you were built to succeed. Have your own pep rally! Buy a 12-month wall calendar and put pen to paper! A timeline is a great way to hold you accountable. These are YOUR dreams, right? Who is going to work harder for them than you? Your timeline is your best friend as a new entrepreneur. You are still learning your way with all this new freedom. Get it under control and have your top three goals done by the time Spring rolls around!

Maximize your Mentor. The purpose of a mentor is to be the one person that can truly relate to your situation. It concerns me when I meet new entrepreneurs and they don't feel the need for a mentor. No one understands your shoes unless someone else walked in them. Therefore, seek a mentor…and fast! But, not just anybody! Identify that person that is doing what you want to do and they are doing it **successfully**. If it is your wish to have your own bakery, don't talk to the manager, get the owner! Tell them your dream; let them feel your energy. I guarantee you if you do, success is sure to follow you. See, that's really a key element. YOU must go to that person and put yourself out there! You must be transparent for them to really take a chance on you. Most people are not willing to do that. It means you have to be vulnerable, and completely honest. I understand why people don't risk it all. Have you figured out the word yet? Yep, you guessed it: *REJECTION*. Who wants to be told that their dream is dumb or unrealistic? No one, but that's part of the package. From Award-Winning Comedian Eddie Murphy to Mega Producer/Director Steven Spielberg they will tell you about rejection early on in their career. But, that didn't seem to stop them. Why should it stop you? Include your mentor in your big ideas and you'll have someone to help you make them come true.

Forge new friendships. Remember those friends who didn't believe in you and don't support your being an entrepreneur? Well, are they really your friends? Only you can answer that question, but my answer would be "no". I make every effort to meet people who don't look like me, talk like me, listen to my kind of music or even dress like me. This is called culture. This is how we learn. If you stick with the same people you've always been around, how do you expect to get ahead in life? Trust me; cliques are easy because everyone knows each other. But, after a while that gets boring. It's no different when you start your own business. It is critical that you align yourself with people who know more than you do. Your old 'friends' won't be much competition with the new ones who show you cool stuff. Case in point; the word *scotoma*. I love this word. It means the inability to see something that's right in front of you. Sorry, the friends you've known since you were twelve don't know this word. The hot-shot new business guru does. If I were you, I'd ask her for coffee and learn more stuff if you plan to get ahead.

Paralyze the past. You quit your job. You turned in your picture identification card. You cleaned out your desk. Your old boss hired your replacement. It's a done deal now. Just because the results aren't where you want them to be does not mean the past was a better option. Didn't you choose to have a more fruitful life on your own terms? Then stop looking over your shoulder like you made some big mistake! You didn't! You can do this! You just have to paralyze the past. It can be very dangerous when people live in the past. Some people do it so much they miss the present and the future. Between you and me, I miss my mother. She was amazing! But, she was also very sick. The year 2005 was a blur. When she finally passed – it hurt. In fact, it was the worst feeling I've ever had in my life. But, I had to make a decision. Was I going to stay there and sulk, or remember her for who she was and move on with my life? I chose the latter. The past can help us and hurt us. When I think of my mother, I smile and laugh. She is looking down on her cloud telling the other residents about her baby girl. Actually, she's got the best seat in the house! You have to do the same. It doesn't matter if your husband left you, your wife cheated, your friends were fickle, your job didn't appreciate you, the bank denied you a loan or thinking you're too old to go back to college. At the end of the day, you have to live with all of it and do your best to make your dreams happen. The past is just that…it has passed.

Whenever I need to feel inspired, I look at those who came before me; especially in the world of business. The folks who have really 'made it' leave something to offer. For example, take our 16th President of the United States, Abraham Lincoln. It is widely known that he ran for many positions and lost most of them, including the United States Senate where he lost twice. Business Mogul Donald Trump knows a thing or two about persistence. Who can go bankrupt twice and still be worth billions? Television Mogul Oprah Winfrey grew up poor in Mississippi. Did she let that stop her? Since so many people made it despite the odds, why can't you? Obstacles are designed like a roller coaster. No matter what you've been through you are still here. You have already WON!!!

I would be remiss if I didn't leave you with this last tidbit of advice. Life is like one giant parade. Many people love to get up early on Saturday and watch a good parade. You see the bands, singers, motorcycles, floats and you get all the candy. Your dreams are your float. It takes time to build them and make them noticeable. The effort you put into your float also requires handlers to guide you along the right path. Then, when you hit that corner, the crowd sees what took you years to manifest. They wait with anticipation because this was the float that was better than the rest! Don't just have a life…Live! I want to see you take the world by storm and leave the crowd wanting more!

Denise Y. Mose, Ph.D is the owner/creator of Simply D Perfume, Beauty Skin Care Line and Daniel, Cologne for Men. She is the host of her own talk show, Urban America Today). Having authored her signature book, Life at 433, and written for several magazines, she is an authority on edu-

cation, business, beauty/fashion, career coaching and etiquette. Her new book, The Guilt-Free Guide to Fashion, will be released summer 2011. The American Image Consultant Association often seeks her advice on wardrobe and fashion seminars. She can be reached through her Agent Monique Mason at 407-456-5624.

ABOUT DENISE

Eager, Effervescent and Empowered are a few words that describe this young lady. Denise Y. Mose is a proud native of Huntsville, Alabama where she graduated from Alabama A&M University with a double major in Elementary and Early Childhood Education. She taught for over ten years, having spent her most recent time teaching at Full Sail University where she was a Professor of Branding/Marketing and Public Speaking.

Currently, she is the Founder and President of Simply D Perfume. Here she houses her signature fragrances: Beauty by DYM and her newest Fragrance, Daniel for Men launched this year in April. She is a Certified Fashion Expert with The Association of Image Consultants International where she specializes in Wardrobe and Corporate Image.

Through her talk show, Urban America Today, she has traveled to The Trumpet Awards, Stellar Awards, The Dove Awards, The Grammy's, ESSENCE Music Festival, Tribeca Film Festival, MTV Movie Awards, Taste of Chicago and The Kentucky Derby. Having interviewed Smokey Robinson, Earth, Wind and Fire, Teena Marie, Stephanie Mills, Kurt Franklin, Fred Hammond, The Clark Sisters, Jay-Z, Little Wayne, Drake, Eminem, Justin Timberlake, The Jonas Brothers, Taylor Swift, Miley Cyrus, Justin Bieber, Gabrielle Union, Lynn Whitfield, Taylor Hicks, Photographer Nigel Barker, Billonaire Bob Johnson, Heavyweight Champion Lennox Lewis, and Dwayne Wade she is a staple at any major event. She is a sought out Red Carpet host and interviews celebrities on a monthly basis. Dr. Mose is the author of two books and serves as Feature Writer for the following publications: ONYX Magazine, Orlando Woman and RYSE Magazine. Her third book, *The Guilt-Free Guide to Fashion* will be released summer 2011.

Recently, she has been honored by the Orlando Business Journal with their Women Who Mean Business Award. The Girl Scouts of America identified her as a Woman of Distinction. She won the Entrepreneur of the Year Award from the Chamber of Commerce in 2008. The Tom Joyner Morning Radio Show (Audience of 10 million) bestowed upon her the Hardest Working Entrepreneur Award in 2008. Currently, she is the 2011 Cover Girl for ONYX Magazine due to her rapid accomplishments as an Entrepreneur. USA TODAY Newspaper (a readership of over 35 million) featured her as their top Beauty and Fashion Expert for 2011.

As a Certified Life Coach, she is an avid volunteer with many organizations where she demonstrates the use of proper Public Speaking, Etiquette, and Social Graces to young people. She volunteers with: Junior Achievement of Central Florida, LBS Foundation, Central Florida Urban League Leaders of Tomorrow, 100 Black Men, Habitat for Humanity, Central Florida Homeless Shelter, Give Kids the World, Make a Wish Foundation, Rollins College Generation Next, Jones High School, Girls Scouts of America and Valencia Community College. She is a member of New Covenant Baptist Church where she serves as a Deacon, Sunday School Teacher, and the Koinonia (Courtesy) Ministries.

She has received post graduate degrees and certifications from Florida Metropolitan University, Walden University, Harvard University and The Oxford University in Oxford, England.

Monique Mason, Agent & Communications Specialist
Contact Information: 407-456-5624
1105 Baltimore Drive
Orlando, FL 32810

CHAPTER 21

REAL ESTATE – INVESTING TO WIN! A SHORT COURSE ON GETTING IT RIGHT.

BY MICHAEL MAZZELLA

(Why most of what you've been taught about
Real Estate Investing is wrong. Why it's really not all about
"Location, location, location," and its not "all about cash flow,"
either! How to do it right, and come out ahead in a bad economy.)

Lets explore and debunk four of the common myths that have poisoned the well of knowledge, and can trip many people up in their endeavor to invest profitably and intelligently in real estate. Then I'll share five 'golden nuggets' that I've learned in my journey as a professional investor in the past ten years – five key lessons that will help you earn higher profits, with lower risk!

MYTH #1:
"IT'S ALL ABOUT CASH FLOW."

The Reality: If your goal is wealth creation, pursuit of cash flow deals is far more likely to derail your financial journey. Believing it's all about cash flow is an 'old school' mentality, however, it is still embraced by the masses. It is my estimate that roughly half of all real estate investors subscribe to this school of thought. Let's look a little deeper...

First, you should know that there are only three possible ways to make money in real estate:

1. Cash flow.
2. Appreciation.
3. Tax benefits.

Regardless of what source the deal came from, i.e., foreclosure, short sale, probate, eviction lead, etc., and regardless of what strategy you used to do the deal, i.e., hold as a rental, flip as a buy-fix-sell, assignment of the contract from another person, or a rent-to-own lease option, the deal can only pay you in any combination of these three ways – Cash flow, appreciation, and tax benefits.

Cash flow is monthly recurring income over a period of time. In a typical rental property, if our total expenses are $1,800 per month, and we receive $2000 in rental income, we have a positive cash flow of $200 per month. The truly wonderful thing about cash flow, is that once we set up the deal, that $200 per month will continue to come in whether we are working on that deal, working on our next deal, or away on vacation. It is automatic income, a check in your mailbox every month. Just as if we had turned on a faucet and walked away, the water would continue to flow. This makes cash flow ideal for retirement income. The problem however, is that cash flow properties frequently have a low return. In the deal we cited above, at the end of the year you will only have $2,400. And that's if everything goes flawlessly. So we would need to own many, many properties in order to be able to retire comfortably with this example. In the world of real estate investing, this is the path the herd follows.

Appreciation. The second way that real estate makes money is through appreciation. There are three basic types of appreciation.

1. Forced. We can force appreciation of value through renovation of the property. This is why real estate investors love ugly houses. We can often buy them cheap, renovate them, and sell them for a nice profit. This works even in down markets.

2. Instant. This is when we buy the property below market value. We are finding a great bargain, from a motivated seller who needs money, then reselling at market value for profit.

3. Market. Market appreciation is the gradual increase in value over time. Market appreciation is the single most powerful wealth creator in history. Because we cannot control the market, however, it is important not to rely solely upon market appreciation as the only profit in your deal. This is known as speculation, and it is just as easy to lose money in a market as it is to make money. If we invest in an emerging market, a wise investor will keep their risks lower by making sure that there are other 'profit centers' in the deal, such as instant appreciation, forced appreciation, tax benefits, or cash flow. This way, even if the market goes flat, the investor still makes money. We treat market appreciation only as a bonus.

Appreciation is good for short-term wealth creation. It requires active investing, and is not passive like cash flow. If the market I am investing in is flat or dropping, my best move will be to flip it for a quick profit. In a typical flip of a single-family home, we will net a profit of at least $50,000, and sometimes as much as $100,000 or more. We are making our money through forced and instant appreciation.

In a rising market, I may hold the property for 12 or 18 months prior to selling. This way I am capturing some of that market appreciation. To keep my holding costs down, I may put a renter in the property during this time, and the property may break even or even carry a negative cash flow for this short time.

Tax benefits. The third way of making money in real estate is through tax benefits. A professional investor can easily save tens of thousands of dollars each year by arranging their affairs in such a way as to pay the least amount of taxes possible under the law. I wont get into details here, but just make sure you hire a good CPA who owns real estate.

So with three different ways of making money in real estate, each of which can have potentially large payouts, why would someone only pay attention to one way of making money?

As an investor, my job is to make the most amount of money, with the least risk to my capital. My focus is to look at all three ways of making money in each and every deal. I am looking at the total amount of money I am making per deal, from all three sources. It is far less important from which of the three sources the money flows. Whether it is from cash flow, appreciation, or tax benefits, in the end, it's all green money!

How to Win: Cash flow deals and cash flowing properties are good for retirement, however due to usually low returns, they are poor as a wealth creation vehicle. Appreciation deals require active investing, so they do not favor retirement, however they are excellent for wealth creation.

So if your goal is wealth creation, focus initially on deals that have lots of appreciation. Pass over the deals that pay $200 or $300 a month in cash flow, and go after the deals that will pay you $40-$70,000 in a single Buy-Fix-Sell transaction. Single family homes are the best platform for appreciation.

After you've created a good amount of capital for yourself through concentrating your investing for wealth creation, and are now looking for a steady stream of passive income, this is the time to focus on cash flowing deals. But we still face the problem of low return. So how can we mitigate this? Here is the answer...

Pay off the mortgage! Simply write a check and pay off the mortgage completely. You have already created wealth because you have been flipping houses during your wealth creation phase. Now you can use some of this to buy your cash flowing properties outright, to create the largest amount of passive income to retire on. Multi-unit properties are the best platforms for cash flow.

Note that we have established a 2-stage game plan. In stage 1, our objective is to create short-term wealth. In stage 2, we are now ready to go for passive income. Because you first went though a wealth creation stage, now you can do the cash flow deals the smart way! You have the money to pay off the mortgage, and buy the property outright. So that same property that was producing only $200 per month in cashflow is now producing $1,000 per month. Now, you'll only need a few of these to retire comfortably and live off this passive income, which now flows freely!

MYTH #2:
MY NATIONAL BOOT CAMP TRAINER, MENTOR, ETC., IS A REAL ESTATE MULTI-MILLIONAIRE.

The Reality: Highly unlikely. From the training company's perspective, their measure of success is whether they can get you to buy more training products. Their success is not based on how good their strategies are, or how successful you become as a result of buying their products. The company values their pitchman's sales ability much more than his success as a real estate investor. As a result, you are usually being trained by people who need a job, rather than those whom have already created their fortunes as real estate investors!

"Most of what we've learned about investing, has been taught to us by a commissioned salesperson."

How to Win: Resist the temptation to buy when your emotions run high. If you are going to a free, or low-cost seminar, remember that they are in business to make money. They need to sell you something to make it all work. In almost all cases, the person standing up there giving that powerful presentation is paid on commission, based on back-end sales. If you like the product, here are some wise questions to ask yourself before reaching for your credit card:

- Am I making my 'Buy' decision on impulse… out of excitement?
- If I sleep on it, will I still want this product a week from now?
- Have I done independent research, or am I buying based entirely upon what the pitchman has told me?
- Is there a lot of pressure to buy right now? Are they discouraging me from thinking it over, and doing some independent research?
- Am I really going to use this product?
- When I Google this company, this product, & this trainer, what have others said about it?
- Are there less expensive alternatives available on eBay, and elsewhere?

"Never ask a barber if you need a haircut."

MYTH #3:
IT'S ALL ABOUT "LOCATION, LOCATION, LOCATION"

The Reality: It's really not. It's much more about the numbers in your deal. This Realtor mantra is centered around retail homebuyers, and for them, it may be OK. A savvy investor operates from a different mindset. So while location does play a role, this will be reflected in the value of the property. As an investor, you could buy a property in a great location, but not make any money because you overpaid for it, or used the wrong strategy; i.e., you held it as a rental, when you would have done much better by flipping it, taking your cash, and moving on.

How to Win: Follow the money! Stack the profit centers in your deal, making sure your deal has as much profit as possible, from any combination of the following: forced appreciation, instant appreciation, market appreciation, cashflow, and tax benefits.

MYTH #4:
THE BEST WAY TO FIND A GOOD INVESTMENT PROPERTY IS TO CONSULT WITH A REALTOR.

The Reality: This is rarely true. A realtor's training centers around transactions, and having them flow smoothly. If they could make good money investing in real estate, many of them would. When a realtor states: "This property is a good investment," your response should be: "Show me the numbers that led you to this conclusion." Many investors struggle to find a good investment property – and this assumes they know what they're looking for. Realtors are far less likely to know about investing. People tend to believe because its all real estate, after all, that Realtors would know lots about real estate investing. Upon closer examination, they are two entirely different businesses within the same broad industry. For the same reason you would not seek out a dermatologist to diagnose a hearing impairment; or hire a probate attorney to defend you in tax court, you should not expect your realtor to know a lot about successful investing.

Recently I bought a property in an exclusive area on Oahu, direct from a distressed owner, for $295k. Similar properties routinely sell for $400k to $450k. I was talking to a local realtor, who's been in the business for over 30 years. When I told her the neighborhood, and the price I bought it for, she thought that was not possible. "No way - how can that be?" she asked, and stated that she'd never seen anything like it. She was surprised when I informed her that I bought the property directly from the owner, it was never listed on the MLS, and there were no realtors involved in the transaction. The Realtor and the real estate investor – they live in 2 different worlds.

How to Win: YOU should become the expert at locating the good deals. I personally know about 50 good realtors here in my local market. Only three of them have been able to find me good investor-quality deals consistently. Realtors can provide a valuable service, though for most of them, investing is just not their area of expertise. Most of my deals are found in the 'hidden market,' meaning properties that are not for sale, and not listed with a Realtor. I deal with the owners directly.

The Way, the Truth, and the Light: Five key points to invest for higher profits and lower risk:

1. **Use a 2-stage game plan**. Unless you are already wealthy, the first stage of your game plan will focus upon wealth-creation deals, NOT cash flow deals! We are bypassing the $300 a month deals, and going for the deals that pay us $40,000 or more per deal. These are usually flips, or they may be a short-term hold (12-24 months) in a strong emerging market. Remember if you do the latter, we don't control the market, so mitigate the risk by ensuring your deal will stand on its own, without any market appreciation.

2. **Understand that there are three ways to make money in real estate**. Cash flow, appreciation, and tax benefits. Use this powerful fundamental to your advantage!

3. **Stacking Profit Centers**. From #2 above, "stack" as many of these into your deal as possible. By stacking profit centers, you can ensure you are maximizing the profit potential in your deal.

4. **Beware, the narrow margin**! This has been the downfall of many. Make sure you have plenty of profit margin built in your deals. This allows for the unexpected, and any mistakes you might make. If things go wrong, you have a safety net,

and you'll still make money.

5. **Due diligence**. Run the numbers! Never delegate this. If you would like a copy of the software I created to accurately analyze our Buy-Fix-Sell deals (aka "flipping houses") contact me through my website at www.TurtleBayLandCompany.com, and mention this book. Ask, and you shall receive a free copy of my excel spreadsheet that will simplify the number crunching!

ABOUT MICHAEL

Michael Mazzella is a nationally known Real Estate Investor, author, and millionaire mentor, who bought his first property in 1993.

After flipping a foreclosure property for a quick profit, Michael gave notice at work and has been 'happily unemployed' ever since. The rest is history. Today, Michael is one of Hawaii's most active real estate investors, and owns residential and commercial properties from the Hawaiian Islands to the US East coast.

Michael invests to *win* – he does not 'follow the herd.' Over the past decade he has developed and refined his own savvy investing strategies, in both up and down markets, and as a result of these techniques, *has never lost money in a deal*.

In 2004, Michael started a training company, Honolulu Mentor (www.HonoluluMentor.com) and began sharing his strategies, which are not taught anywhere else. Michael is also a highly sought-after speaker and mentor, and has trained thousands of students across the nation. Graduates of his *Millionaire Mentor* course enjoy a high success rate, and include an expanding list of real estate millionaires.

Rather than using banks, Michael uses cash from private individuals to fund his investing operations. His private lenders earn up to 12% while their investment is secured by real estate. If you would like more information about joining Michael's elite team of private lending partners, contact him at: Michael@TurtleBayLandCompany.com.

Michael lives in Honolulu, HI, with his wife and 3 children. He hosts a weekly radio & television show, and enjoys working out and playing with his children.

CHAPTER 22

DUPLICATE YOURSELF

BY FRANK LAPLACA

T he # 1 Marketing Strategy to take your business to the next level.

When was the last time someone contacted you and wanted to buy your products or services and you never met them before?

When was the last time someone contacted you and asked that you contact a family member or a friend of theirs or someone that they knew who needed or wanted your product or services?

If the answer to the above is all the time, then you probably have been to one of my workshops or are a member of our organization.

I would like to share with you a marketing strategy that I believe is the # 1 strategy for taking your business to the next level and will help you be more successful.

As a business owner for over 40 years, I realized that the traditional ways of getting, wanting and increasing my business just like everyone else was doing was not working. Should I increase my hours during the week and perhaps open on Saturday, thinking that the added hours in the office would bring more clients? The business plan I developed each year would allocate more and more dollars for advertising in print, radio, TV, mailings, yellow pages, flyers, organization fees and the Internet. I did the meal seminars that everyone else was doing. When a couple showed up with chair cushions and their own personal name tags and then took a nap after they ate, I decided there had to be a better way. I needed to get in front of the right people.

THE PHONE CALL

Ten years ago on a Monday morning at 9:00 AM the phone rang and I answered. The caller introduced himself as Jeff and mentioned that Paul, a good friend of mine, was telling him about the work I was doing for him and that he wanted to get together with me and do the same thing. I arranged a time that was convenient to meet and after several meetings with him he became one of my largest clients. He was not only one of my largest clients, but he asked me to contact his parents and brothers and sisters as well as his wife's parents and sisters. He contacted them in advance and told them about me and how I had helped him and could probably do the same for them.

THE "AH-HA" MOMENT

Jeff's reason for wanting me to meet with people that he cared about was that he understood about the benefits of my products and services and how it could help them. We got to know each other pretty well. He liked and trusted me to do the same for the people he knew. I did business with every one of the family members and friends he referred me to. Jeff knows the value of what I bring to the table and is aware of the problems I can solve. (Duplicate yourself # 1, Jeff) His parents have introduced me to friends of theirs. (Duplicate yourself # 2, 3, Jeff's parents) His brothers and sisters now refer me to people they know. (Duplicate yourself 4, 5, 6, Jeff's brothers and sisters...) Are you starting to get it? When your clients start to tell the people they know that you are the person they should contact, you have just duplicated yourself. The success I've enjoyed in my business is due to solving problems or satisfying a need or want. I strive to provide excellent service and deliver a quality product.

THE EDUCATION PROCESS

Most sales people are trying to sell their products or services to potential clients rather than educate them about the benefits. When you educate someone about how your product or service can solve a problem you have just duplicated yourself. When you educate someone about how your products or services can satisfy a need or a want you also create another you. Can you imagine creating this new "Sales Team" of twenty-five, fifty, one hundred people or more, that understand who you are, know what you do ,and know how you can help solve problems. This sales team is now working for you. What a great way to do business. Each one can then introduce you to people they know. You can build a sales team of one hundred, five hundred or a thousand or more by providing excellent service. Everyone knows three hundred or more people. That is the potential market you have to do business with. Would this concept take your business to the next level? Ten years ago, I developed this type of relationship with a group of 25 clients; today, over 1,200 business owners and salespeople know who I am, what I do, and how I can benefit others.

YOUR PERSONAL BOARD OF DIRECTORS.

I advise all salespeople and business owners to put together a Personal Board of Directors. This is a group of individuals that potentially compliment your business. Your Personal Board is comprised of individuals from different professions who understand you and the value and benefits of your products or services. You should meet with them on a regular basis to educate each other about what is going on in the market place. With changing tax laws, interest rates, the economy, government, the investment area etc., it pays to be aware of how these changes may effect your clients' situations.

DUPLICATE YOURSELF

So now there are hundreds of 'me' ready to direct family, friends, clients, or patients back to the 'original me' to solve problems or satisfy their needs or wants. Does it stop there? The answer is no. Duplicating yourself requires that you be proactive in your business and requires that you stay in touch. Remember to communicate with your sales team on a regular basis. The internet is probably the least expensive and best way to stay in touch to deliver information to a large number of people. But nothing beats a face-to-face meeting. **Exceed your clients expectations and they will refer you to everyone they know.**

DUPLICATE YOURSELF ACTIVITIES

Be different to the competition. Find ways that you can help your clients with other issues that they are facing. Be a resource in the community as someone who can refer them to other professionals that you know will do a fantastic job. Probably one of the most beneficial events I host during the year is a client appreciation luncheon or dinner. I also make my clients aware that they can bring a guest. This is the informal process of duplicating me through my clients. The dinner is not a sales event it is an appreciation dinner. I have never had anyone show up with cushions and name tags. I introduce myself and give them an update on our business and how well we are doing because of them. I thank them and make them aware that we wouldn't be able to do it without them. I have my business information displayed and available. Everyone receives a packet of information to take with them when they leave. I follow up with clients after the event to get feedback. I also ask what their invited guests thought of the event and always receive positive comments. My reason for doing follow up phone calls is to cultivate our relationship. If you are not staying in touch – they are not thinking of you.

Be creative. For example, on their birthday, rather than send a card, I call when I know that the call will go to their voice mail and I sing in my worst voice 'Happy Birthday.' I usually get a call back with the response something like, was that you? We laugh and they thank me for remembering. If they are having a baby, I deliver a sterling silver bank with a silver dollar inside. Inside the bank is also a note that says, "This is the first dollar being saved towards your college education". On Thanksgiving, I deliver pumpkin pies to their office and send thank you cards to their home. I e-mail what I think would be topics of interest to them with a note in the subject line that says, "I thought you might be interested in the following article, Frank". By exceeding their expectations they know that I care about them and they tell others.

SUCCESS STORIES

I look at myself as a resource in the community. If someone needs a doctor, accountant, attorney, real estate agent, mortgage broker, investment advisor, banker, business equipment supplier, or someone to get the squirrels out of the attic they call me. I've established business relationships with some of the best professionals in their industries and I know that when I refer them, they will do an excellent job. The Business Network that I oversee understands this concept of duplicating yourself. They meet each week to educate each other as to the benefits of their products or services and who their target market is. Here are some of their success stories.

A credit processor shared with his team that one of the benefits of his company's services was that they paid interest on the monies that were left in the account prior to transferring the funds to their business accounts. His team shared the information with business owners that they knew and he received thirty-six new pieces of business the next time they met.

Meeting frequently with your sales team, your board of directors and your clients will get you the desired results you are looking for.

A financial planner shared with his group a profile of the ideal client. He stated that the client should be someone married, in a white collar profession, earning between $75,000 and $150,000 per year, between the ages of thirty and forty-five with two children and a home owner. This profile would most benefit from the planning he had to offer. A real estate agent that he knew went back to his data base, searched for three years the clients he did business with, and the next time they got together the agent passed ninety six referrals to the financial planner. He also sent letters to everyone on the list why he thought it would be beneficial to meet with the planner.

Cross marketing is another way to duplicate yourself.

Another success story that is a result of duplicating yourself was when a health insurance agent teamed up with an event planner. The event planner was currently working with a nationwide business association. The association's business owners had been notified by their current insurance carrier that they were pulling out of the health insurance market and that they had twelve months to find coverage elsewhere. The next time they met she gave the health insurance agent a printout of seven hundred fifty-six names, addresses, phone numbers and the person to contact to give a quote for health insurance.

Educating people about who you are, what you do, and staying in touch, can bring business to your door.

IT IS ALWAYS MORE THAN ONE THING

I don't know of any "one thing" you can do in business that will continue to help your business grow. I do know that focusing on the concept of 'duplicating me' and by educating people about my business has been the number one activity and one of the major reasons for my success.

I sense that people know that I have a passion for what I do, and that I am willing to help them be as successful as they want to be in their chosen professions. I still advertise and am involved with several local business organizations. On occasion, I will do a seminar and at the end of the presentation will give everyone attending an inflatable seat cushion and professional name tag.

Frank La Placa is the Executive Director of Business Network International's North East Kansas Region. BNI is the world's largest business networking and marketing organization. You can contact Frank by going to www.BNIKansas.com or by e-mail at BNIChapters@aol.com.

ABOUT FRANK

Frank La Placa is the Executive Director of Business Network International's North East Kansas Region. BNI is the world's largest business networking and marketing organization. He is also a sought-after speaker and sales trainer. His workshop on "How To Take Your Business To The Next Level" is delivered in an interactive style incorporating humor and promoting activities that businesses and sales people should do to be successful.

His past activities include:

• Managing partner of a financial consulting firm.

• Served on the Board of Directors of one of the country's top financial services organization.

• President of a local Chamber of Commerce and President of Friends of the Library.

• Frank was one of fifteen master instructors nationwide chosen to train and educate members in the financial services industry regarding planning and meeting their clients needs.

His interests are diverse. He is an amateur magician and musician. He plays the guitar, saxophone and drums. He collects magic books and 45 rpm records from the 50's & 60's.

Frank is veteran of the United States Navy. He lives in Kansas with his wife Catherine. They are extremely proud of their two children, Tamara and Michael, and of their grandchildren, Wyatt and Easton, who they know will make a difference in this world someday.

You may contact Frank by going to www.BNIKansas.com or by e-mail at BNIChapters@aol.com.

CHAPTER 23

LIVING A FEARLESS LIFE BY CHOICE

(HOW 'HAND MEDITATION' CAN TAKE YOU THERE)

BY ANGELIKA CHRISTIE

Are you frustrated when all of your good intentions only bring forth mediocre outcomes?

Have you read about tools that are available today that promise great results and still are not achieving what you desire?

You are not alone. In fact, most of us have been there at some point. You may have exhausted your willpower by trying to overcome old patterns of beliefs and behaviors and you may feel defeated and disappointed in yourself. But let me tell you: It is not your fault! Willpower and positive thinking alone are not enough to have it All. We are just not wired in our brain for radical change. Or are we?

Why do we encounter so much discomfort, fear, anxiety, and even terror on the path to success? It is the sum of all negative imprints, because over ninety percent of your life is on automatic, according to the learned behavior from your earliest time of existence, yes, even before you were born. Your brain uploaded everything you experienced from post-conception through your formative years. Surely, you were not consciously aware of this. Together, with the inherited traits from your parents and ancestors, your program was pretty complete early on. Unfortunately, it only guaranteed your survival on this planet. As a species, we have evolved and became more conscious of our latent ability to achieve anything we desire. If you are in the middle or the 'autumn of your years', you know what a stretch this may be for you. The truth is, that you experience your life according to your beliefs, and early imprinting. But you can change anything at any age; it is never too late.

Instinctively, I knew since my childhood that I was part of something bigger. My search to find what it was took me into an unconventional life. I found that I always got what I wanted, because I could visualize and feel what I desired so clearly, and consequently, my private life looked glamorous and happy. After my five children had left the nest, I realized that even with the free time and all my knowledge, I felt terror show up in a big way. What was my problem? What was the missing piece? I had overcome the fear of public speaking (surveyed to be more feared than death). I stood up for my beliefs and feelings, even if they were unconventional. I trusted my instincts; this alone brought interesting and mostly fulfilling life experiences to me. And yet, whatever I manifested still left me with a yearning for what I still needed to learn, understand and give birth to.

The compliments, admiration and perception of others created an ever-tighter wall around me. Most of them were certain that I had it all. In my visualizations, my image easily expressed what I wanted: stepping fully into my power and bringing my gift to the world. I could see myself being a sought-after speaker and teacher, traveling to all the sacred and mystical places on earth. These visions excited me to a point that involved all of my senses; I felt elated and inspired for most of the day…but it waned. Why? Because whenever I thought about it rationally, it triggered a tension that turned into a feeling of terror. What if I achieved great success? How radically would my life change? Do I really want to be that successful? There was this Jo-Jo between excitement and anxiety.

I did nothing for a while, except thinking that I needed some more training, more books, and even more seminars, which I enrolled into. Of course, I knew it was my racket for hiding and not fully stepping into and expressing my soul's purpose. In my soul, I knew my connection to the unlimited wisdom and creativity of the universe. I just did not trust myself enough; and then, **I had a major break-through.** It came in a moment of my greatest despair. I cried out to God, and, simultaneously attempted to quiet my racing mind. As if guided by an unseen force, my hands gently touched, and I felt a surge of tremendous energy coming from my heart into the palms of my hands. I dropped into a deep relaxation, where I connected with my unique power, which burned like a fire, through my fears and limitations.

As a woman in my early sixties, my life changed that moment. I knew that a whole new life of purpose, success and prosperity was seeded; and I was ready. I could see my empowerment to teach, especially women, how to re-create their later years. Too many of us believe that it is too late to shine and create a life of joy and abundance after children have grown, and partners may not always share your vision for yourself. But this is far from the truth. And yet, new situations create their own stressors.

Stress and anxiety are triggered by an ancient mechanism that sits in a small gland, the Amygdala, which is just above your ears. When danger is approaching, stress-chemicals are released into your autonomic nervous system through neurotransmitters and create a reaction faster than the speed of light. It is mostly beneficial. For example, when you don't see a car approaching as you step onto a busy street; a flash of terror makes you jump back faster than you can think!

Anxiety is widespread but it is not always talked about on your path to success. You may have experienced it in different situations in your life, whenever major change is anticipated, even if it is just in your mind. This primal instinct to avoid risk served your ancestors well for their survival; otherwise, you would not be here to read this chapter. This primal instinct is deeply seated in your subconscious mind and runs at least ninety percent of your life. It is outdated, and in dire need of upgrading.

Manifesting your greatest success for anything you desire is already programmed within you. You see, you are capable of manifesting anything in your life. God, or whatever you call this creative power from which the universe sprang and you are part of, resides within every cell of your body. It is my belief that the mystery of knowing who we truly are, lies within the reservoir of our awakening consciousness. We become more conscious of consciousness itself at an ever-increasing speed. You can experience it in a state of deep listening; deep listening can only happen in silence and meditation.

Today we know without doubt (confirmed by latest scientific research), that we are capable of changing any program in our subconscious mind and consequently, we can change any condition. It does not matter whether it is in the realm of physical health, emotional health, relationship issues, success, or money. All current situations you find yourself in are according to what you think, feel and acted upon. This is true for unconscious negative thoughts and feelings from the past and present, as well as for thoughts about the future.

In computer terms, it is like deleting old programs and downloading new ones onto your hard drive, the most powerful processor within you. There is nothing as fast and powerful as your subconscious mind. Nothing. Not even all the computers on this planet combined. Their combined power is only a fraction of what your subconscious mind is capable of processing. So, the question is how do you access this powerful part of your brain?

We know that you can reach it through deep meditation and breathing techniques. But, let's face it – it is much more difficult to get into this peaceful quiet state of mind in our busy world of mental stress and information overload. Technology unleashes constant electronic noise to your mind, polluting and congesting your nervous system. Is it any wonder that emotions like fear, anxiety and terror are on the rise?

It is like driving a racecar in first gear at high speed. Dropping into a relaxed state is like shifting into a lower gear, which calms down the engine, but speeds up the wheels that bring you faster to your goal. Every time you shift into the next lower gear, your body uses less energy to reach a faster result; the engine stays calm, but the wheels turn faster and faster. Isn't this great? It works for you just as it works in your car. What you need is an easy-to-learn tool that can do just that: calm down your body, quiet the external noise and internal chatter, so you reach that part of your brain where new programs can be installed. Then you can see clearly that all the negative emotions from the past were only illusions.

There is so much I would like to share with you, but I have only one chapter here. I will introduce you to the first step in my *"Five-Step-Program-to–Living-a-Fearless-Life."*

I will give you an easy tool to get into a deep meditation, even if you have never meditated before, or have a hard time shutting up your "monkey mind". For the beginner, the intermediate, and advanced student of meditation, my "Hand Meditation" is an excellent tool to travel the path through your heart to your subconscious mind, leaving all stress, anxiety and chatter behind. You reach a deeply relaxing Alpha/Theta brainwave by using: **your hands**.

Your hands play a major role from the beginning of your life. Watch an infant exploring space with his/her hands or recall small children's primal instinct to touch **everything**. Your hands are involved in every action at all times – they caress, enforce, teach, negate, approve, pat, point, give, take away, and so on. Your hands carry out manual labor like preparing food, holding the cup you drink from or the utensils you eat with, doing housework, earn money, and other countless tasks. "Hearing-impaired" people use their hands as the main tool for communication – but so do you.

YOUR HANDS ARE THE BRIDGE BETWEEN YOUR HEART AND YOUR BRAIN.

What does this mean? They move differently when you speak from your heart than when you express from your brain. The amazing thing is that over ninety-eight percent of all tasks your hands are involved in come from your subconscious mind. You don't have to think about how to use your hands; they know, because it is accomplished without your conscious direction.

Remember that the first step in clearing the path to your desired dream of success is: eliminating your stress, your anxieties and negative internal dialogue. I have to show you via video or in person, how to get deeply into a meditative state using your hands.

Here I can only give you a quick exercise, so you can get a glimpse of what is possible.

Sit in a comfortable position with your spine upright and your legs uncrossed. Allow your abdomen to become soft while taking a few long deep breaths. Just imagine a gentle wave of golden light flowing through every part of your body, from the top of your head to the tips of your toes, softening and releasing any tension, warming and relaxing your entire body. Feel this for a moment while you slowly bring up your hands, palms facing each other and touching slightly.

Bring all of your attention to the sensation in your hands while you slowly explore one hand with the other. Trace your fingertips along the inside of one palm, and then the outside of your hand. Repeat a few times and switch to the other hand exploring the same way. You may rotate your palms toward each other and explore the space in between your palms. Feel the sensation! A tingling, an energy or heat in your hands are a sign of surrender to the creative force within you…

If you do this for a few minutes while being fully involved in the sensory experience, you will have slowed your breathing. This will naturally and easily bring about a state of deep relaxation and focused attention. Slow down the movement of your hands even further. Explore the space in between your hands, and sense the warmth and energy increasing.

When you feel deeply connected to your inner Self, start visualizing exactly what you want. Feel it, taste it, see it, and know that this laser sharp focus creates the mold or vessel into which your desired dream can be physically manifested.

Use my "Hand Meditation" often to quickly and easily calm your mind, see clearly, and step into the power of your Unlimited Self from which you can create all that you desire. As an additional benefit, it is enjoyable and builds an intrinsic relationship with your body. I know it works. I have done it, and so can you.

Copyright: Angelika Christie 2011

ABOUT ANGELIKA

Angelika was born in Germany right after World War II, and moved to the Bahamas in 1978, where she lives with her Bahamian husband. Although she is blessed with 5 children (and 8 grand children), she only sees them now occasionally, since they are all grown and left the nest.

Angelika studied mystical teachings and health sciences for the last 25 years. She studied with many teachers in the health and energy medicine field. Her thirst for knowledge brought a wide horizon of possibilities into her field of awareness, together with a large toolbox of modalities and applications. She is an ND, a Nutritional Therapist, a Reiki Master Teacher (for 18 years), a Hypnotherapist, a Writer and Speaker on Health issues, a Coach, a Yoga teacher, and an avid reader of books related to the New Quantum Science of Biology and Spirituality.

Angelika loves the works of Gregg Braden and Dr. Bruce Lipton. Recently, she studies "Evolutionary Life Transformation" with Craig Hamilton.

She is the Author of "Your Intelligent Cell" and co-author of 2 other books, which will be available later this year. She teaches meditation and programs on how to live your best life after 45 and create the life you chose to live.

All of her activities -- her health articles in the local newspaper, the radio shows on health issues, her speaking presentations to Service Clubs and Medical Discussion Panels -- all were stepping stones to what she brings forward now and in the future.

Visit her blog: www.radianthealthbahamas.blogspot.com

www.angelikachristie.com
www.meditatinghands.tv
www.reikibahamas.com
www.breath-of-peace-yoga.com

CHAPTER 24

YOU'VE WON BEFORE YOU'VE BEGUN.

BY JEFF PEOPLES AND DAVID ELLZEY

How to live and prosper from your inborn success now.

Ponder this simple question: *Are you aware of these words*? If your answer is yes, you've won. I know this may sound too simple, but let me explain why it's true and how this radically simple recognition can profoundly transform every aspect of your life with no effort on your part except for making a simple choice.

Whether you'd like a more loving relationship, a more rewarding job, a more successful business, a healthier body or you simply wish to feel a deeper purpose to your life – this simple realization is essential. It is the key to a lock that most of humankind has never unlocked. You can.

YOUR COSMIC MOMENT

Travel with me now to that cosmic moment: A microscopic meeting of one of three million sperm and a lonely egg. From out of that encounter, your physical form began its journey to where it is at this moment, trillions and trillions of cells later, right here right now, reading these words.

Between then and now, you have walked this planet 'experience by experience' – first learning to eat, sleep, and walk, falling in love, being hurt, falling in love again. Whatever roles you've played, including son, daughter, student, executive, entrepreneur, artist, chef, wall street analyst, mother and countless other roles that are played on the great stage of this world, the question is, "Are those experiences or roles the totality of who you truly are?"

Experiences and roles, people, relationships, your body, nations, the weather, the value of money – they all change. Yet through this change, there is something that has always been present. It has watched the events of life come and go, including the thoughts and feelings that come and go in you like fish in the ocean. Do you know what I am referring to that is always here? It is mostly overlooked because it never leaves.

I am referring to the essential *you*. The awareness that is the background of all the roles you play, and all the feelings and thoughts that frequent the landscape of your life.

KNOWING WHO YOU ARE AND WHY IT MATTERS

This idea of you being here all along seems obvious. Of course you were here all along. So what is my point? I am proposing that even though this is obvious, you still have identified more with what comes and goes than with the reassuring awareness of your own self, that has patiently been here all along.

Is it possible that the main component of who you truly are is this awareness, rather than the transient items that you watch come and go? For example, you are reading these words now and later you'll do something else. Things will change and yet you remain present through it all. Why is this essential to understand? It isn't – unless you want a more fulfilling life.

THE DIVIDENDS OF RECOGNIZING AWARENESS

Let's look at how this realization can be invaluable in everyday life and even in the world of business. We feel dissatisfied with life because we seek happiness not in this constant self, but in the items of life that appear and disappear. Additionally, we suffer as we attempt to control the coming and going of the unpredictable contents of life.

To be more succinct, we look for fulfillment and success in the world, a world that is transient and eternally changing. Can you see the dilemma in this? How can we find lasting happiness based on things that don't last?

What's the option? I propose that success and happiness are even more possible when living with an expanded sense of awareness and self, I will explain more "why" in a moment. First, let's complete this idea with an analogy.

This habit of seeking fulfillment in all the wrong places is similar to the story of Dorothy in The Wizard of Oz. After her journey of trials and tribulations, she finally locates the Wizard who was supposed to have the secret to her returning home. Instead, she discovers that he is not a wizard, but simply a gentle man behind a grand façade. In his own way, he reveals to her three friends that they had the special gifts of wisdom, heart, and courage inside all along.

Similarly, Dorothy learns that she always had the ability to go home. Had she looked inside herself and not at the outer world for the answer, she'd have recognized her own power. To make this story more meaningful, the movie points out that Dorothy never actually left home. She only dreamed that she did.

YOUR LAND OF OZ

What is the false dream you are living? Your quest for happiness, success, or a fulfilling life is likely based on the idea that they exist somewhere other than inside you now. Have you been focused outside of yourself seeking some wizard or imagined perfect Land of Oz? Perhaps you've been postponing your happiness until you find the perfect life-partner, the perfect job, or the perfect home.

Let me be very clear here. Having these things is certainly of great value and I recommend you allow yourself to enjoy them. However, it is when you believe that happiness is based only in those things and that who you are is dependent on them, that you suffer. You can never be permanently fulfilled with them, because those things all come and go.

Like Dorothy, your ability to return home or to a more permanent state of grace, peace, and contentment is dependent on your recognizing what is already here. Awareness itself. This *you* needs no fixing, no finding, no search. This is the reason it is overlooked. St Francis of Assisi said it best, "What you are looking for – is what is looking."

However, according to much of society, religion, and our childhood we are often told that this is not enough. Supposedly, we are inherently imperfect: not educated enough, good enough, worthy enough, tall or short enough, old or young enough. And we must do many things to become a "better me." What if all of this is a lie?

LIVING THE LIE

Do you find yourself feeling that you need to make a million, be enlightened, have the perfect body, or a great sex-life, before you let yourself be happy or feel successful? As we've said, having these things is not the issue. The question is, "Do these things guarantee lasting happiness?"

Even when you achieve things that you desire in the world, do you notice that soon after there is an inner restlessness? Do you notice that these things never quite seem to be enough? Our soul seeks more than temporary fulfillment. That is the reason for our restlessness. The soul knows.

As we've already said, we are well-trained to believe that we are not enough as we are now and need to either get "more" or be "better." This is a never-ending road and can create that pervasive disease called *self-doubt.*

AN EXPERIMENT FOR YOUR LIFE

Let's look beyond all self-doubt and limiting beliefs. In this very moment, as your eyes rest on this page, can you see that awareness is here? Does this awareness require any fixing, altering, or improving in order to exist? In this simple and clear way, you are complete. There is nothing to change, no more to get, and nothing to make "better." Your mind may fight this a bit. It might ask, "Shouldn't I always be striving to achieve more success?"

For just this moment, can you see how the habits of being "an achiever, a doer, a hard worker" are not required in order for you to exist here and now? It is great to achieve and create a successful life that you love and enjoy. However, we are speaking here of endlessly striving to succeed based on the unconscious belief that who you are is never enough. The option is to live and achieve your dreams based on realizing your inherent greatness and the simple miracle of your existence. This is being a true winner in every moment of your life.

If you strongly believe that you are not enough, no matter what you do, have, or achieve, you will always have the feeling of not enough. Unconscious self-sabotage becomes the norm. On the other hand, if you are willing to question that self-destructive belief and see through it, the relief can be like nourishing water in a scorching desert.

Let's make this more real for you. Take a breath, relax and just be here. Take another breath, lower your shoulders. Seriously, try this. Breathe deeply. Simply be aware of this moment. There's a good possibility that your blood pressure is lowering as you do this. Your overall health and well-being can improve because you are showing up in the here-and-now the only place where health can actually happen.

The current moment is the only place that health, creative thinking and problem solving can actually occur. When we let go of filling the present with our past or future concerns, we find the possibility of recognizing the love that is here now. When you allow this moment to be more open and you allow awareness to simply be, each moment holds more potential for riches and wealth. That can mean more money, health, or simply resting in love, acceptance, and appreciation right now.

This awareness, in this moment, is the infinite fountain out of which the wealth of life flows. Think of it like the ocean. You can always focus on the fish and how small they appear, and thus you mostly experience the limitations of life - or you can focus on the expanse of the ocean and experience the vast potential of existence and of yourself. From this expansive view, opportunities can arise that you never expected, because you are open to them.

This is a radically simple proposal that as the ocean of awareness you have already won. You exist. A fulfilled life must be born from here:

the success, the love you seek, everything. If you overlook this *you*, can you see that you're building your life on the ever-shifting sands of the mind and imagination, rather than on the constant foundation of the *you* that is forever here?

HOW THIS AFFECTS YOUR EVERYDAY

Example One: You are preparing for a meeting and you feel a history of anger toward the others coming to the meeting. This means a majority of your creative resources are redirected to your emotions and replaying the story of the events in the past that stirred up those feelings. Your attention is not present. After the meeting you say to yourself. "See, it was just as I thought. Nothing got done and they didn't listen to a word I said."

Can you see how you contributed to the outcome? You expected a certain behavior and that it would be an unproductive meeting, Thus you weren't available in any real way to participate in a fresh outcome. You weren't present. You were reliving the past and projecting it into the current situation. There was no room for success or a win/win outcome.

Example Two: Your age and your body are angling toward the final stages of life. Whether you have a few days or a few more years, you are filled with regrets and unresolved emotions. Let's look at this closely. Do you see how in this case fulfillment is based *only* on how the *outer* world could have been different? Can you see how this approach guarantees disappointment and regret?

In both cases, your life is impacted by your unconscious habit of focusing on life's events and not on who you truly are. Notice, who you are in this moment needs no changing of the past in order to be present. And it is only in you that the fulfillment you seek can be ultimately found here and now. Nothing in the world will give this to you. Nothing today, yesterday or tomorrow. All things are temporary. It is only the awareness that you are – that remains constant and the ultimate source for having and creating continual happiness and success.

THE FINAL TREASURE

Here is the gold. In any realm, whether you have difficulty with work associates, are in the final stages of life, or you're simply trying to move beyond the weight of self-judgment, when you see through the false perception that you are not enough, your life transforms. By seeing yourself as the completeness of awareness itself, you have more potential for acceptance and love. You are free of the limiting confines of self-judgment and doubt. This contributes to the possibility of healing relationships and producing more rewarding results in life and business.

You have won before you've begun because *who you truly are* is vast and a success through your mere existence, even before you have set out on the path toward worldly success. Who you truly are has never wavered regardless of what you've achieved or not achieved. The profound and radical simplicity of this is the unshakeable foundation upon which a more fulfilling life can be built. Moving beyond self-doubt and the perception of lack can powerfully pry open the door to greater achievement, prosperity, love and happiness.

Your task now is to live knowing that lasting happiness is found not in the ever-changing external world or the imagined Land of Oz, but <u>in the constant essence of who you truly are here and now</u>. In this way, success and achievement can certainly occur, but along the path even before you initiate any new project or phase of life, you can say with certainty, "I've won before I've begun."

ABOUT JEFF

Jeffery Peoples has created six successful entrepreneurial companies. Currently he is the founder and CEO of Window Book, Inc., a company with an incredible team that has enabled thousands of people in business to mail over $39.5 billion in postage – generating aggregate profits of well over $395,000,000.00 by mailing and shipping more intelligently since 1989.

Jeffery has a BA in Economics from the University of Colorado, Boulder. As a leader, Jeffery strongly values people seeing their inherent greatness, generating wealth, and learning life-skills that transform their lives. He was awarded a Sedona Method Certified Coach in 2010 and coaches people one-on-one to discover their innate gifts and potential for success.

Jeffery is a requested speaker at direct marketing, mailing and shipping industry events nationwide. He has been in a loving relationship with Liz Peoples for over 30 years and is the proud father of two spectacular children. To learn if your company can increase its profits by $50,000 to $1,000,000.00 or more, go to www.WindowBook.com/demo

Contact Information:

Jeffery Peoples
Cambridge MA 02139
617-395-4520
jpeoples@windowbook.com
www.jefferypeoples.com

ABOUT DAVID

David Ellzey is a transformational speaker, author, and coach who has inspired over a quarter of a million people worldwide. He is co-contributor with Dr. Deepak Chopra and Jack Canfield to the upcoming book, *Stepping Stones to Success.* His own book, *The Ocean of Now,* will launch in 2011.

In addition to being a requested motivational speaker for The World Bank, Future Business Leaders of America, and more, David recently lead a strategic planning retreat for the United Nations Bureau for Development Policy, which operates in 166 countries and is the United Nations' global development network.

His private coaching clients include global executives, people of all walks of life, and entrepreneurs who seek clarity of vision and success with a deep sense of purpose.

Using ancient principles, modern techniques, and his special brand of humor, David inspires an inner alchemy from fear to courage and profound clarity. He has an unshakeable passion for people's awakening to their magnificence. Dr. Christiane Northrup, Norman Cousins, Susan Jeffers, and Rev. Michael Beckwith have all endorsed David and his transformative work around the world.

Contact Information:

David Ellzey
New York, NY 10128
212-996-5159 office
david@davidellzey.com
www.davidellzey.com

CHAPTER 25

MASTERING THE 12 KEY AREAS THAT DRIVE BUSINESS SUCCESS

BY VICTOR HOLMAN

What makes a great entrepreneur and high achiever? This question has been asked and answered throughout time. But it wasn't until my personal journey of studying successful business owners and entrepreneurs that I was able to transform my life and build a successful business. I'd like to share these powerful lessons I learned with you today.

I. DO AS SUCCESSFUL PEOPLE DO

Since I was a kid, I've always admired people who could overcome obstacles and always come out on top. I was an average student at best…I definitely wasn't the kid you wanted to cheat off of. In college, I constantly struggled to fully grasp the readings and lectures and to execute good grades on exams. I used to always get frustrated when I'd see somebody who I knew wasn't any brighter than me get much better grades. So, I started observing and focusing on why some students were able to get A's while other students (like myself) struggled. I spoke to several top students and found out what they did, how they studied, who they studied with, and how they managed their time. I learned that, well, cramming the night before the test was not a good practice. But I also learned that these students that got good grades studied differently than those that did not. They understood what they needed to focus on, and where they needed to study more. I applied what I learned from my research, and was able to get A's on my last two report cards. I was onto something.

II. BE COMFORTABLE BEING UNCOMFORTABLE

I went on to work for a top international consulting firm, where once again, I was average at best. I was scared. I lacked confidence. I was afraid to fail. It was then that I found a mentor who taught me a lesson that today still gets me through the challenges I face with my businesses. He was a senior associate with the firm and he told me "Victor, in business you've got to learn to be comfortable being uncomfortable". Think about that. We often shy away from our dreams or from greatness because greatness often involves putting ourselves in situations that are out of our comfort zone. Working as a management consultant, where every project is different, definitely forced me to step out of my comfort zone.

III. SET YOURSELF APART FROM YOUR COMPETITION

So, from that point on, I began to take risks. I took on projects that I had no clue how to complete. I learned that I had a passion for business performance, for helping clients understand why they perform the way they do, and helping them turn their businesses around. I studied hundreds of high-performing organizations. I surveyed their CEOs and top managers, I wrote books, articles, and created a business model for high-performing organizations. What I didn't realize I was doing at the time, was establishing myself as an expert in this field. I soon became the go-to guy in my company for business performance. And because I wrote articles and a book, my company started putting me on all of their proposals as a key personnel member to help them win contracts. What I had done was set myself apart from the rest of my colleagues. I climbed the ladder so fast that I surpassed my mentor within a year and a half. As the saying goes, "There's no traffic in the extra mile." Most people do just enough to get by. *People who stand out are simply those who do a little more than most, who set themselves apart or go that extra mile.* Many businesses that are very successful go that extra mile for their customers.

IV. TWO KEYS TO BEING A SUCCESSFUL ENTREPRENEUR

I've gone on to start a coaching business, I've developed several business mastery systems, I own several profit generating websites, and I've developed frameworks for running successful businesses. Most of my achievements came from what I learned from studying successful entrepreneurs. What I learned was that people that are able to overcome huge challenges and achieve great things share two common traits:

1. They determine what areas, if they were to improve, would have the greatest impact on their success, and
2. They take immediate action to improve those areas.

They step out of their comfort zone and take that first step. And once they take that first step they take the next step, and the next step and they stay fully committed and steadfast to improving, and they refuse to give up no matter what happens, and before they know it, they reach their goal. My study of high performing businesses showed that successful owners refuse to fail.

V. THE GAMERS MENTALITY

Successful entrepreneurs remind me of my little cousin who can beat any video game. He plays these games over and over again. And when his character dies, he simply hits the continue button and continues playing until he eventually beats the game. Now, while I don't agree with playing video games all day long, we can learn a lot from the mentality of the video gamer. When they begin a new game, it may be awkward. The controls of the game, the layout and the rules are often unfamiliar. They may be completely awful the first few attempts. But with persistence and the will to win, they overcome these challenges (rather quickly, if I might add), and complete their goal of conquering all levels within that game. Does this mean that they are the most skilled, the most ambidextrous, or the most talented? No. It simply means that they made the decision to not quit until they accomplished their goal.

We have to be like these gamers, when it comes to our businesses. As you begin to conquer your weaknesses, your doubts and your fears get less and less. You begin to pick up momentum and soon it's IMPOSSIBLE to stop you. And that's where the magic begins. This is where we become the type of entrepreneur that can overcome any challenge, any obstacle and any set back that crosses our paths.

VI. YOU'RE ONLY AS STRONG AS YOUR WEAKEST SKILL

Perhaps the toughest attribute of a successful entrepreneur is learning those skills that most people aren't comfortable with – such as sales, financial management, and marketing. I come from an Information Technology Management background. In IT systems you are only as strong as your weakest component. In your home, you can have the newest, fastest computer, and the best computer software and peripherals, but if you are accessing the Internet through a dial up modem, your performance will be poor. Your business works in the same way. You can have the greatest products and sell them at the lowest prices, but if you don't have the marketing skills to get those products in front of the people who need them, your business will struggle. Simply put, being a successful entrepreneur requires that you be rounded in key business-success areas.

VII. THE 12 KEY BUSINESS SUCCESS AREAS

In order to run a successful business you have to master skills in the 12 key business success areas.

1. You have to have solid strategic planning skills to define your future business and develop a clear plan to get there. Your ability to articulate your vision and translate it into action is critical to business success.

2. You must have solid products and services that satisfy customer demand and needs. When your products and services are aligned to your customers needs, you become a business based on providing value.

3. You must have solid pricing skills to ensure that you are competitive, but at the same time maximizing your profits. Knowing which pricing strategies to apply throughout the various phases of the product lifecycle is a key to staying competitive.

4. You have to have people skills to get the best out of your employees and partners, and to take advantage of joint venture opportunities. The people that surround your business are your best allies, and the more you understand what drives them, the harder they will work for your business.

5. You have to have sound finance skills to understand what all the numbers and financial ratios mean to your business, and to ensure that you can get financing from banks. The ability to manage cash flow effectively is the blood line of your business.

6. You need customer skills to ensure a great customer experience and to ensure repeat business and referral business. It only takes one unhappy customer to damage your business reputation. Developing a process to manage customer satisfaction is essential for growing your business.

7. You need marketing skills to get your message and products out to the public and to manage your potential customers. The ability to get the right products to the right people at the right time is the key to ensuring a successful marketing campaign.

8. You need strong sales skills to keep the revenues coming in, to create a solid sales force, and to constantly grow your business. Developing an effective sales program built around the key phases of the sales process enables you to identify more opportunities, and thus close more sales.

9. You need distribution skills to make sure your products are in stock and getting to your customers in the fastest, most convenient way. You can have the best products, at the best prices, but if you can't manage inventories or ensure fast delivery times, your business will suffer.

10. You need technical skills to make sure you are taking

advantage of the systems that help you reach your goals faster. You don't have to be a technical wizard, but you do need to be aware of the tools that can enhance your services and the tools that your competition is taking advantage of.

11. You need analytical skills to ensure that every aspect of your business is operating at peak performance, and to make sure that you understand the obstacles that are keeping you from reaching your goals. Understanding what's working and what isn't, and being able to make fast, informed decisions will keep your business on the path to success.

12. You need personal development skills to make sure your business goals are in line with your personal goals. This is needed to ensure that you, as a businessperson, are constantly growing as an individual, and making a positive impact in your world. Being able to balance your business and personal life is one of the greatest challenges for thriving entrepreneurs.

These are the 12 key skills that drive business success. If you lack processes and skills in any of these areas, your business is likely to suffer. Conversely, if you are strong in all of these areas, or making improvements to become strong in them, your business is destined for success.

VIII. MASTERING SKILLS IN THE KEY BUSINESS SUCCESS AREAS

Mastering skills in the 12 key success areas may sound like a daunting task. But the truth is that all of these skills are learnable. You can master them quite quickly if you know the formula and simply make the decision that you are going to overcome all challenges, and then dedicate the time to master them.

My Small Business Mastery System provides a systematic approach to learning these key skills and applying them to your current business. It walks you through a series of business assessments to help you find out exactly what area you need to focus on to build your business in the shortest amount of time. It then walks you through a series of business plans that provide a step by step blueprint for you to implement powerful business growth strategies. It provides videos, audios, templates, training programs, guides and other valuable resources to help you achieve your business goals. But before you can achieve this, you have to overcome the two things that hold most entrepreneurs back from huge success: fear and doubt.

You have to learn how to be comfortable, being uncomfortable. And when you begin to master these skills, you become the type of person that can grow any business and overcome all obstacles.

ABOUT VICTOR

Victor Holman is a successful business coach, consultant, international speaker and entrepreneur. His passion for business performance and process improvement is unsurpassed. Victor has provided his expertise to over 50 government agencies worldwide and hundreds of corporations of all sizes. His goal is to help small businesses outperform their competition by applying business growth strategies that large, successful businesses use. He has developed a series of Business Mastery Programs that help business owners apply simple, powerful, cost effective techniques that deliver quantifiable results.

Victor's Performance Mastery System is an innovative, turnkey approach for achieving huge performance gains by applying best practices, leveraging strengths and implementing measurement systems that drive business success. It includes an online analysis tool which identifies strengths, weaknesses, cost savings opportunities, and provides a custom, step by step roadmap for maximizing profits, performance and productivity.

Victor's Small Business Mastery System is a fast-track roadmap for mastering the 12 key business success areas. It includes 10 business assessment tools, an online action planning tool, a Small Business Makeover tool, business skills training, and over 200 business growth strategy videos that deliver fast results.

His Internet Mastery System is a powerful program that teaches entrepreneurs step by step how to create products, establish credibility, and develop websites that generate huge traffic and converts high sales.

Victor has delivered his Internet Mastery Workshop worldwide. He authored "The 120 Day Performance Plan: A Step-by-Step Guide to Implementing a World-Class Performance Solution". He also has developed several business related guides that tackle just about any business obstacle you can imagine. Victor has developed video seminars, which have been delivered to over 400,000 prospective customers worldwide. And his Business Management Portal, http://www.lifecycle-performance-pros.com, provides free assessments, videos, management strategies, illustrated methodologies, articles, guides, templates, and advice on business growth and performance optimization.

Victor provides business consulting for small and large size organizations, business coaching, team performance workshops, and in-depth on-site business assessments for business owners trying to take their business to the next level.

You can take Victor's FREE business profitability and website assessments at: http://www.lifecycle-performance-pros.com.

CHAPTER 26

KNOW WHO YOU ARE AND DO WHAT YOU LOVE!

BY LAURA TREONZE

What do you do? Isn't it funny how often we use this question to start a conversation and yet it's not a topic most people enjoy talking about. Research shows approximately 55% of working adults surveyed are dissatisfied with their job. Why?

We spend countless hours and thousands of dollars taking classes to train us for a "job," then we chose a career based on what we learn instead of based on who we are. Most of us don't know who we are or how to harness our passion to create wealth. Often, the sense of dissatisfaction with work doesn't happen until our 30's and 40's; it's then we start feeling there must be more to life than a "job," but we're trapped by life's responsibilities and fearful of change.

Working for money may make you rich but true wealth comes from abundance within.

Although my credentials say Realtor, I am an entrepreneur, coach and speaker passionate about real estate. I love my work. My job does not define me and yet my attraction to the industry has helped me create a career and mission that perfectly describes me.

Your work should be about living a life style that creates the outcomes you desire. While most people are working their job as "a means to an end," I started asking myself, …if it all ended tomorrow, did I spend my time wisely?

We balance our budgets and evaluate our finances, but most people don't balance their energy or evaluate their sense of fulfillment at work. Knowing who you are and understanding what excites you allows immense creativity, and opens opportunities to unimaginable success and wealth.

I didn't realize that until seven years ago – when I read Jack Canfield's Success Principles – which asked the reader to write a mission statement. Mine said, "It is my mission to help people do and be more than they thought possible physically, emotionally and spiritually through real estate."

Until I wrote those words, I hadn't thought of my occupation as a means to live my mission. I have been blessed by great opportunities, had very interesting jobs, and yet I always felt like I was meant to do more. I assumed that "more" would happen outside work. Even when I created the statement I didn't fully grasp its meaning; and yet when I said the words aloud, they penetrated my core and I knew intuitively they would guide me to an amazing life that encompassed my career.

THE PATH

Today I say the words aloud and the meaning is crystal clear, but my journey to this point took many turns and resulted in countless moments of self-doubt.

I bought my first multi-family home when I was single and 23. A year later I met my boyfriend (now my husband) and convinced him to buy a multi-family property in New Hampshire. Two years later we were married, and moved to Connecticut through his job. We continued to manage the properties as rentals while I served as a fundraiser with a local division of a national non-profit. Ready to embark on motherhood, I knew I wanted a more flexible schedule so I could stay home with the baby. I decided to become a full-time real estate investor. With that decision, I knew I needed education, so I studied to get my real estate license.

A great real estate market and a connection through a friend gave me an opportunity to work as a buyer's agent for a local top producing broker. It was interesting and fun and seemed to fulfill my mission. Working with buyers was a great introduction to the industry, and I was thrilled to make money in my first year in the business.

In the meantime, we sold our rental properties out-of-state and decided to purchase properties closer to home. The investment transactions and subsequent fixing of the properties kept me in the investing game, although it was not at the forefront of my day-to-day activities.

As the market slowed, my broker's volume decreased, which meant he could no longer justify a buyer's agent. This change forced me to get my own clients, which proved to be a challenge. The previous market and working as a buyer's agent didn't teach me how to generate leads, maintain a database and manage my time. So, learning and building my new business was financially and energetically exhausting. I was working twice as hard and producing half as much.

I was very unhappy. I started questioning everything. Do I stay in real estate? Was I supposed to live out my stated mission? Should I go back to fundraising?

While the path may lead you down unexpected roads, your internal compass will keep you on track.

After a couple of years as a solo agent, I switched real estate offices and decided to revisit my reason for getting licensed – investing. Upon meeting my new broker, I boldly informed her I would not be practicing traditional real estate. I declared myself an investor and merely needed a place to "hang my license."

She said, "How can I help you achieve your goals?" That question opened the floodgates of opportunity.

I started learning about negotiating short sales for the purpose of buying investment properties. A *short sale* is when the bank allows a homeowner to sell their home for less than is owed. The process can be time consuming and challenging, but I found it very rewarding. After completing my first *short sale*, the seller said, "You were like an angel. You took an embarrassing situation and gave us our dignity back." I was speechless. I thought, "This is it, this is how I am meant to fulfill my mission." It all started to make sense.

My focus was short lived. Being in a new office brought an abundance of education. I quickly became over-educated. As a result, I jumped from niche to niche looking for 'the magic bullet' to create instant success in my business. After all, *short sales* took a long time to close, clearly there had to be an easier way to find success. At this point, success had changed meaning for me - I was tired of struggling in this business; spiritually rewarding work was no longer the focus. I wanted to make money. I paid a coach and was making cold calls for traditional business. As a result I was making more money, but I did not feel fulfilled. By definition I was living my mission - helping people buy and sell real estate - and yet the part that felt most rewarding (investing) had once again been put on the back burner.

Meanwhile, I met up with a local investor who had gained national acclaim on a popular house flipping show. Together we created a couple of educational workshops which had me recognized as the Realtor of choice for investors. I started speaking at the local Real Estate Investment Association and began to teach investor workshops through my brokerage.

After two years of trying build a business that fit someone else's definition of success, I revisited my mission and went back to working *short sales*. In my heart, I knew my sense of fulfillment was more important than a fast payout. I took a course and became certified to help homeowners faced with mortgage troubles. The class helped me systematize my business and allowed me to close deals faster. With each step and greater clarity, my mission brought me back to the core of who I was, and what I was meant to do.

Finally I could define my business. I declared myself an Investor Specialist and created my brand The Gold Coast Investment Group at Keller Williams, where our focus is "Enriching lives through real estate." After more than six years in the industry, I had established a business model that incorporated my passion for investing, the experience I had as a traditional agent and my goals for helping people through education. Was I finally living my mission? Yes and it doesn't end there...

THE DESTINATION

The path to my destination taught me it's easy to be influenced by others goals when you aren't clear on your own. Life is about trusting your inner voice and declaring yourself more important than anyone else. It's about making your goals and dreams your top priority. You can't give to others if you don't fill yourself first. You can't fill yourself up if you don't know what makes you full.

It is also about surrounding yourself with people who support you. Dreams are often lost through "reasons" in the guise of..."my mother always told me", "my husband won't allow me", "my kids need me to", ... STOP with the excuses! You have control of your destiny. You can live your life based on the past or you can create your future based on your dreams. Once you know who you are, the excuses go away because you set the path. There is no one to blame and the people around you will either start to support you or they will filter themselves out of your life. Either way you win.

Each year, my declaration of self gets clearer and the rewards greater. Following the path and reaching a destination offers new beginnings and unexpected opportunities. This year, I became a national instructor for a class that teaches real estate agents how to work with investors. My real estate business is flourishing and now I am blessed with an opportunity to be paid to speak to agents across the country about my passion. None of this could have happened without knowing who I am, and going back to a mission that reminds me to do what I love.

When you decide to live your authentic self – success happens!

Finally, follow me to the ten steps that will take you on the path to *SUCCESS* and *SATISFACTION*.

TEN STEPS THAT TAKE YOU CLOSER TO KNOWING WHO YOU ARE AND DOING WHAT YOU LOVE

1. *Decide who you are.* If money were no object what would you be doing today?
2. *Write your mission.* Name three times in your life when you felt most successful. What do they have in common?

3. ***Determine YOUR goals.*** What are your top five goals? Are you working toward them each day?

4. ***Affirm your goals.*** Review your goals multiple times a day – put them where you eat so you are sure to see them at least 3x per day.

5. ***Surround yourself with support.*** Who do you spend time with? Do they bring you energy or deplete your energy?

6. ***Surround yourself with inspiration.*** What/who inspires you? Bring inspiration to your space through quotes, music or decor.

7. ***Focus on growth.*** Create a growth plan that includes training related to your passion – include everything from books and audio to webinars and live training.

8. ***Take daily action.*** Do one thing each day that brings you closer to living your passion.

9. ***Inventory your time.*** If you think you don't have enough time to live your dreams, take an inventory of your time tracking in 15 minute intervals what you do.

10. ***Celebrate YOU!*** Celebrate successes and milestones. Be sure to reward yourself and the ultimate reward will be a fulfilling life.

ABOUT LAURA

Laura Treonze is "Enriching Lives Through Real Estate" as an investor, Realtor with the Gold Coast Investment Group and public speaker. She holds a Bachelor of Arts degree from Stonehill College.

Laura possesses more than 15 years of real estate investment experience and has been a REALTOR® since 2004. She is a Certified Distressed Property Expert, Certified Investor Agent Specialist and has her e-pro designation. Laura is a national instructor on real estate investment and personal development. Laura's success in real estate has been featured in the book "Living The Law of Attraction".

Laura is a member of the National Association of REALTORS®, Connecticut Association of REALTORS®, Greater Fairfield Association of REALTORS®, Women's Council of REALTORS® and the Connecticut Real Estate Investors Association.

Her prior professional skills include marketing and fundraising.

Laura currently resides in Connecticut with her husband Todd and their two children. When Laura is not "living" real estate she is studying human nature or observing the world through a camera lens.

www.GoldCoastInvestmentGroup.com
Laura@kw.com
203-513-9331

CHAPTER 27

HONESTY ... THE FIRST STEP TO SUCCESS

BY WILLIAM GOLD

"Honesty is the first chapter of the book of wisdom."
~ Thomas Jefferson

Many times we are challenged with questions of honesty. Full disclosure is always the best policy. "Whatever happened to the personal guarantee?" I cannot sufficiently express the importance of doing business with honest, open people. If someone appears dishonest in any manner, pick up your planner and run away as fast as possible. I personally have hired many attorneys, contractors, and brokers. I ask them explicit questions that they may or may not reveal. "Will you sign the TRO, lawsuit, or ex-parte?" …"Will this amount cover the response to demur?" …"What does your quote include on the contractor's estimate?" …"Specifically, what kind of marketing and promotions will you do and when will you do those events?" Important questions that need honest answers. Let me add that it is OK to demand results. But you will have 'to pay to play.' "You only get as much justice as you can afford in America."

Here is an amazing story about honesty. Brian is my granite guy and he installs granite counter tops. I overpaid Brian $2,500 to encase a

Jacuzzi tub and shower in granite. I cut a check to Brian for $5,000. Brian could have issued a change order for $2,500 and not returned the money. And I would have still been happy with his work because it was excellent. Brian returned the $2,500. Brian honored his original agreement even at a loss. People like Brian are successful because they over-deliver and under-promise their services.

Sometimes you get the opportunity to see people go through amazing peril and stress without lowering their dignity and honor. I have a story about John, John does not make a great deal of money and he is a family man. In this past year, John's mother was murdered and he also received news that he was gravely ill. John pays me for services every month, even though he doesn't have enough money to pay for his mother's ashes at the cemetery. John has a hard time making the payments and sometimes he is late. Yet John is honoring his agreement. "I don't know John very well, but he has more credit worthiness than some of my family members." This is yet another story of a normal person doing extraordinary things.

We started off talking about the importance of trust and honesty. The second piece of advice would be the establishment of being the problem solver. If you look at your job as a counselor, rather than a sales person/business owner, people trust you with their business. Communication is always an important part of problem solving. First, take notes and then follow up with mail and email. Second, people want options, so give them the options. Your job is presenting yourself as the only option. Third, get to the point. People don't have any patience for long-winded conversations. They want to hear the <u>bottom line</u> and its impact on them. Fourth, always have a clean desk and a clean car. Lack of organization is a very dangerous quality, which could lead to losing files or worse, loss of your paperwork. It sends a message that you are too busy for details. Last, be inquisitive. Less than 5% of the population has an inquisitive nature. In other words, ask as many questions as possible, in order to identify values and goals.

Remember, people don't care about you or your story, until they know you care. They only care about the way you make them feel. "I think most of my success can be attributed to my knowledge of the client's needs and wants."

After you get a grasp of honesty and start understanding your role as a problem solver, another integral component of success would be …"hanging around people that are successful." Successful people are attracted to other successful people. Sometimes success is based off proximity. "Believe it or not, 'successful' rubs off." I have always made it a practice to work or train with only the best professionals in any industry. Successful people are wealthy and have a positive attitude. Stay away from people that have a negative presence. Healthy competition always pushes people to be better at home and work.

The fourth and most obvious advice I could give someone would be "Hang with others that give freely." You do not want a relationship with someone that does not understand reciprocity of shows greed. So, go to charitable events and meet people that are genuine and authentic about helping other people. I have a quote on the wall "We are each other's Angels." Give back to your community. I promise that it comes back in many other ways.

The last ingredient of success is obvious. "Do not do business with someone that you do not genuinely like." I know many people that are desperate and needy. They always take the low cost provider. Generally speaking, most people have a tendency to gravitate to the lower cost product or service. "Do not be one of the people that swims at the bottom of the pool." Remember you get what you pay for in this life. I would recommend you take the highest priced guy vs. the lowest priced guy. "Go forth with vigor and follow your gut feelings."

Now, I cannot stand people who are "data miners" or "time wasters." Those are people who over-analyze everything and get nothing done. Remember and write this down -- "Invite people not to call you back." Basically, tell them that your time is very limited and politely request that they get everything organized before you invest time and effort into their proposition/idea.

You want to be with people that appreciate your time and effort, so set the stage properly at the beginning of the relationship or project. For example, I invited a real estate agent not to call me unless it was a 'screaming' deal. I told him that I reviewed only 'screaming' deals. I told him that I just can't find the time to review anything less than a 'screaming' good deal. This technique is a huge time saver. Consequently, he sent me a complete package with all the requested details and we were able to do business. Most agents will give you bits and pieces and hours later, you still don't know the full story about the asset.

In closing, be honest, do business with people that you genuinely like and appreciate. Make sure you hang out with successful people that appreciate your time and effort. If you always ask the question "what if?" …You will always get a new answer.

Here is one of my favorite quotes on wisdom from Ecclesiastes 9:15 *15But there was found in it a poor wise man and he delivered the city by his wisdom. Yet no one remembered that poor man.*

ABOUT WILL

William Gold is an Orange County, California-based visionary in the real estate industry. He started on his path to success by helping to build a global communications company from 50 to 6000 employees – and with the acquisition of a key European internet firm – developed it into the largest internet company in the world at that time. William's real estate/finance expertise is regularly sought out by the media, which he's shared on NBC, CBS, ABC and FOX affiliates, as well as in USA Today and Newsweek.

His ongoing realization that banks were not working hard enough to help keep property owners in their homes – combined with his desire to help people beyond the *pro bono* financial work he was already doing – led Gold to launch REAL, a full service national company that could be dubbed "Foreclosure Fighters." While matching buyers and investors with sellers across the country, REAL specializes in stopping foreclosures via all the available legal avenues to help facilitate short sales that are ultimately great deals for new buyers.

Working with high caliber CPAs and litigating attorneys, and drawing on the classic broker/attorney business model, Gold's company can stop a bank from foreclosing on a property just minutes before foreclosure on any property.

REAL has a 'friendly force' approach with the banks, which includes an amazing equity share program, for homeowners to negotiate with the bank and maintain tenancy, while the agent still gets a commission on the transfer of title. The program allows the homeowner to stay in the property at a significantly reduced rate. The bank becomes a 50% co-beneficiary in the property. In this program, the bank takes no write offs.

"Bottom line, we are delivering candy to the bank, not medicine," he says. "We can show the banks and investors that this option is far better than a loan modification or foreclosure. I am amazed that we only have a few politicians and economists that have looked at our white papers on this subject matter."

To learn more about William Gold, and how you can receive free special reports and other invaluable real estate information from one of the country's leading experts, visit www.endallforeclosures.com or call 949-394-7438.

CHAPTER 28

HOW CAN WE EMERGE STRONGER IN TIMES OF CRISIS?

BY FRANCISCO YANEZ

"Tough times pass, but strong men remain"

In difficult times, some of us get weakened and in danger of succumbing to the storm. But don't be scared, "A calm sea does not make good sailors." We must mature above adversity and show the kind of mettle of which your heart is wrought. I remember those times of great adversity when everything was dark, and there wasn't a way out of my economic problems. ...nor out of the anguish, despair and grief.

I was without money, without work and without any possibility of feeding my family that was already hungry and demanding results. My intentions were good, but my results were poor. I wanted to get ahead, but **I COULDN´T**, I despaired that others didn't understand the difficulties and the bad moments I was living.

Now I understand. I understand that thoughts condition our emotions, and when you DO NOT control your emotions, you couldn't have positive results, which means that emotion is equal to results.

Thoughts = Emotions

Emotions = Results

So, start by changing the root of the problem: change your thoughts, and your results will be different. Never be a victim, you would be better off to become a creator of powerful circumstances to get out of the problem.

If you think that things are terrible and that your problem has no solution (negative thinking), then the (negative) emotions will be of anguish and despair (emotional limitations), which would lead to results of the same nature as the thought that created them. On the other hand, when you **focus** on the **POSITIVE,** you receive something positive as a result.

Think about it for a moment. When you're in trouble, your mind instinctively seeks answers unconsciously and then you ask: "Why is this happening to me?" Or we blame God, "Why is God making me do this, or not giving me that?" With these questions we're blocking the unconscious mind, and simply become victims of the circumstances or of God, but we don't find answers to our problems. To err is human, but to blame others or God is nonsense!

And mourning isn't good, so when you are in trouble you'd better avoid crying and focus on creating opportunities for solutions and stop talking nonsense. When you find yourself in trouble, ask yourself: "What can this problem be useful for?" or "What can I learn from this situation?" Maybe the answer for your unconscious mind could take several days or weeks to come, but once you find the answer within yourself, you'll grow tremendously and evolve to the next level.

When I understood that by controlling my thoughts I could also change the way I act, I discovered that it is better to live in peace than to live in anguish. You can always have a reason to be angry, anxious, unhappy, but it's much better to have hundreds of reasons to live happily and enjoy life.

In the following paragraphs, I'll teach that when you fall deeper into the well, you only have two alternatives, one is to die in the mud, or two, emerge stronger from the well with a wisdom that you didn't know you had. Miracles do happen, and anything is possible when one drives, stays on focus and remains insistent until you get it.

Listen to this carefully; the answers are in you...

Once upon a time there was an ordinary man living in an ordinary city. His life was completely average. Macfran had an ordinary family, lived in an ordinary neighborhood, and had a regular job, just like you.

One day, which was typically like any other, he suddenly lost his job. At first it seemed bad news, because he didn't know what to expect. He always thought it would be easy for a person with his background to find another job and relocate immediately. He was accustomed to the security of having money even though he didn't live with excess, and his life was comfortable, rather than wealthy.

As weeks went by without him finding a job, things changed. Macfran began to despair over his lack of money; he became concerned with the needs of feeding, clothing, taking his children and wife to the doctor, and not having a job. The little money he had saved started to dwindle.

Nights gave him moments of greatest anguish; his dragons of anxiety grew and looked invincible. In the early morning, these dragons reminded him of all the problems he had, and which seemed impossible to resolve. Macfran was uptight and distressed, he felt that he couldn't face the problems that grew more and more every day. The relationship with his wife seemed worse than ever, his problems were unresolved, and his irritation began to surface. His mental state didn't let him see that he was destroying everything around him that he loved. He was himself becoming a dragon.

Then it happened. One night Macfran woke up wrestling with the dragon, and in great distress. His heart was beating so sharply that he felt it in his throat. His teeth were clenched and both his jaws caused further pain in his neck. Macfran, in the middle of his anguish, covered his face with his hands and thought: **"I CANNOT HANDLE IT ANY MORE, ...I WANT TO DISAPPEAR, ...I WANT TO ESCAPE, ...I WANT TO RUN!"**

Macfran thought at the same time: "My wife doesn't care what happens to me, God doesn't care what happens to me, nobody cares." Desperately, he put on his clothes and went out running into the middle of the dark night. His tears ran down his face. As Macfran was running, the night was becoming colder and colder.

Passing by the temple where he said his prayers every morning asking for work, this time he desperately yelled to God, asking for an answer: **"Why me, Lord? Why have you abandoned me? How can you say you love me, when you see that I have small children and you can't give me a job? Why doesn't my wife understand me? Why, if you say you love me, you leave me?"** His anger against God and his cries grew louder each time.

He continued to run into the darkness of the night, without knowing where to go. He ran down the mountain, and aimlessly he kept running, just like the tears on his face, trying to flee his dragons.

At dawn, he found himself at the center of the old city, and far, far away from home and the warmth of his family. The intense cold of dawn and tiredness of the long road played havoc with Macfran; he needed a little warmth and rest. Suddenly he heard the ringing of the bells from an old church on the horizon that he saw as a strong castle. "It's time to rest", he said. He crossed through the carved wooden door of the old church, and looked for a bench away from the eyes of the people to find some peace.

There were just a few faithful people who flocked to the temple at that time, most of them were elderly and homeless. When Macfran leaned to meditate, a ragged, barefoot man sat beside him and, before thinking or saying anything to Macfran, the ragged man said:

"Don't be afraid, I know what you're going through, you and the many other men and women who suffer and find no answer... that's why you're here today – I want you to go and give a message to all those who cannot find answers to their troubles and think they are alone."

Macfran couldn't understand what was going on. He didn't know this ragged man who was talking to him, and whether or not he was crazy, or just what was happening there.

The ragged man, with a soft, sweet voice that filled him with peace, continued:

"I want you to know that *you are not alone*. You have me, I am your Father in heaven, I hear your prayers and your troubles, and I know them, every one. I let things happen. And I know that you're wondering, ... Why me?"

An enormous silence permeated the temple; at the same time Macfran experienced a strong chill running down his body, from the top of his head to the bottom of his toes.

"Son, I'm giving you the chance to be a better human, this is your big opportunity to mature and grow. Only the most beloved of my children have this great opportunity, and because I love you in a special way, I'm giving you this gift. Don't disdain it, my son, this time I give you to grow, because only the mature trees with firm roots will bear rich and abundant fruit.

One day you told me that you had faith in me. And faith is belief in what you don't see, to believe in the unseen; so sometimes it's so hard to understand me, because you don't see me.

But, you know? I have faith in you, because I see unique talents in you, which no other being in this world has, because you, my little son, you are unique and unrepeatable, you are beautiful in my eyes and I love you, there's no other like you.

I have faith in you because I know what you're made of and what you are capable of achieving. I'm sure you can achieve your dreams, although you sometimes fail and lose control, as if everything was over, but you always think about it and carefully get back up, as only the great ones know how to do.

When I thought about you, I said I will create a beautiful creature, an excellent, perfect, infinite, unique and unrepeatable being – to fight for his ideals and achieve his goals, ... one that knows how to reach and conquer the top of the highest mountains and the world, ... how to take the stars in his hands and help with the creation of the perfect and unique.

And I know that I am not wrong with you, because you can count on the talents that only the best have, you have gifts, and special and unique strengths. It is time, then, to show them to you, that you discover them, that you realize how valuable you are, that the best of you is within the depths of your being, because I put it there myself, and you're about to discover it.

Your greatest treasure is within you, it's on your mind. Look closely, now is the time to act, nothing stops you. It's time to give yourself the

WINNING STRATEGIES FOR HEALTH, WEALTH & SUCCESS

time: stop and look in the silence inside you. It's time that you understand that if you're in this world, it is not by chance; it's simply because I've given you a mission **HERE AND NOW**, and until that happens, I won't call you to be by my side. Look inside yourself to see what your mission is in this world, and be sure to comply with it.

While you discover it, I'll give you seven keys that let you see the light in the darkness.

1. Put the magic ingredient in everything you do: **love**
2. Live intensely every moment of your life, do not waste a moment looking for excuses for not being happy.
3. Make the ordinary things count in an extraordinary way.
4. Say thanks every day for what you have as well as for what you still do not have, because only the grateful in poverty will be square in wealth.
5. Seek to serve others, because only those who live to serve, serve to live.
6. Prepare yourself with the power of knowledge, and come closer to learning from those who already went along the same path. If your vocation is to be a great architect, look for the best architect in the world. Learn, imitate and go beyond.
7. Have faith in me and what I'm doing with you. You have to understand that the changes and adjustments I am making in you are painful, and I understand it, but this is the only way to end my masterpiece in you. So take each difficult moment, every anguish, every pain as a step to be overcome, and face it with determination to transform it into something positive – with the strong conviction of knowing that all pain and agony will get the best out of you.

Now, my son, I give you an order as I gave to Lazarus in the tomb... **STAND UP AND WALK!** *And that's an order –* **UNDERSTAND IT, STAND UP**. Can't you see that I need you to be strong? Didn't you hear that your family needs you? Don't you know that this world needs you?

You can't go on defeated, you can't go on hurting yourself and others. Stop blaming yourself and whining now.

STAND UP AND WALK! You are a great being with unique strengths, so **GET UP**, stand up. It's now time to take out the best of you and fight for your ideals, it is time to reach the top and take the stars in your hands; it's time to have faith and understand that what comes now is **THE LIGHT,** is the most intense sunrise of your life.

Finally, my son, I want you to know that I'm with you and I always will be, you must only have faith and learn to listen. You will go through times that you won't see me, you won't hear me and think that I have left, but this is where your character will be tempered and your faith will shine, because now you know I'll be there, holding you inside my heart."

An enormous silence filled the temple. Macfran, kneeling, remained surprised and his tears covered his face.

The ragged man rose from his seat and left the temple. By then, Macfran was practically frozen in an ecstasy of love at what he had just witnessed. When he reacted and realized what had just happened, he ran from the church to frantically seek out the man who had spoken to him. It was less than a minute, and when Macfran came out to look for the ragged man, he discovered that he had disappeared. The earth simply had swallowed him up. He looked in every corner of the town, but he never saw him again.

From that day on, Macfran traveled the world to teach and inspire the world's leading companies. As you can understand, what matters is not the size of your problems, the really important thing is how you react to them. You decide if you wish to escape from them, or face them with determination and mature action.

And remember, it doesn't matter how much knowledge you acquire, what counts is what you do with your knowledge, so act now and consider each problem a ladder to reach your dreams.

Sincerely,
Macfran
Francisco Yanez
www.seminarios.com.mx
Changing Lives Speaker

ABOUT FRANCISCO

Francisco Yañez is an international speaker focused on psycho-therapy of the deep change. He´s the author of several books including "Work for an unemployed," "Youngsters with courage," and "The power inside you." Yañez is also the producer of a unique film LA LUZ (The Light) which has quickly gained success around the world.

He has recently been awarded as "The Best Hispanic Conference Speaker" by the Hispanic Conference Teller Association; and has also received the the award for "The Best Conference Speaker" in 2011 by Latin American Quality Institute.

Francisco Yanez has lived with so much passion in his own life that he has been able to transform his life from being a Bricklayer into one of the most important international coaches. He has been able to help hundreds of people through his books, his movie and the conferences. A great change from the conformism to the total expansion is the reason why his clients identify with him.

"WOW... Francisco Yáñez inspires so much passion, energy and privileged information as I ever saw in an orator. He Is simply dynamic and incredibly intense. You have to live him."

~ Jim Cunningham – Disney University Coordinator for 14 years

If what you require is to create a lasting impact or you are in search of happiness and financial success for yourself and your family, business or your employees, Francisco Yanez is the guy www.seminarios.com.mx - francisco@seminarios.com.mx

CHAPTER 29

HOW TO PAY FOR COLLEGE WITHOUT SPENDING YOUR LIFE SAVINGS

BY CLIFF MORGAN/TODD THOMAE

"Beware of little expenses; a small leak will sink a great ship."
~ Benjamin Franklin

I f a small leak can sink a great ship, imagine what a huge leak will do! Many people we talk to daydream of retiring while they "plan" to send their children to college, often thinking that doing both is just a dream. At US College Planning, LLC, we know that the two are NOT mutually exclusive.

True, the expense of sending even one child to college can be as much as the price of a home, depending on the school the child selects. Whether a family makes $50,000 a year or $500,000 a year, the cost of a college education for their child is one of the largest drains the family budget will ever have. Even if your family's budget is so large that college seems like a small leak – and you think, "I can afford to pay for my child's education without help" – beware! *Here is the big question to ask oneself, "If you CAN pay for college but you don't HAVE to, do you still want to pay for it?"*

Let us ask you this: Did you purchase your home by offering the asking price without negotiating? Would you rather purchase your car for the sticker price at the first dealer you stopped at? And would you purchase a car or a home without giving any thought to it being the best fit for your family or the neighborhood that best suits your commute to work?

Most likely you would not purchase a home for the asking price or without researching the neighborhood, and you wouldn't try to put your six kids into the two-seater, sports car either. So, you should take care when planning for your child's college education to make sure that you are getting the best deal possible.

We work in the Financial Services industry, but what we do is fairly unique in that we help people find money they may be giving away unknowingly and unnecessarily. Think about your family's finances as a bucket. You fill it with the family's income. Whether that income comes as a gush or as a trickle, the bucket is not going to fill if there are holes in the bottom. We begin by working with families to plug the holes in their financial bucket, thereby allowing them to use more of the income flowing into the bucket to support both their lifestyle and their retirement goals. Unfortunately many advisors in our industry only focus on getting high rates of return. Although a higher rate of return is important, if you are transferring away more money as a percentage than you can possibly gain, it is irresponsible to only look at one side of the balance sheet.

Our firm specializes in strategies that encompass stocks, bonds, mutual funds, hedge funds, insurance, business planning, college strategies and legacy planning. We come from a background of business owners and own several businesses ourselves. We are driven to help other business owners and self-employed people to maximize their finances. We specialize in filling the holes in the businessman's bucket; often it is more important to figure out how to save money than it is to make more money.

For most families, what it really boils down to is this: "Will we be able to retire, and will there be any money to retire with after we pay for our house, our children's college, etc.?" Many people feel they must choose between retirement and education. Our firm finds the most efficient way for our clients to live in the present, while still providing enough money to save for a great retirement. Our most important asset is our children.

Although we want to do everything for them and will sacrifice for them, we shouldn't have to forfeit our retirement in place of their education.

Our firm begins with one of the biggest expenses of the family budget – college tuition. The average public college education costs about $25,000 a year for a state school, while a private college education can average $40,000 a year. Our strategies focus on four primary disciplines to find the means of paying for college without money coming from your checkbook. The first is to use the tax code to your advantage (especially for the business owner/self-employed/professional). Second, we make the most of the financial aid system; (remember, it is written by the same government who wrote the IRS tax code). The third is to utilize innovative funding strategies such as real estate, trusts, retirement planning and estate planning, etc. Finally, we offer admissions assistance and counseling to make sure your child is at the right school so that they have the best chance at getting through college in four years.

USING TAXES TO YOUR ADVANTAGE

Our first step in creating our client's college plan is to utilize the tax code to their greatest advantage. Did you know there are 153 tax strategies for the college years alone? Working with advisors who know, understand, and stay current on these laws can save your bottom line and save you some headaches.

If you are a business owner/self-employed/professional, there are some very helpful, but little-known, tax-planning strategies to help reduce your bottom line. This, in turn, will help you and your child qualify for more money and lower your taxes. One strategy is to hire your kids. Wages paid to your children are a valid business deduction if they are doing real work and are compensated fairly. And while the IRS suggested minimum age for employment is 7 years old, there are some jobs such as business advertising where you may be able to employ a child even younger.

CASE STUDY: ADVANTAGES TO HIRING ONE'S CHILD

I remember as a child, my dad had to go out and inspect houses, and I would go along to assist him. I started out in charge of the clipboard with all the important documents or maybe the big tape measure, and after a while I graduated to the Polaroid camera, and was allowed to take photos at the inspections. I remember what a great time I had with my dad – being able to learn what he did, learn about work ethic and the value of what it took to earn a dollar. I have even done this with my kids today. For one of the businesses that I own I also have had to inspect houses. My children love to go with me to inspect the homes. We have even trained them to be able to go through the entire inspection process; paperwork, measurements, and photos. The fact that they love to be out with their dad is perhaps the best benefit of all." Obviously there are more and better benefits to employing your child than just tax advantages.

Your children can use their income to build a savings account or a retirement account. The tax benefits of hiring your child come primarily from shifting income from your higher tax bracket to your child's lower tax bracket. Better still, if you are business owner/self-employed/professional and your child is under the age of 18, you don't have to pay Social Security or Medicare payroll taxes on them. This can be a huge tax savings (currently 13.35%). Setting up such agreements with your children has lasting value, as this intentionality allows for many years of hands-on, practical business training and could be the best education they ever receive.

CASE STUDY: VETERINARIAN/BUSINESS OWNER

Let's begin with a case study of one of our recent clients, a veterinarian/ business owner. His income is $302,000 with assets of $450,000 (excluding his home). There are six members in his family, including one child who is applying to college. We began by looking at the FAFSA form. By helping to position their student to be "more valuable to one school" over the other, we were able to save the doctor and his family $113,446 in total Expected Family Contribution (EFC)/FAFSA savings. Next we took advantage of some tax strategies on the doctor's income to save an additional $21,996 per year (assuming their family is in the 31% Federal, 5% state and 2.9% Medicare brackets) in addition to the $113,446 we had already saved. Because of the above tax and income savings, we were able to save the doctor $18,205.20 per year in additional EFC/FASFA savings.

MAKING SENSE OF THE FAFSA
(FREE APPLICATION FOR FEDERAL STUDENT AID)

As "holes" in the family finance bucket go, one of the biggest is caused by families who think they make too much money to qualify for financial aid, therefore, do not ever fill out the FAFSA form at all. Making the most of the federal financial aid system is the first step in plugging a hole in your family bucket. It costs you nothing to fill it out, but it is the portal through which all assistance, even merit based, is procured. Let's face it, you check for ways to save money all day: finding the cheapest gas, online searches, looking for 'buy one, get one free' at the grocery. Why would you not at least entertain the idea that you might be able to save money on that $100,000 college investment?

We show our clients how to avoid the three critical mistakes families often make when filing for financial aid. First of all, don't pay to file the FAFSA. Go directly to the U.S. Department of Education's only financial aid website (www.fafsa.ed.gov NOT www.fafsa.com). By going to the latter site and similar sites, you might pay anywhere from $65 to $100 to file. That's a waste of money. Secondly, file on time.

You can begin to file on January 1st of each year. Federal student aid is awarded on a first come, first served basis. If you wait, you may lose out on free money.

Finally, we make sure financial aid forms are completed correctly. For example, line #89 of the financial aid form, which asks what your net worth is, if answered incorrectly, can keep your child from receiving their full amount of aid. A form completed incorrectly will usually get "bumped" adding another 4-6 weeks of processing time.

Again, ask yourself: If you CAN pay for college but you don't HAVE to, do you still WANT to pay for it?

WHERE IS YOUR MONEY?
– INNOVATIVE FUNDING STRATEGIES

Most people spend more time planning their next vacation than they do planning to pay for college or for retirement.

Unfortunately most families do not understand the difference between "includable assets" and "non-includable assets." Certain assets are counted much more heavily in the financial aid formulas than others. For example checking and savings accounts, trust funds, UGMA/ UTMA accounts, money market, mutual funds, CD's, stocks, bonds, commodities, qualified educational benefits/savings accounts are asked about on the FASFA form. However, it does not ask about the value of life insurance, retirement plans, 401(k) plans, pension funds, annuities, or IRAs anywhere on that same form. Another misconception is that people believe that it doesn't matter where you keep your money; they believe it is all counted the same. The truth is where you keep your money can mean the difference of thousands of dollars in financial aid or merit-based money. For example, money in the student's name counts against your Expected Family Contribution significantly more than it does in the parent's name.

For some parents, real estate strategies can actually save them money on their kid's college bill. If you own property in the state in which your child wishes to attend school, you might save money by allowing your child to pay in-state tuition at that school. It might also offer you tax advantages. Once again, even if you have all the money saved for your student's college, wouldn't you like to save some more of your hard-earned money?

HELPING YOUR CHILDREN SUCCEED

The last way we help you save on college eduation is by working with your most important asset – your student. We make sure your child can complete his or her education in four years and not the nearly five years it takes some students to finish. We do this through interest inventory tests that will help make sure that your child selects the right school and program to give the best odds that he/she will complete school in less time. School guidance counselors were once the primary source for such information, however, today's guidance couselors are often overworked, underpaid or both. Your student deserves to have someone take the time to assess what he or she wants for the future; someone who can help create a plan of how to get there. We can help your student improve their SAT and ACT test scores which will ultimately improve the chances of getting into their school of choice, as well as increase the amount of merit aid available to them. Recently we had a student who had a score of 31 on the ACT and was offered $60,000 in scholarships. Re-taking the ACT after the right test prep course increased the student's score to 32 which seems like a small increase, until you realize that a 32 ACT score was worth $128,000 in scholarships! By taking the courses to improve ACT skills usually equals a 2-6 pt. increase, which is a 5-15% increase in score.

Did you know that a "bombed" admissions interview can make or break your efforts to get into a chosen school? Did you know that some colleges require several essays for admissions and that there are over twenty different genres of essays for college admissions? For one school, they measure levels of creativity, whereas another school may require more self-reflection. It pays to know your audience. We can coach your child through both processes to maximize his or her potential. We work with college professors who match and edit the style of essay with the school to which it is being sent; they suggest ways in which your student might improve his/her essays. Your child's essay is their resume. Well-written essays will articulate how your child will be a benefit to the college or university. Your financial package will generally be better from the right-fit school that really wants your child and sees the value in what your child brings to the school. Also, the right school will be a much better experience and value for your child overall.

Selecting the right school isn't just about picking a school that offers the program your child wants. Some schools meet 100% of need for students while other schools with similar programs may only meet 30% - 50% of need. This is a lot like choosing the car dealship with the same car at a lower price! It's imperative for families to keep an open mind and to shop around for the best school. Schools meet needs in different ways. You want to know the percentage of Gift Aid (or free money) versus the percentage of Self Help Aid (loans that you have to pay back) the school offers. Some schools meet most or all of a student's need with Self Help Aid such as work/study or loans. Who wants to learn in June that your student will be receiving all LOANS? We predict with a reasonable level of accuracy what your financial aid packages will be.

CASE STUDY– POSITIONING

What's the real benefit of "positioning" your child to their best advantage when college shopping? When we combine the aforementioned strategies of selecting the right school, crafting essays to highlight your child's most sought after skills, and helping to increase their test scores, the family bottom line can change dramatically. Take for example this comparison of family A and family B.

Family A		Family B	
Income:	$85,000	Income:	$85,000
Assets (excluding home)	$90,000	Assets (excluding home)	$90,000
Real Estate:	$150,000	Real estate:	$150,000
Number in family:	5	Number in family:	5
Number in school:	1	Number in school:	1
Financial Aid Award:	$15,185	Financial Aid Award:	$ 7,766

That's a difference of $7,645 a year because Family A got help to Position their Student, making them "more valuable to one school" over the other!

I hope that your eyes are opening to the fact that there is a wider pool of college choices available to your family through the financial savings listed above. The schools that were once out of reach can be brought that much closer to your child's dream education.

Consider the short-sightedness of going through the college admissions and financial aid process by yourself because you think it could be cheaper. Most people wouldn't represent themselves in a court of law without legal training or perform surgery on their child just to save a few hundred dollars. It would be nearly impossible to educate oneself enough to do this job effectively. The same is true with representing yourself and your child through the financial funding process. Is it worth saving a couple hundred dollars on a $10,000-$60,000 annual investment and risk your child having to "settle" on a less desirable school because of cost? Don't try to be "penny wise" and "dollar foolish". You can obviously go through this process on your own, but I would recommend that you find a professional to help you get all the money to which you are entitled.

No family should feel like they have to choose between college for their children and retirement for themselves. US College Planning, LLC can strategize with you to plug the leaks, both large and small, in your total family financial plan so that you can have it all. Our strategy, focusing on the four primary disciplines, might mean that even though you can afford to pay for your child's education – you might not have to!

In addition to all of the strategies above clients that work with us receive scholarships ranging from $1,000 to $40,000. To learn how receive your scholarship and to work with our team please call 1-219-476-3435 OR visit our website and make an appointment at www.uscollegeplanning.com

ABOUT CLIFF

Cliff Morgan is a nationally sought after speaker and author. He specializes in working with families during the college years. His expertise has helped families across the United States save tens of thousands of dollars off the college bill while helping students enter the schools of their dreams. Cliff is also a personal mentor to many financial planners around the US.

Mr. Morgan focuses on helping his clients save significant amounts off the college sticker price thus allowing families to maintain their current lifestyle and save for retirement at the same time.

He was born in Rhode Island and raised in the mountains of New Hampshire. He attended the University of New Hampshire and graduated from Chicago's Moody Bible Institute with a degree in Church Theology. Cliff has worked with Strategic Wealth Advisory Group and has be a as a trusted advisor for the past nine years. He is passionate about serving people by helping them and their families to build and achieve their short and long term financial goals. Cliff is married to his wife Amy and they have 2 children; William and Charlotte. He is actively involved in his local church, plays soccer recreationally, participates in a bicycling club and is an avid skier. Cliff and his family reside in Chesterton, Indiana.

Cliff's accomplishments include:

- Founder and Partner of US College Planning & Strategic Wealth Advisory Group
- Author of the upcoming book "WIN"
- Member of the American College Funding Association
- Working as a Wealth Strategist in the financial planning industry since 2003
- MDRT – The Premier Association of Financial Professionals
- 2010 Named to by Chicago Magazine Five Star award for wealth managers
- Member of the National Association of College Admission Counseling
- A nationally recognized speaker on wealth accumulation and preservation
- Named to America's Premiere Experts as a wealth strategist
- Member of the National Institute of Certified College Planners

ABOUT TODD

Todd Thomae is a nationally sought after speaker and author. He specializes in working with professionals, business owners and the self-employed by helping them address their current Tax and debt reduction strategies.

Mr. Thomae focuses on helping his clients save significant amounts of their current monthly income by avoiding voluntary taxes and expenses. Todd understands the importance of both traditional and non-traditional planning.

Todd and the Strategic Wealth Advisory Group team educate clients on how to increase their retirement income by 50% or more with little or no tax, with no market risk, and with 90% or more liquidity.

He was born and raised Valparaiso, IN. Todd is married to his beautiful wife Michelle and they have 3 children; Autumn, Lincoln, and Elle. He is actively involved in his local church and youth organizations. Todd can also be found fishing with his children on rivers throughout Northwest Indiana and Western Michigan in the spring and fall.

Todd's passion is to make a difference in his client's lives by finding significant amounts of money by eliminating unknown wealth transfers on things like reducing/eliminating interest payments, voluntary taxes, and making sure clients are being efficient with their money.

Todd's accomplishments include:

- Author of the upcoming book "WIN"
- Member NAIFA, National Association of Insurance and Financial Advisors
- Working as a Wealth Strategist in the planning industry since 1993
- MDRT – The Premier Association of Financial Professionals
- A top 5 planner with the largest captive agency company in the world
- A nationally recognized speaker on wealth accumulation and preservation
- Named to America's Premiere Experts as a wealth strategist
- Certified Mentor with one of the largest financial planning organizations in the world
- Graduate of Mount Vernon Nazarene University with degrees in History and Business.

CHAPTER 30

SEVEN FUNDAMENTALS OF A HIGHLY SUCCESSFUL FLIP

BY BRANT PHILLIPS

Buying, renovating and selling a house for profit, known as Flipping, is one of the most exciting ways to make money in Real Estate. As we all know, there are potentially <u>HUGE PAYDAYS</u> with only a minimum amount of time invested, *if* you do it the right way! As an entrepreneur, I am always looking for ways to effectively utilize my cash and time by locating opportunities that can provide the greatest ROI for my dollar and my time. For me, flipping houses was appealing not only for the money that could be made, but rather, the lifestyle you could live. You see, when I started investing in real estate, I was dead broke while working <u>long</u> hours at a full-time job I couldn't stand! My wife and I were raising our children in an apartment and had ZERO CASH!! As a matter of fact, I bought my first investment property on a credit card while we were still living in that apartment! Nowadays, I'm living the life I dreamed of as a full-time investor, speaker and entrepreneur, and most importantly, in control of my time and finances! I found my freedom through real estate investing, and I know that you can too, if you follow the Seven Fundamentals of Highly Successful Flips that experienced investors utilize.

SO, LET'S GET STARTED!

FLIP FUNDAMENTAL #1
DEVELOP A WINNING MINDSET

When flipping houses, as with most things in life and business, there are going to be obstacles along the way. All great achievers in the past have had to overcome obstacles at some point in time in order to achieve success. Real Estate is no exception to this rule. If I had to point to one thing that separates those who will *thrive* and those who will *dive*, it would all come down to <u>Mindset</u> <u>Determination</u>. You see, if you have a mindset that is determined to accomplish a goal NO MATTER WHAT, then you will achieve success.

I want you take a few moments to think about what your current mindset is for achieving success by flipping houses… What if you run into troubles along the way? …because you will. Will you give up? Or, will you push through and find the solution to the challenge at hand? I will tell you from experience, there is no challenge that is insurmountable. Commit yourself to developing and strengthening your mindset to promise yourself that you will not give up when you meet challenges, and commit to achieving success!

FLIP FUNDAMENTAL #2
CREATE DEAL FLOW

If you are limited for time like I was when I started flipping houses, it is important you do not waste time looking for deals. I have seen a lot of new investors spend way too much time looking through classified ads, local real estate magazines and even worse, driving all over town spending hours and hours searching for a deal. This is NOT what successful flippers do!

You must make the deals come to you! It's critical to utilize OPT (Other Peoples *Time*) to bring you the deals. This is what we call "Deal Flow" and the more deals that are flowing to you, the more opportunities you will have to flip houses. This doesn't mean that you buy every deal that comes your way; rather, this means that you create an abundance of deals that flow to YOU so that you can pick out the very best deals to assure you see a nice profit at the closing table!

The most effective way to bring the deals to you is by building a team of 'investor-experienced' Real Estate Agents and Wholesalers that know exactly what types of deals you are looking for. In case you've never heard of a wholesaler, a wholesaler is an individual who utilizes different marketing strategies to locate discounted investment properties, and the best part is they specialize in working exclusively with investors.

FLIP FUNDAMENTAL #3
USE THE FORMULA

If you're going to make money on a flip, then you must make a promise to yourself…You must swear to NEVER buy a property unless it meets and/or exceeds the buying formula that I am about to share with you.

Here is the formula:

Maximum Offer = 70% of ARV - Minus Repair Costs
(ARV Stands for <u>After</u> <u>Repaired</u> <u>Value</u>)

This means that if a house would be worth $100,000 <u>AFTER</u> it is all fixed up, then $55,000 would be your Maximum Offer <u>IF</u> the property needed $15,000 in repairs. Basically, you take the ARV multiplied by 70% ($100k x .7 = $70k), then subtract the estimated repairs, $15,000 from $70,000 to arrive at our final Maximum Offer, $55,000. Of course, if you can get deals for less than the 70% ARV, then the more profit you can make!

I want you to understand using this formula is Absolutely Critical. If your maximum offer price exceeds 70% of the ARV, you are putting yourself at risk of not making a profit. It's as simple as this: When you input the numbers into the formula, if the numbers work, you can proceed with the deal, if the numbers don't work, then WALK AWAY!

FLIP FUNDAMENTAL #4
QUICKLY ESTIMATE REPAIRS

If you followed my steps from earlier and become good at creating Deal Flow, then you are going to have to learn how to quickly analyze the cost of repairs. I see too many investors walk away from good deals because they get scared off from some repairs they were unsure or un-educated about. Well, allow me to make your life a whole lot easier by going to this website:

www.FreeRehabEstimator.com

FreeRehabEstimator.com is a simple-to-use spreadsheet that will quick-ly give you the capability to accurately estimate repairs. Estimating the cost of repairs is a serious issue so make sure that you fully complete the FreeRehabEstimator.com form. And, if you're uncertain about any particular item, be sure to call a contractor in your area to help you find out the information that is needed to accurately determine the cost of that repair. It's a good idea anyways to get multiple bids from qualified contractors when you're analyzing a flip.

FLIP FUNDAMENTAL #5
PROPER FINANCING

Perhaps the most overused excuse given for people failing to invest in Real Estate today is,

"I can't invest in Real Estate because I don't have any money."

If a lack of funds is your personal excuse for not flipping, let me break it to you: It's not a good excuse! I realize that many of you reading this are like me when I started, and you don't have *"2 nickels to rub togeth-er,"* but don't lose faith my friend, there is light at the end of the tun-nel. We discussed earlier about using OPT (Other People's Time), well now, you're going to learn how to use OPM, **O**ther **P**eople's **M**oney!

The two most common ways to finance flips are utilizing Hard Money Lenders or Private Money. Hard money loans are high-interest loans given to investors for properties in need of repair. These are the types of loans I used when I first began buying houses, and they're probably the most common form of financing for flippers, especially beginning investors. However, as you progress in your investing expertise, you will want to find ways to finance your deals with more favorable terms, and that's where private money can tremendously impact your invest-ing ease and profitability.

Private money is relationship-based lending, where people lend you the capital you need – to buy and fix the houses you flip. There are a lot of great advantages for you and your private money lender, and the biggest is that you can structure the terms virtually any way you like! Including no money down!

A lot of investors think it is difficult to raise private money, but this couldn't be further from the truth! I finance all of my deals with private money lenders. Basically, private lenders are 'everyday people' who are looking for places other than the stock market to invest their money and still earn a nice rate of return. This is a true 'Win-Win' opportunity for you and your private lender, and it's an extremely simple financing option to integrate into your business once you know the steps. If you're looking to raise some private money for your real estate deals, check this site out when you get the chance: www.SimplePrivateMoneySystem.com.

FLIP FUNDAMENTAL #6
FIX IT RIGHT

This is "Make It or Break It" time, so please realize this: Fixing things yourself is one of the most common Flipper mistakes that occur! Trust me, I know this from experience! By doing 'handyman' work, you will only slow down the project and limit yourself from bigger opportunities.

Now that that's out of the way, let's talk about the cosmetics of a rehab. First, understand your flip needs to be attractive to buyers, not to you. So, you should define your scope of work by checking out comparable properties that have sold quickly in that market/price range, not based on your personal preferences! The key here is to make sure your property is as nice, or slightly nicer, than your competition in the neighborhood, while at the same time being priced competitively.

If you can make your home look similar in color combinations and upgrades to new construction homes in a similar price range, then chances are you will find your flip positioned nicely for a prospective buyer. It's wise to consult with a Realtor who knows that particular market prior to beginning the rehab.

I could write a whole book on how to work with contractors and how to avoid the many 'pitfalls' that a lot of investors run into by working with contractors, but rather, let me give you some of the basics:

- ✓ Obtain Bids From Qualified "Turn-Key" Contractors
- ✓ Have A Clearly-Defined Scope Of Work
- ✓ Use Written Agreements & Payment Draw Schedules
- ✓ Establish A Work Completion Date
- ✓ Don't Forget To Budget-In ALL Items

FLIP FUNDAMENTAL #7
SELL IT QUICK

If you carefully follow the first six Flip Fundamentals correctly, then you're going to be feeling pretty good about your Flips at this point. So PLEASE, don't blow the whole thing at this point by getting greedy with your asking price! This is painful to watch, but I see it happen all the time. Price your property to sell fast, and don't get stuck holding a house that is overpriced. And just in case it doesn't sell quickly, you should have multiple exit strategies available so you don't get stuck holding a house.

Here are a couple of alternative strategies for selling properties in our current financial market:

✓ Sell to Investors

- When we go through downswings in the market like we have experienced recently, it becomes a great time to flip deals to investors. This is an approach I've been perfecting recently. Basically, we look for deals in neighborhoods that make good 'Landlord' properties. Then we rehab them 100% to get them 'Rent Ready,' so they can put a tenant in.

✓ Owner Financing

- This is a really nice way to flip houses, especially with the way banks are hoarding all the money and not loaning it out. Basically, you can get a higher asking price and expand the number of potential buyers.

The main points here: follow the first six fundamentals correctly, and then make sure you price the property right, and offer it to the greatest number of potential buyers. By increasing the number of potential buyers, then it is more likely to get an offer/sale. …And don't get greedy. A friend of mine has a good quote I like to use when it comes to pricing flips, "Fast Nickels over Slow Dimes." There's nothing wrong with discounting the price if you are still going to walk away with a profit.

CLOSING THOUGHTS

I know how you feel. I was scared too when I bought my first property. But you know what, when you step out and take action, it's like God and the universe all line up and conspire to step in and help you out, because you acted on faith. At least, that's been my experience. Even when things haven't worked out exactly the way I planned, I am still able to feel good about myself at the end of the day, because I didn't let fear come in and determine my future. Sometimes that's what we have to do in life: *Overcome FEAR and Take Action!* Yes, you should continue to educate yourself, and learn and train, but sometimes you just have to act on faith and go out there and do it!

I will tell you another thing, there is nothing like finding your passion in life. When you are able to do something you really enjoy and get paid to do it, life becomes so much more enjoyable. I really want to encourage you to pursue what you are passionate about in life, and learn to monetize it while helping people at the same time – and you'll find that your whole future is going to start looking very, very sweet indeed. I have found this through flipping houses, and I know you can experience the same success!

That's All I Got... Now, Get Out There And Start Flipping Some Houses!

All The Best For Your Future, Brant Phillips

ABOUT BRANT

Brant is a full-time real estate investor, business owner (www.RentReadyContractors.com)**, entrepreneur, author & speaker. He has been featured on Fox News** (www.rentreadytv.com/investing-interview/), hosts local seminars (www.FlippingHoustonLive.com) and is even being considered to star in one of those "Flipping Houses" TV shows (http://rentreadytv.com/a-day-in-the-life/).

Brant is a proverbial 'rags to riches' story, while living in an apartment and having no money, was able to purchase his first investment property on a credit card! He went on to buy 10 properties that same year with no money down; and within only a mere few years later, has rehabbed hundreds of homes and now owns a portfolio of rental properties worth millions and routinely flips houses for fast cash.

Brant is a former police officer who prides himself on integrity and serving others. He is a husband and father of three and enjoys helping and teaching people to experience the freedom and success he has achieved through successfully investing in real estate.

"I want to see you succeed and I don't want to let you down,

I hope you take action today and see incredible results soon!"

You can learn more about Brant and flipping houses here:

www.BrantPhillips.com
www.RentReadyContractors.com
www.RentReadyTV.com
www.HoustonCapitalGroup.com
www.SimplePrivateMoneySystem.com
www.PartneringForProperties.com

CHAPTER 31

HOW TO WIN BY CREATING SOLUTION-DRIVEN PRODUCTS

BY GREG ROLLETT

The stage had been set for over a week now. The promotional emails had been written, edited and finally sent out. The registration page was working, steadily collecting names and emails for days.

I decided to pre-record the webinar so I could be live on the call, looking at any technical glitches and answering questions *real time* without any side issues taking me off-path while presenting.

The slide deck and the copy were formatted with 30 minutes of groundbreaking content –followed by what I considered to be a very hard sell. Harder than anything I had ever put online in the past.

Then the 30-minute mark hit. My heard stopped. Would they bite on the pitch? Would they click out as soon as I mentioned price? Would anyone buy?

The moment was so built up in my head that I was an emotional rollercoaster. Firefox was open with tabs for Gmail to immediately see when orders came in; PayPal was used to ensure the correct payments would come in and for the webinar screen, so I would know if my entire year's worth of work in the music marketing niche would finally pay off.

The next 20-30 minutes were a blur. My inbox was full with new orders. PayPal was sending the right amounts and people were redirected to my new product, The New Music Economy. My first big win as an online product creator.

SELLING IS LIKE WALKING. YOU HAVE TO DO IT BEFORE YOU RUN.

One of the biggest lessons I have learned in business is that no matter what you do, you cannot create income without first selling something. Even in finding a job, you are selling yourself to be paid a specific wage. Then once you have the job, you are selling your time to the company for said wage.

As an entrepreneur or a small business owner, you are always selling. And the sales of those products and services create the lifeblood of your business, cash flow.

The problem that I have seen is that most new entrepreneurs struggle with getting their product to market. They have hundreds of ideas, they know that they want to change the world and they even know what they are going to do with their future fortunes. We've all been there – constantly daydreaming and staring at our email inboxes wondering why no money is flying out of it like a shiny silver ATM machine. Didn't my email service just hear my million-dollar idea?

We have all heard the million-dollar idea, but when it comes time to put pen to paper and start, many stop. …Or at least get stuck.

THE INFORMATIONAL PRODUCT MINDSET

Before I created The New Music Economy, I had toiled with hundreds of ideas in my head. ...some brilliant. ...some made for the garbage bin. ...and some not even worthy of the recycling bin (metaphorically speaking).

The discoveries I made during my transition from cubicle dwelling marketing director to online entrepreneur were nothing short of 'eye-opening' and extremely exciting. For starters, the market for selling information is as vast as the oceans – from free reports to cheap eBooks to extensive and expensive research papers, to full-blown multi-media courses.

These products ranged in price from $1 to $10,000. But there was one thing that stood out more than a purple, polka-dotted elephant, …the margins!

My high school math skills were suddenly playing tricks on me. I could create a few videos that helped my marketplace clients reach a desired outcome; ones that cost me nothing but time, and I could charge $50 each, and never have to deliver anything, print anything, or incur overhead of any kind (other than a few cents on my merchant account).

It was music to my ears, literally. …But I was still riddled with doubt.

OVERCOMING YOUR FEARS IN DEVELOPING INFO PRODUCTS

During the planning and development of the New Music Economy, I toiled with many of the same fears, doubts and questions that many of you are facing when trying to develop something for the world not only to see, but to purchase, consume and ultimately produce results from. Questions like:

- How much work am I really getting myself into?
- Do I really have something to teach that people will pay money for?
- How do I put it all together?
- How much should I charge?
- Do I need case studies and testimonials?
- How does all the technology work?
- And so on and so forth…

To get over these fears, I decided to dive head first into my market. I wanted to know who the players were. What were they selling? How much were they selling? Were there reviews? Could I buy copies to sell the material first hand? What was available in stores and mainstream outlets? Who was paying for keywords in Google and Yahoo? What were the popular Facebook pages?

Once you do this for your market, you instantly start to see what is working and what people are demanding.

You also begin your own mental consumption and internal thinking to see what is missing from the market.

In my case, I noticed that most people in the music business and music marketing niche were focused on either helping musicians get recording contracts, or giving them an intro to social media and social networking, with courses on developing Myspace pages (this was a few years ago when Myspace was cool), Twitter accounts (a new tool just coming onto the market), and the like.

So, based on my experience, I saw a huge gap that I could tap into and create my own lane via information products. The product I would later create was a multimedia course teaching musicians how to leverage Internet Marketing and Direct Marketing strategies to build their fan base and create their own business, so they didn't need to rely on a record label or fancy social networking tools.

I would never have known this had I not understood my industry. Once I learned a significant amount about my industry, as you must do, my fears were put to rest almost immediately. I could now spend my time getting to work and creating my products that would add real value for the people that purchased them.

BUILDING A WINNING PRODUCT FRAMEWORK

Getting started is always the hardest part of the process, right? Just like writing this book chapter. The first 20 words are the toughest to write down.

When building your first informational product, creating the first video or writing the first words in an eBook are the hardest to move from your mind to consumable media. But before we get to that first step, we can set ourselves up to succeed by planning out our product path and development.

I like to use mindmaps, or giant whiteboards, and create the largest brainstorming session I can. You may like traditional outlines using a notebook or Word document. No matter your tool of choice, your goal is to build a framework of what your product will look like.

- Will there be 4 modules? 8? 10? 12?
- What is the process you want to take your customers through?
- What is their ultimate goal?

- What are the main problems that you can solve?
- What can you think of that people will pay for?

What you are looking to do is what I like to call <u>a framework</u>. Wikipedia refers to a conceptual framework with the following definition: *"A **conceptual framework** is used in research to outline possible courses of action or to present a preferred approach to an idea or thought."*

To give you further insight into a framework, take the work of some other successful authors and product creators. Stephen Covey wrote his famous book, *The 7 Habits Of Highly Effective People* to highlight the "7 Habits." Those "7 Habits" are the framework for not only his book, but also his consulting practice and his high-level training.

Tim Ferriss has now written two best sellers that take on a slightly different framework. In the *The 4-Hour Body* and *The 4-Hour Workweek*, Tim uses the 4-hour framework to teach his readers how to live a better life. In *The 4-Hour Body*, he uses short bursts of body 'hacks' to live healthier, lose weight and gain muscle, which are the results he wishes for his readers to obtain. In *The 4 Hour Workweek*, Tim uses the same quick techniques to effectively manage our time, because getting more time to do the things we care about is the result of the problem most people face – not enough time.

In legendary marketer Frank Kern's *Mass Control* home study course, his framework is based on *30 Days to Mass Control Millions*. His framework takes the customer through 4 weeks of videos and workbooks to achieve their desired results, which is to build their Internet Marketing business.

In my New Music Economy course, the framework I created is a 4-week video course designed to help musicians become more entrepreneurial through learning direct marketing strategies.

Taking these examples and compiling your own product framework will give you the perfect starting place in getting your product together and to start winning in your marketplace.

CONSTRUCTING YOUR PRODUCT

Once you have your framework, you now have a blueprint to guide your readers and customers through to achieve their desired result.

For example, if you want to create a product to help someone lose weight, what is their optimal goal? To lose 50 pounds? If this is the case, your product should help them gradually get to that goal. We use a 4-module system to illustrate our point.

1. Your first module may be on grocery shopping and changing their mindset towards food.
2. The second module may be to lose that first pound by walking around the block.
3. Your third module builds upon this and helps them get to maybe 20-30 pounds of weight loss through exercise routines, strict meal choices and getting consistent rest.
4. The final module should be your advanced strategies for losing those last 5-10 pounds and give a plan to continue getting into optimal fitness shape. If your product can deliver these four sequences of information, you are providing real value to your marketplace and actually helping people achieve their desired results.

This potent combination will reward you financially as well as internally. Your product has changed someone's life in a positive way and that value is returned to you with an increase in your bank account.

Your product should speak directly to your target market, which you should now know inside and out. You should know if they like audio or video consumption, text or live Q&A with you. You should know the target market flaws, such as laziness or chasing opportunities without focus, but also be able to provide them the magic bullet to get their desired results.

For my New Music Economy product, I knew that independent musicians were usually struggling to make ends meet, great with certain types of technology (like guitar pedals and recording software) and did not have the means to pay large deposits for thousands of CD's or t-shirts.

So my product played off their weaknesses and turned them into strengths. I showed them how to create instant online income by recreating an old product and repackaging it, then selling it using PayPal. I walked them through the drop-shipping process for ordering CD's and t-shirts, so their fans paid them before the CD was printed and shipped. And I gave them the resources for technology that enabled them to use drag-and-drop visual cues to manage the technical side.

In order to create a winning product, you need to know the psychology of your market clients and help them to overcome their weaknesses and turn them into strengths. This is the key technique for creating a product that not only gets sold, but gets attention from the marketplace, stands the test of time and helps you create a long-term business – by using your knowledge and creating a platform to help people change their lives.

It is a big undertaking, but as a digital entrepreneur, it is your responsibility to use your knowledge to help people.

One last piece of advice that I will never forget is that you don't need to be a 'perfect 10' to teach a '1.' You only need to be a '2.' You always have someone that you can help and they will reward you for that help. Over time, as you teach and help others you will likely grow into a '10' out of the sheer fact that you are living and breathing that industry daily, gaining experience and touching so many people's lives with your product.

So get out there and start making products. Once you set your first product into the market, you will want to continue and increase the value you provide. To this day, I get no greater joy than creating something where someone tells me it helped them elevate their business, their life or their relationships.

That's winning to me.

ABOUT GREG

Greg Rollett, the ProductPro, works with authors, experts, entertainers, entrepreneurs and business owners all over the world to help them share their knowledge and change the lives and businesses of others. After creating a successful string of his own educational products, Greg began helping others in the production and marketing of their own products.

Previous clients include Coca-Cola, Miller Lite, Warner Bros and Cash Money Records as well as hundreds of entrepreneurs and small business owners. Greg's work has been featured on FOX News, ABC, the Daily Buzz and Greg has written for Mashable, the Huffington Post, AOL, AMEX's Open Forum and more.

Greg loves to challenge the current business environments that constrain people to working 12-hour days during the best portions of their lives. By teaching them to leverage technology and the power of information Greg loves helping others create freedom businesses that allow them to generate income, make the world a better place and live a radically ambitious lifestyle in the process.

A former touring musician, Greg is a highly sought after speaker having appeared on stages with former Florida Gov. Charlie Crist, best selling authors Chris Brogan and Nick Nanton, and at events such as Affiliate Summit.

If you would like to learn more about Greg and how he can help your business, please contact him directly at: greg@productprosystems.com or calling his office at 877.897.4611.

You can also download a free report on how to create your own educational products at: www.productprosystems.com.

CHAPTER 32

DON'T JUST MAKE A LIVING, MAKE A LIFE!!

– CHOOSE TO LIVE YOUR BEST LIFE EVER!

BY GLENNA GRIFFIN, REMARKABILITY EXPERT & COO SPEAK AMERICA

In a world of schedules, responsibilities, deadlines, commitments and the never-ending task of trying to make 'ends meet', we often lose sight of our personal power of choice. It's easy to feel like we're running on a hamster wheel and are powerless to stop it and step off! The power of choice is alive in each one of us! Once we make the choice to choose, we truly begin to live the life we're meant to live!

Often we are caught up in the idea of 'making a living' and we forget that while we're earning a living we're supposed to be 'making a life'! We can 'make a life' through the simple idea of choosing to make a life! I believe this is accomplished through making the choice of choice, the choice of purpose, and the choice of principles. *The Power of Choice!*

Every day when we wake up, we have choices to make. We have 'daily choices' and then at times we are faced with more 'life choices.'

Daily choices are those choices we make almost instinctively…..what to wear, what to eat for breakfast, which way to travel to work, when to walk the dog, etc. Daily choices are choices more focused on 'making a living.' These are choices that are built into the routine of our days. At times we make them so instinctively we don't remember making them! Have you ever driven home and once you arrive don't even remember the drive? Often, our daily choices become so routine we overlook their subtle power. The challenge comes when a daily choice becomes a routine choice that is detrimental to our overall well being; it's often difficult to stop the cycle.

For example, we could make the daily routine choice to arrive home from work every day, fix a double martini, and sit in front of the TV for hours. We may not recognize it at the time, however we are choosing to not address people or other needs around us. When this occurs, we are inadvertently choosing to make a life choice. We're choosing to incorporate a daily negative choice into our lives.

A more positive life choice would be if we arrived home from work, changed into exercise clothes, leashed up the dog perhaps, and headed out for a walk around the block, perhaps encouraging our family to join us! In this scenario, we are making a positive choice to exercise our bodies and spend time with our families! This daily positive choice has positive ramifications for all involved!

Life choices are those choices that are focused more on our core values, principles, and purpose. Life choices are more about 'making a life'! Life choices are about making choices about how to treat other people, ethical decisions at work, value-based decisions. How we work, how we play, how we interact with others, ...all need to be aligned with moving our lives forward toward our greater purpose and living the lives we are meant to live!

The choices we make are intentional. Whether they are daily choices or life choices, each and every choice is intentional. Whether we intend to make a choice about something or let the choice be made for us, it is still an intentional choice of direction. It is a mystery how some go through life stating they 'didn't have a choice' for a behavior or action. There is always a choice to be made! A choice of action, a choice of non-action, a choice of reaction, a choice of being proactive, ...all are intentional choices. We are fortunate to have the ability to make choices!

Every moment of every day we have the ability to utilize the power of Personal Intentional Choice (PIC). Are you making PICS that add and multiply to the value and essence of your life or are you making PICS that divide and subtract from your life? The choice is yours!! What PIC do you make every day?

REALIZE THE POWER OF CHOICE

"Each of us has been given a spirit of power …of love and self-discipline, not of timidity. Not making a choice is a choice. Choose to choose. Choose yourself! Sometimes we feel like we don't have any choice. There is always a choice. Choose your value. Choose to believe in yourself. Choose to exercise the power you've been given." (Remarkability Key #1 / www.SpeakAmerica.com / 10 Keys of Remarkability)

Often times we make choices in an effort to please others and forget that we need to choose ourselves, our happiness, our well-being, and what's best for ourselves first! This is not a selfish act! This is essential for the ultimate ability to provide for and give to others! If we are not solid in 'who we are' and 'what we stand for' individually, there is no way we can effectively and positively give to others. We do a disservice to ourselves and to others to function in a 'pretend' mode and not truly be who we are and pursue who we are meant to be! Each and every one of us is called for a specific purpose. If we don't choose to act on our true purpose, the world misses what only we can offer.

There is truth in the old adage of "You must love yourself before you can truly love others." This is true with choice as well. You must choose yourself and what is right for yourself first before you can make choices that involve others.

One such example in my life of doing for everyone else before taking care of myself is when several years ago I was told by my doctor that in order to be healthy as I got older I needed to lose some weight. Fifty pounds of weight to be exact! I had for so long been busy taking care of everyone else and running around to meet everyone else's needs and schedules that I had put my personal fitness and health on a back burner. I had to make a life choice. Did I want to improve my health so that in the future I would be healthy and active for my children or did I want to continue giving all of myself and my time to everyone else and compromising my health and well-being for the future? After much deliberation and second-guessing, I made the wisest decision for me! I chose to make the time to 'work out' daily. I chose to make better food choices when eating. I chose to prioritize my schedule around things that were healthy for me. As a result of all of these choices, I was rewarded with not only losing the weight, but also gaining a much more healthy perspective and preparing myself for the future!

I realized after I succeeded at reaching my goal, and since have succeeded at maintaining my goal, that there is so much power in the choice of choice! Realizing we have that power to make the choice is such a strong step! It's powerful! It's essential! It's enabling! It's a choice!

ACCEPT AND ACKNOWLEDGE YOUR GIFTS AND YOUR VISION

"I was not disobedient to the heavenly vision. Everything that has happened to you in your life up to this very moment can be used to help someone else. What you have experienced is what someone else is going through. These pains or painful experiences now become your gift to others. If you don't share what you have learned the world will lose. Share what you have learned and show how much you care. This is your goal. Strive for it. The impact will be incredible!" (Remarkability Key #4 / www.SpeakAmerica.com / 10 Keys of Remarkability)

We all are capable of making a choice toward our true purpose. When we stop trying to be something we aren't, we become whom we're meant to be, and life flows effortlessly!

So many of us deny our talents, our callings, our truth. Yet when we acknowledge our gifts and truths we truly are able to share ourselves with others and the world benefits! Believing in ourselves is the first step! Many of us get so caught up in living a life we are told we should be living that we miss the gift of living our true life!

Have you ever wished you had followed a different path in your career? Did you pass up on what you really wanted to do because you focused on doing what others thought you should do? Did you focus on doing what you thought was the 'right' thing to do but passed up on doing the 'true' thing?

I know a young man who for years tried to be an athlete, and ignored his musical talents. He tried out for every team and sport to make others happy ...not to fulfill his own goal of being an athlete. In every situation he was unhappy. He dragged himself to practices, dreaded the eventual games, and denied himself the true pleasures of dedicating time to his music. Eventually he got to a place where he could go no further.

When he let go of trying to please everyone else with his attempts to be an athlete, and acknowledged his musical talents and gifts, he began to flourish. Music had always been his life, his dream, and his passion. Once he stopped trying to be something he wasn't and embraced his true purpose, his life began to flow effortlessly. He learned that the choice to pursue who he was, and not who others wanted him to be, was really the way life was intended to be lived.

Too many people wait too long to pursue the life they want to live. What typically prevents us is an overall fear. We become consumed with a fear of failure, ...and sometimes a fear of success! What we must realize is that the fear disappears when we are actively making choices for ourselves, about ourselves, and in our own best interest. When we are making personal intentional choices, the fear disappears and it is replaced with an excitement and passion toward our future!

KNOW YOUR INTENTIONS

"Purity of intentions – give with the intent of getting nothing in return. I promise you it is harder to give it away than to sell it. Share your gifts with a pure heart and intentions. People may question you, they may wonder about your intentions. They may doubt you! They will eventually see your acts come with no strings attached. The rewards are 100 fold. Do your best to not let one hand know what the other hand is doing. Question yourself. Be honest. Be truthful." (Remarkability Key #6 / www.SpeakAmerica.com / 10 Keys of Remarkability)

If your intention is to live your life according to your core values and principles, you will discover that it can be a challenge. Yet it is a challenge that reaps many rewards. The process of making choices based on your intentions is something that gains strength and momentum with each choice you make!

Make choices to do the right things without an expectation in return. Living a life without expectation prevents potential disappointments! So many times we get caught up in making choices and decisions with an expectation in return.....and if that expectation rests on someone else's actions and choices, we open ourselves up for disappointment should the results turn out differently. Give freely. Make the right choices for the right reasons.

Someone many years ago said to me, "Always tell the truth, it's easier to remember!" That saying goes toward the power of positive choices for the right reasons too. If we are making choices for the right reasons, we have nothing to fear. When we make choices for the true reasons - and in line with whom we truly are - we have nothing to fear and our lives will flow....effortlessly!

Every choice is a step toward more powerful living. Every choice is a step toward living the life you are meant to live! Every step is a choice toward making a 'life' and moving beyond just 'making a living'!

Positive choices. *Positive Intentional Choices*. Make the choice and live your most powerful life ever! Stop making a 'living' and make the choices to live a 'life'!!!

ABOUT GLENNA

Glenna Griffin is driven to encourage others to make positive choices and changes in their lives! The power of choice and the power of change can result in outstanding personal and professional success!

As seen in USA today, COO of Speak America and Remarkability expert, Glenna Griffin is a sought after speaker and trainer. Speak America is a national resource organization for remarkability, dedicated to helping people create and live lives of "Intentional Legacy." Through personal and professional experience, Glenna encourages the development of personal communication skills for the discovery of an individual's true "voice." When someone finds their 'voice' and purpose, and has the ability to share that discovery with others, the world truly benefits from the gift.

Speak America is dedicated to helping people achieve their full realization of that gift. Speak America helps individuals through three key focus areas :

1- ULTIMATE BUSINESS SPEAK,
2- ULTIMATE LIFE SPEAK &
3- ULTIMATE YOUTH SPEAK.

The result of finding your voice and sharing your gift allows people to find their vocation. Glenna believes when you are living out your vocation, then and only then, the result is letting your life speak! When your life speaks, you will be living a life of true "joy!

As co-founder of the Let Your Life Speak Foundation, Glenna travels the world sharing her communication gifts. Her most recent journey on behalf of the foundation was to Kenya where she shared the ULTIMATE POWERSPEAK communication skills as she worked with a political caucus group in Nairobi, and children in an orphanage in the remote village of Wikondiek. This effort has now lead to the goal of reaching 5 continents in 5 years and the launching of the national Youth Speak program.

When your life speaks, you are on the path to remarkability. The Speak America tagline is... "BE REMARKABLE, GIVE ME A PLACE TO STAND AND I CAN MOVE THE WORLD!"

Speak America will move the world one voice at a time, one gift at a time, one person at a time!

CHAPTER 33

THE POWER OF YOUR CORE STORY –

HOW TO WIN BY CREATING THE COMPETITIVE ADVANTAGE AND THE COMPETITIVE DIFFERENTIATOR

BY BART QUEEN, REMARKABILITY EXPERT, CEO SPEAK AMERICA & ULTIMATE POWER SPEAKER

The situation today for most individuals/entrepreneurs and business owners is how do they separate themselves from the pack. How do I gain the continuous edge in everything I do?

Most business owners will race out to buy the newest piece of technology, fancy process or system. Some will invest thousands of dollars in the shiny new thing, believing it will give them the new edge. They keep missing the most powerful tool and concept they have at their fingertips.

I have seen large corporations send their sales people through fancy training courses to learn new strategies of gaining customers. Most employees look at it as the 'flavor of the month.' They never embrace the training. It eventually falls to the wayside. They go back to doing exactly what they have always done. The end result is getting the same thing they always GOT!!! Sales people have a natural way of doing their selling. We never teach them how to tap into it. We force them into processes and systems that don't allow their authenticity to come forward! We don't teach them how to leverage their most powerful tool in every interaction and selling situation. This is a global condition. This is not a local problem!

The complication is that entrepreneurs, business owners and VP's of sales organizations are missing the mark with their customers. Cost of sales keeps going higher, customer loyalty becomes an abstract idea, customer service becomes a process, not a reach-out personal relationship.

> Business becomes TRANSACTION-BASED, NOT RELATIONSHIP BASED!

> Business becomes PROCESS-BASED, NOT AN ONGOING EXPERIENCE!

> Business becomes a ONE WAY FLOW, NOT A MUTUAL EXCHANGE OF SERVICES!

> Business becomes a CONSTANT HUNT-AND-CONQUER, NOT A DEVELOPMENT AND NUTURE FOCUS!

The question then becomes: How do I separate myself from the pack of the masses? How do I win the race in business not once, not twice, but every time? How do I create the experience where people seek me out? How do I become the magnet people want to do business with? How do I create the relationship with people that exceeds loyalty?

HOW DO I BECOME THE GURU OF MY TOPIC, AREA, BUSINESS AND NICHE?

I believe your core story is your competitive differentiator. Your core story creates uniqueness that only you have. Your core story gives you the competitive advantage that no one else has... IT SETS YOU APART FROM EVERYONE ELSE! Your core story allows for authenticity. Your core story is your secret weapon!!!

Through this chapter I want you to do two things as you read: (1) become aware of the benefits of a core story, and (2) begin to visualize using your core story in every aspect of your business!

Here is what I know you will find: You will find you can approach your business from a total different perspective – "a purpose-driven" perspective. You will find you have uncovered an untapped natural market that demands only you. You become the magnet. You will find people seek you out - referrals become a marketing machine on steroids! Most importantly, your uniqueness and authenticity is your competitive differentiator! GURU STATUS IS ACHIEVED!!!

In this chapter, I will cover the concept of *people buy from people*, the mindset shift of empowering others, not impressing others, and the three levels of selling.

Here is what I have found in my twenty-three years of helping people communicate their messages. Three principles drive my discussion on your core story. This is the foundation information to build your core story.

1. Understand the concept of *people buy from people*, people buy from people they like!

In your business strive for three major goals:

   A - build trust

   B - build relationship

   C - build engagement

Everything you do should drive to one of these goals. In the book, GOD IS A SALESMAN, the author, Mark Stevens, makes the comment "...people buy trust before they buy a solution, tool, or product!" Think about people you do business with. You have a mechanic, a barber, a hairdresser, a dry cleaner, a plumber, a doctor, realtor or car dealership that you only do business with! You trust them.

I raise Clydesdale horses as a hobby. I wanted to buy a wagon for the horses to pull. I found one on the Internet in Canada. I spoke with the gentleman for 45 minutes. We had a tremendous conversation. I bought the wagon. I sent the man a check. I trusted him. The day my wagon arrived from Canada to my home in North Carolina he called me. He built both trust and relationship!

Our number one goal every day should be to build trust with our family, friends and customers!

Build relationships:- people do business with people they like! Your question is how do I build the LIKEABILITY FACTOR? Your core story builds the likeability factor! This links to the second level of my selling model, *ME TOO*!! Think about those times when you met someone, had a brief conversation, walked away and said, "WOW! I am just like them," …or "We have so much in common." Certain fraternities create this: the Marines, attending the same school, having a similar experience such as cancer, or families with special needs, etc. These things create automatic relationships and *ME TOO* factors!

Remember "people want to be a part of something bigger than themselves." We all have a natural place, fit, or connection to give back. One of my favorite old pieces of wisdom is … "comfort those with the comfort you have been comforted with!" Much like today, businesses want to do business with companies that have a green initiative. This is the same principle. People want to do business with people with whom they share a common experience, concern or philosophy. One of my clients does a huge amount of work in education. My commitment to reaching youth, to giving them the belief of following their vocation, makes for a solid partnership. At one of my consultations last year, the gentleman in question was involved in the Big Brother-Big Sister program. This again made a perfect link with my youth program. Today we are doing business together! The result - high likeability factors on both sides, being a part of something bigger than our selves, high engagement factors, and a lot of *"ME TOO."*

Build engagement - here is my definition of engagement! "Engagement is the ability to get the listener, customer, guest, client, student, and prospect to listen, respond and interact!" This should be done through our face-to-face meeting, over the phone, and web presence.

If our customers are engaged they should be saying… "TELL ME MORE!" …**NOT**, … "IS IT OVER YET???"

2. Work from an approach of EMPOWERING OTHERS! People do not care what you know. This is working from a mindset of IMPRESSING. They care about how much you care and what you have learned. No one can argue with what you have learned

through your experience. Develop the philosophy of "share and service" not "sell!" This creates an experience of trust and relationship! The end result is – becoming a Trusted Resource!!

Become aware of the three levels of communicating and selling your business.

A. "SO WHAT"

B. *"ME TOO"*

C. "I NEED YOU!"

Understanding these three levels will revolutionize your approach to examining and doing your business! Lets take a look at each one.

SO WHAT - This is the hardest level to sell at. This is where 90% of most people work their business. Selling at this level creates two major hurdles to get over. One, the conversation isn't even in their head. Your basic rule is to always "continue the conversation in their head." Two, we sell in the wrong direction. Most people try to sell in this order - first the company, second the solution, tool, product and third themselves. If you believe in anything I have said so far, if you grasp the concept of *people-buy-from-people*, then you realize this order will not work! The correct order is: one - yourself, two - your solution, tool or product and third - your company.

Think about the average conversation you might have standing in line at Starbucks while you're getting your coffee in the morning. Some small talk begins between you and another individual. You ask, "What do you do?" The person responds with, "I work for IBM, Microsoft, Oracle, or Yahoo." Your next question tends to be, "What do you do for them?" You get, "I am an accountant, engineer or analyst." Your response is typically, "Great, have a good day!" This is the standard approach. You hear this every day!

This is selling at the "so what" level.

Now notice the difference if I sell myself first. This would be how I would answer the question. Same conversation, same place:

"Morning!"

"What do you do?"

"I am a Remarkability Expert!"

"What is that?"

"I help people create and live lives of intentional legacy!"

Now the individual is saying, "Interesting, tell me more!" ...engagement is achieved!!!! From here in the conversation, I get to share more. This concept is called verbal ping pong – back-and-forth, back-and-forth, etc.

This is selling yourself first!!

The second is *"me too"*. There are thousands of ways to create the *"me too"* factor. One important way is to share some type of vulnerability or painful experience. I do not mean share your therapy. I mean share what you have learned!!! This allows you to be real. The result is a higher trust, a stronger likeability factor and people saying "Me too!"

I recently worked with a young man to identify his core story. As we worked through the process, he said the main thing he has learned is... "no excuses, no regrets." It was fantastic!!! Now everything he talks about in his company is to help others have no excuses, no regrets. He signs his email with his name and his concept... Bill "NO REGRETS" Jones.

There is not a person alive who wants to live their life with regrets. Right now you are thinking, you're right! Right now you're thinking... what can I learn about having no excuses and no regrets. Right now you're thinking, ...who is this guy? Right now you have no concept of what type of business he is in! What you are saying is... "tell me more," and *"me too."* You can do the same! You have not even begun to realize how much value you bring to the table of business, how powerful you are, or how your uniqueness is being untapped!

Now for the final level... "I need you!" This is what we all strive for! This is where all our concepts and ideas come together as one!

Trust is high
Relationship is high
Engagement is high

Likeability factor is high
Empowerment is high
"*Me too*" factor is high

The result is "I want what you have!" … "I need you."

The strongest results of developing and sharing your core story are three-fold! You reach a market that you didn't even know existed. Your core story does not have a shelf life and your uniqueness is your key differentiator! *People buy from people.* People buy from people they like. People buy from you!

We have taken a look at the key concepts of understanding the power of your core story. We highlighted the concept of *people buy from people.* We changed your focus to empower others, not impress others, and we shared the three levels of communicating about your business.

Your core story is your unique differentiator! Everything that has happened to you so far, both the good and the difficult, allows you to connect in a unique way. I see the power everyday with folks I work with. They discover a purpose-driven approach. They realize a laser focus. They become the magnet!!! People search them out! I believe you can have this too!!! I believe your core story will make the biggest difference in your business.

My challenge to you is two fold! First, look at any successful business or successful business person today and find the elements I have described in some way. Look at the people you do business with everyday, and identify the concepts that make up a core story. Whether it is in politics, religion, Corporate America, small to medium business or the individual owner, you will find the core story.

Challenge number two... If any of these ideas are important to you, email me at: bart@speakamerica.com and put in the subject line WIN – CORE STORY. I will be happy to send you details about developing your core story!

I had an opportunity to hear Rolf Meyer speak on a trip to South Africa. He was a key individual in the rewriting of the constitution of South Africa. He shared how there was a point of transition and the process of transformation. The point of transition was when he emotionally and intellectually decided things needed to change. The process of transformation is the ongoing experience since that point. The story continues! People want to be a part of something bigger than themselves.

WHAT WILL BE YOUR POINT OF TRANSITION TO SHARE AND DEVELOP YOUR CORE STORY?

WILL YOU TAKE YOUR BUSINESS TO THE NEXT LEVEL?

OUR GOAL IS TO GIVE ONE MILLION PEOPLE THEIR VOICE. WHAT NUMBER WILL YOU BE?

I DARE YOU!

ABOUT BART

In today's global economic environment it has never been more important to have the competitive advantage. The ability to communicate your message clearly, concisely and powerfully is your "silver bullet". Bart is a highly sought after speaker, communication expert and trainer. He is a valued asset and resource in helping individuals and businesses around the world develop solid communications skills for their professional and personal success.

Bart's communications training company, ULTIMATE POWERSPEAK operates across industries and with executives, IT professionals, salespeople and individuals in any capacity that are communicating face-to-face or in the virtual world. The result of his training helps them articulate their message more clearly and with greater impact, results and influence.

Bart and the ULTIMATE POWERSPEAK team truly turn the art of communication into the science of REMARKABLE results.

Bart is now dedicated to expanding his efforts to helping people take their communication to the next level and "Letting their Life Speak". Bart's team recently took the ULTIMATE POWERSPEAK communication skills to Kenya and worked with a women's political caucus group and with junior and seniors in a high school. This effort has now lead to the goal of reaching 5 continents in 5 years and the launching of the national Youth Speak program.

As seen in USA today, Bart founded Speak America based on people's longing to make a difference yet not knowing how. Speak America inspires, develops and helps people realize that difference! Bart, author of "THE 10 KEYS TO REMARKABILITY" shows others how to create and live remarkable lives.

Speak America is a national resource organization for remarkability. Speak America is dedicated to helping people create and live lives of "Intentional Legacy." Bart has determined through his years of helping people with their communication skills, that when people find their voice, they find their purpose and gift to the world. Speak America is dedicated to helping people achieve their full realization of that gift.

Speak America helps individuals through three key focus areas:-

ULTIMATE BUSINESS SPEAK

ULTIMATE LIFE SPEAK &

ULTIMATE YOUTH SPEAK.

The result of finding your voice and sharing your gift allows people to find their vocation. Bart believes when you are living out your vocation, then and only then, the result is letting your life speak!

Bart's goal is to give one million people their "voice."

When your life speaks, you are on the path to remarkability.

The Speak America tagline is ... "BE REMARKABLE, GIVE ME A PLACE TO STAND AND I CAN MOVE THE WORLD!"

Speak America will move the world one voice at a time, one gift at a time, one person at a time!

CHAPTER 34

NICHING

MAKE MORE MONEY BY FINDING NEW (NICHE) MARKETS FOR THE THINGS YOU ALREADY DO.

BY WILLIAM R. BENNER JR.

Within the book Game Changers, I taught you how to take an idea you had in your head, turn that idea into a product, and then take that product to market by starting your own small business.

Within my own field of endeavor, I've turned dozens of ideas into products that are the basis of multi-national company operations. If you've ever seen a professional laser show, then you've probably seen one of my products in action, since they are used to create shows at the world's top theme parks and major events like concerts, the Super Bowl and the Olympics. Because of how long we've been in business and our success, I know how to bring brand new products to market. However, most recently we've been using a technique that I call "*niching*", which involves much less effort and risk, and whose payoff could be far greater.

Within this chapter, I will teach you my niching process – how to make more money by taking your existing products, identifying new niche markets for those products, and modifying those products to meet the needs of the new niche market.

CLASSIC WAYS TO MAKE MORE MONEY

Before going into the exact formulation of niching presented in this chapter, let's first look at a two classic ways of making more money from your existing business endeavors.

The first way to make more money is to increase the marketing efforts for the products you already make. This includes improving Internet search-engine ranking, increasing your presence at tradeshows, increasing advertising within trade-journals and within various on-line spaces, and other techniques to improve top-of-the-mind awareness (sometimes called TOMA) of your product. I am going to make the assumption that you are already doing this as much as you can, and as we will see later in this chapter, there are circumstances under which increased marketing efforts can have very limited results.

The second way to make more money is to use the techniques presented in the book Game Changers, and develop an entirely new product. However, there is a lot of effort and risk involved in making an entirely new product. You will need to make sure your new product idea isn't already protected in some way (e.g. protected by copyright, trademark or patent). You will need to perhaps get additional help, such as consultants or specialists to make the new product. You will need to manufacture or otherwise acquire the components to make the new product. You will need to make a prototype of the new product and make sure it functions properly. You will need to produce completely new documentation for the new product, along with the new packaging, new web pages, new marketing materials, etc. In a very real way, this is like starting another business all over again.

As an alternative to increasing your marketing efforts, or to creating an entirely new product, we will discuss a third way to make more money from your existing business endeavors. This is niching. It involves examining the products you already make, identifying a new (niche) market that might be served by your products, and then modifying your product to suit the needs of the new niche.

Before discussing how I have applied niching within my own business, I'll discuss my observation of two other companies, and how they have used niching within their business. If nothing else, this will provide food for thought, by helping you to see how the process works, and it might also give you ideas about how you can apply niching within your own business.

HOW VOLKSWAGEN APPLIED NICHING

The first company that I will discuss is the German automobile manufacturer Volkswagen. Throughout the '60s and '70s, Volkswagen was best known for the Beatle – a low-cost two-door coupe which developed a cult following. The Beetle was certainly moderately successful on the market, but it was never really considered to be a serious competitor to the 'Big Three' automakers in the United States.

Well, as the decades went by and with the changes in perception of what a low-cost car should look like, fuelled by success of Japanese automakers, Volkswagen eventually got away from the shape and style of the Beetle, and came out with hatchback models such as the Rabbit, the Golf and the Polo. These cars never reached a degree of market penetration of the Japanese autos, nor did they ever reach a degree of ubiquity of their original Beetle design.

In an effort to increase their market share within the '90s, Volkswagen came out with the advertising slogan "*Fahrvergnügen*". However, aside from being fodder for a slew of T-shirts and bumper stickers which tended to make fun of the slogan, it's not clear that this marketing effort motivated people to buy Volkswagen automobiles in greater numbers.

Then in 1998, Volkswagen released The New Beetle – a car whose shape was reminiscent of the original Beetle.

There is no question that The New Beetle has been very successful in the marketplace. In fact, when The New Beetle was first released, people were on a waiting list for many months and, because of this, it was not uncommon for people to pay higher than U.S. suggested list price for that car, just to gain priority on that list.

Now, let's take a look at lessons we can learn from The New Beetle. First, The New Beetle appealed to a true niche – the people who would drive The New Beetle were not the same as the customers who would drive a Volkswagen Golf, and vice-versa. Second, it is important to note that this really wasn't an entirely new product for the Volkswagen company. What I mean is, Volkswagen didn't make more money by starting a new line of sewing machines. The New Beetle was based on the chassis of the Volkswagen Golf – a car that Volkswagen had manufactured many of in the past, and therefore many of the parts, and even much of the documentation (user's manual, etc.) could be reused with only little modification. So by expending a minimum of effort, Volkswagen was able to make more money by basically modifying an existing product (the Volkswagen Golf), which allowed them to access a new niche market – a market that had not been served by anybody up until then.

HOW DAVE RAMSEY APPLIED NICHING

Niching can work not only for tangible physical products such as automobiles, but also for softer products such as information products. With this in mind, the second company that I will discuss is The Lampo Group, more commonly known as Dave Ramsey's company.

In case you've never heard of him, Dave Ramsey can best be described as a financial advocate. He has authored several books on the topic of personal and business finance. He also has a radio program, a television program, and he occasionally does public speaking on financial and business-related topics.

Dave Ramsey's main products are books such as The Total Money Makeover and Financial Peace, and a virtual classroom product called Financial Peace University. Within these products, Dave teaches people how to get on a budget, how to get out of debt, and how to save for retirement.

I attended one of Dave Ramsey's public speaking events in 2010 and, for me, I can certainly say it was very educational and inspirational. At this event, Dave spoke about how the economic downturn of the last few years was affecting his business. In his words, Dave said, "The cheese moved – time to find more cheese".

Although Dave didn't use the word niching, where did Dave look for more cheese? Teens! Dave Ramsey created a series of financial products just for teenage kids, including Generation Change, and Foundations In Personal Finance. And let's face it, who needs advice about money more than teens!

It's important to note that, to make more money, Dave didn't create an entirely new product. What I mean is that Dave didn't start a chain of fast-food restaurants. Instead, Dave took the information and lessons taught within his books and virtual classroom products, and re-formatted them for consumption by a new niche market – a market that had not been served very well up until then.

HOW MY COMPANY PANGOLIN APPLIED NICHING

Let me now turn to how niching has been applied at my company, Pangolin Laser Systems. We are the world leader in software and control hardware used for creating and displaying professional laser light shows. It can certainly be said that we've been serving a niche market all along, because for the past 25 years, we've concentrated on producing products for professional show producers and, as a result, we have garnered an estimated 85% market share. However, one thing that we discovered is that just because you already serve a niche market, doesn't mean you can't access additional niche markets by modifying an existing product.

At a tradeshow in Shanghai, China, we were displaying our main software product called Lasershow Designer. Although we didn't know it at the time we signed up for the tradeshow, the attendees were really far less sophisticated than our typical clientele. By the second day of the four-day tradeshow, it became obvious to us that Lasershow Designer was really way too complicated for the people attending the show, and also that the price was a bit too high for this particular market. However, it was also apparent that there were many people at this tradeshow who were interested in doing laser shows if we could make the process more simple, and the price more appealing to them.

In an effort to use the tradeshow as a learning experience, we made a log of all of the questions that had been asked by potential clients, and also the answers to questions we asked about their needs and the price-point that would be acceptable.

After that, we went about making modifications to Lasershow Designer, to make it much less sophisticated and much easier to use. (It might surprise you to learn that most of the changes were actually made by reducing feature complexity and by completely eliminating certain options.) Also, based on feedback from the tradeshow, we eliminated the printed user manual, putting all of the written material in PDF files. We also changed the hardware configuration to a much easier to connect, USB format. The result is QuickShow – a product whose emphasis is on quickness, simplicity, and low cost.

Well, this exercise in niching was certainly very successful for us. We introduced QuickShow in late 2009, and by the end of 2010 Quick-Show sales represented 25% of Pangolin's gross revenue! During the year 2010 we ran out of QuickShow packages for 11 out of 12 months, despite doubling production every single month. And as a result of the lessons learned in creating QuickShow, we have rethought the way in which we craft and deliver laser software.

As was the case with Volkswagen and Dave Ramsey, we did not make more money by creating an entirely new product. Instead we took our existing product, modified it, and as a result, we were able to access an entirely new clientele – a clientele that had not been served by anybody up until then.

BENEFITS OF NICHING

By now you should see a few themes emerging. One of the themes is that there is less effort and lower risk involved in taking an existing product and modifying it, when compared to the effort and risk of creating something entirely new. By modifying an existing product, many of the existing parts, documentation, web pages, and marketing materials could be used directly and thus, the time-to-market can be very short. Because of this, the monetary investment is smaller, and so the time required to get a return on the investment is much shorter.

Another theme is that niche markets have fewer (or perhaps zero) competitors, which gives you more freedom in how you access the market, and even the price you charge for the niche products.

WHERE TO LOOK FOR NICHES

While trying to identify niche markets, there are several places you can look.

One obvious place is lower-cost markets. There are almost always more clients to be found by reducing the price of a product. The challenge is to find a way to reduce the cost of manufacture and delivery of a product while not cannibalizing your existing products and clients.

A corollary to reducing the price might be reducing the product complexity. By reducing the number of buttons, user-controls, gadgets, etc., it makes a product more limited, but also easier to use. Sure, specialist users need all of the features and benefits of a full-blown product, but easier-to-use products can appeal to a broader customer base.

Another place to look for niches is other cultures or ethnicities. For example, if your products are related to cosmetics, then hair and skin types certainly vary based on ethnicity. It may be possible to change a product formulation to serve an entirely new clientele.

Another place to look for niches is to look at different client demographics, such as higher or lower age brackets. We've already seen how Dave Ramsey successfully adopted his products for consumption by teenagers. Think about how cell-phones with few features, and yet with very large buttons and a large, easy-to-view LCD display are more appealing to senior citizens.

Yet another place to look for niches is pets. Think about how pet stores are chock-full of products that are simple, then think about how in Beverly Hills, California, some pets are actually adorned by diamond necklaces!

As a final note on where to look, I will mention that it is possible to create products that deliver a greater degree of exclusivity and charge a higher price. For example, a few years ago Motorola made a limited number of their model V3 RAZR phones – they were gold in color with the brand Dolce and Gabbana printed on the outside of the phone and as part of the background artwork. Because of the gold color, the branding and the limited number available, these appealed to an upscale clientele, and were of course sold at a much higher price than their other RAZR phone models.

MY CHALLENGE FOR YOU

As I conclude this chapter, I call upon you to apply the lessons taught in this chapter. Examine the products that you already make, and identify other potential markets for modified versions of these products. After that, create modified versions of your products to access new niche markets. The end result is more money earned with less effort expended.

ABOUT WILLIAM

William R. Benner, Jr. is President and CTO of Pangolin Laser Systems – a multi-national organization with offices in the United States, Central Europe and Mainland China. As President, he sets the general strategic direction for the company and oversees all company operations. As CTO, he is in charge of all hardware and software, as well as research and development on new products, which tend to strongly influence the future direction of the laser- and SMS-display industries.

In addition to having received more than 20 international awards for technical achievement, Benner's products are used by some of the best-known companies in the world, including Walt Disney World, Universal Studios, DreamWorks, Boeing, Samsung, and Lawrence Livermore Labs.

Beyond his work at Pangolin, Benner has served as a director on several boards as well as Technical Committee Chairman for the International Laser Display Association. He has also consulted for companies outside of Pangolin including NEOS, Cambridge Technologies, RMB Miniature Bearings and many others.

Benner holds numerous Patents, and has received personal letters of commendation from President Ronald Reagan and Florida Governor Bob Graham. He has also been published in the SMPTE Journal, The Laserist, LaserFX, US Tech magazine and Motorola's Embedded Connection magazine. He is also co-author of the best-selling book "Game Changers", and was selected as one of America's PremierExperts™ as well as being featured on NBC, ABC, CBS and FOX television affiliates.

He represented the state of Florida in the United States Skill Olympics and represented the U.S. in International Skill Olympics trials, receiving gold medals for each. Benner has also received the International Laser Display Association's highest accolade, the Career Achievement Award.

CHAPTER 35

THE BUSINESS TRIFECTA & THE MAGIC FORMULA FOR MEDIA SUCCESS

BY NICK NANTON, ESQ., JW DICKS, ESQ, & LINDSAY DICKS

"Success is simple. Do what's right, the right way, at the right time."
~ Arnold H. Glasgow

Imagine a new movie studio starting up with modest means. Anxious to get off on the right foot, they put every dollar into making the most amazing feature film anyone has ever seen.

Note two critical words in that last sentence:– "every dollar." Because when the studio finishes this amazing movie, they have no money left to market it. They can't get anyone to see it because they don't have any funds to tell anyone about it.

Anxious not to repeat that mistake, they raise more money and put a bundle into hiring the best movie marketing company in the country to sell their next very-modestly budgeted film. The marketing company delivers to them an amazing film trailer and TV commercials.

Except, again, they've spent everything. Now they have no money to do the P.R. to do the all-important press junket and get the stars on the late night talk shows.

The moral of this story? You can't properly grow your company without the right "business trifecta" – the perfect combination of media, marketing and P.R. Over-emphasizing one or the other leads to an imbalance, just as if you tried to sit on a stool with two legs.

First let's walk through all three of the elements we're talking about here, so you can better understand why each is important. We'll start with…

MEDIA

Entrepreneurs and professionals create media to sell an aspect of their businesses – it could simply be an image-booster, useful information or more of a hard-sell pitch. Media can be in the form of a brochure, a video, an audio CD, a book, etc.

This kind of media is usually not a client's main business, even though media can be sold just like any informational product. For instance, a tax specialist could write a book on tax secrets. That book could then be sold on Amazon, even though the specialist's main business is, obviously, helping his or her own clients with their tax issues. The book serves as an indirect advertisement for the specialist.

Of course, it's sometimes more worthwhile to give the media away for free to generate leads, establish expertise and grab contact info for future marketing. Downloadable information on company websites that require an email entry for access to that kind of media is a prime example of that.

When producing media, it's really important to look at your target market and your distribution method to make sure that your media is produced in a fashion that will be in-line with the distribution method and target audience.

Note here we're not saying that it all has to look like it came out of a Hollywood studio, because, even *with* a Hollywood studio, sometimes you want it to look "home brewed" (think "The Blair Witch Project"). Whatever your creative approach, the presentation of the media and the packaging can be the first step in establishing the critical elements of credibility and trust.

But again, no matter how good your media is, you still need…

MARKETING

How do you let your target group and/or customer base know that your media, which is probably of great interest to them, is out there and available? Well, that's where marketing comes into play.

Marketing can involve everything from low-cost viral videos to highly-polished TV spots, from free emails to expensive direct mail campaigns, from simple robo-calls to sophisticated referral programs. Marketing is how you get prospects to either buy what you're selling or, at the very least, get them to take a good look at you.

The purpose of your marketing, of course, can be multi-faceted. You may want to drive people to your website…and then, have your website convince them to leave their contact info…and then generate an email sequence designed to get them to buy. Or you may want a simple, targeted campaign with just one end result in mind – a simple sales letter designed to get people to buy your product, for example.

But either way, once you've done that, it's time to employ…

P.R.

P.R., or Public Relations, is all about creating *awareness*. You know the age-old question: if a tree falls in a forest and nobody's around, does it make a sound? Well, P.R. doesn't really care about the answer to that question – it just wants to make sure somebody *is* around to hear when that tree hits the ground.

That awareness comes primarily from press releases and media appearances. When your business has sold its one millionth widget (or whatever it is you sell), that's impressive to people – so you want them to know about it, because it boosts the image of your company. That's why you want to put out a special press release about that special widget, both online and offline.

If that press release hits at the right time, it could land you a story in the newspaper, in a magazine, on the radio, TV or online. It can also get you invited on radio and TV interview shows to talk about that special millionth widget. Or, if it's an online press release, it could just drive more traffic to your website - which, if you've got your ducks in a row, could end up being far more profitable than any media appearance you could get!

(By the way, that's why we mostly concentrate on the online press release, rather than the old-school offline variety. Online press releases boost your internet presence and, since they're written in the third person, also act as powerful online testimonials to anyone Googling you or your business – and its ROI is pretty much guaranteed.)

Should you nab those special media appearances, stories, and the traffic to your website, the great thing is you got it all *totally free*. Your main cost might come from hiring a P.R. company to help you make all of that happen. But, unless you have a legitimate story that really *does* stand out, that P.R. firm might be hard-pressed to get you much of an afterlife beyond that initial press release.

As a matter of fact, that's one of the biggest mistakes I see companies make – hiring P.R. firms when they don't have the marketing or media to back it up. When you try to get P.R. and you don't really have a story to tell… well, let's get back to that tree falling in the forest fable. In this case, there *are* people around to hear it – but nobody really bothers to listen.

Which is why we came up with….

THE SECRET FORMULA

How you put all three of these elements together – media, marketing and P.R. – is critically important. If you don't allocate enough money and resources to each one of them - and/or if you don't use each of them in the right way – you'll end up spending a lot of money without much to show for your efforts.

What we'd like to do is walk you through our "secret formula" for using all three in an orchestrated and effective system for our Celebrity-Press™ authors. We're not doing this to toot our own horn, but, quite honestly, it's one of the few all-in-one campaigns that we know of.

First of all, as we noted before, we produce a great high-quality hard-cover book that's got an attractive eye-catching cover, powerful overall theme and the participation of a lot of great authors. Those authors usually only have to worry about contributing a chapter rather than generating an entire book – making it much easier on their end. They still get credit for authoring the book, however, and can order special customized copies of the book with their picture on the cover. That takes care of the **media** portion of the program – because our client now has a terrific product around which he or she can build the marketing and P.R.

Next, comes the **marketing**. We've created a targeted marketing system that guarantees each one of our books becomes a best-seller on Amazon. The other half of that marketing formula is that we give our authors *over 30 ways* to use their new best-seller to market their business. Having a book is a great attention-getter, but having a *best-selling* book is impressive on a whole different level. So, again, we're handling the marketing to make the book a Best-Seller, which will get it lots of attention, and at the same time, our authors are using more than 30 of our marketing strategies simultaneously to market the book to their own audiences to create a far greater impact.

And that carries over to the **P.R.** Remember when I said you needed to have a real story to tell when you put out press releases (another way to think about it is "you've got to *find* the news in what you're doing)? Well, a best-selling book gives you that story. Our P.R. starts by putting out a press release that says so-and-so has signed a publishing deal with CelebrityPress™ - and then, after publication, the all-important follow-up press release that proclaims our author's book has achieved best-selling status. Those press releases spur media outlets to pursue any one of our authors for stories and interviews about their new book and, of course, their business.

Everything feeds into each other – but all of it springs from the fact that we have created a *real* media product as well as a *real* story about that media product. Which brings us to the magic ingredient of our special formula....

MELDING MEDIA

What we left out of our discussion of media earlier in this chapter is the fact that there are *two kinds of media.*

Mass media is the type most people know about. We're talking about commercial TV networks, national magazines, radio stations, etc. that are operated specifically to bring in consumers of all stripes. Mass media is about numbers – they want to attract the most users, so they can't really mess around; they *must* produce content that's genuine and interesting to the most people or they lose money.

All of us put the "mass" into mass media – we seek it out every day by watching our favorite shows, reading our favorite newspapers, listening to our favorite music and so forth. And because it has no other visible agenda than to entertain and inform the most people, mass media automatically brings two things to the table – awareness and credibility. If there's a story about you on CNN, people (1) see it and (2) think more of you because of it (unless, of course, you just murdered somebody or something...but we won't get into that here!).

This is why people hire P.R. companies - to get them on mass media outlets. The problem is, you can't "eat" awareness and credibility – in other words, if there isn't a direct solicitation involved with a mass media appearance, it's not really a big revenue generator. You're a story for a day and then it disappears (another reason we prefer online P.R. – it pretty much *stays* online forever!).

Now, let's talk about the second kind of media, known as "direct media." This is more of a targeted informational sales tool that takes the form of a CD, DVD, newsletter, direct mail piece, website copy, etc. The business distributes this direct media to an audience it selects (or in most cases the audience has identified itself by "opting in" on the website) with the sole purpose of selling to that audience – and it's created by that business for that specific purpose.

The problem? *Direct media lacks credibility.* There's a reason direct mail campaigns only have an average response rate of between 2 and 3 percent. Whenever anyone knows that a business is directly trying to sell to them, they immediately put up their guard and get suspicious. They don't know if what the sales piece is telling them is true because they know that the company is mainly interested in their money.

One way around this credibility gap is to use testimonials and product reviews, and other third party verification that appears objective. But there's still another way around it that takes the cake....

...and that's melding *both* kinds of media – mass media and direct media - into one.

For example, when you talk about having a best-selling book (mass media) in your direct media, that gives you an awesome level of credibility you wouldn't otherwise have. We also often place our clients on shows that appear on NBC, CBS, ABC, FOX and other national outlets. They can then talk about those *mass media* appearances in their *direct* media. If someone sees those network logos on your direct mail piece or your website, again, you're suddenly elevated in their eyes to a national expert (which you may already be – but would have a hard time convincing a stranger of that fact otherwise).

But any business person can do the same thing. For example, you use P.R. to get on mass media – television, radio, newspapers/magazines – the fastest and easiest way you possibly can. Then you take your direct media, stuff you can easily control the cost and distribution of, and put your mass media credibility in the direct media.

In other words, say you managed to get a spot on CNBC talking about your business. You trumpet that fact on your website, your newsletter, your e-zine, whatever direct media piece you create. That mass media "stamp of approval" can mean the world to a potential customer and can mean the difference between them paying attention instead of throwing it in the trash—and we all know the ROI on the trash can!

Even better is if you post a copy of that mass media appearance on your website, or put a copy of your newspaper article into a direct mail piece. We even hang ours up on our office walls – and our clients will invariably comment on them, which inevitably leads to us telling those clients how they can get the same coverage for themselves.

So ask yourself - don't you think that kind of mass media "stamp of approval" will get you taken a little bit more seriously? We can tell you, based on literally hundreds of case studies, it absolutely will get people to pay closer attention to you and what you have to offer.

So get yourself some mass media credibility – and insert it into your direct media. Don't spend all your time and money trying to get on TV or in the paper without having a plan for using that mass media exposure in conjunction with direct media for your marketing.

When you successfully combine media, marketing and p.r., you're guaranteed business growth and increased revenues   Correctly using the business trifecta raises your enterprise to the next level – and trust us, you'll enjoy the view from up there!

ABOUT NICK

Nick Nanton, Esq., is known as The Celebrity Lawyer and Agent to top Celebrity Experts for his role in developing and marketing business and professional experts, through personal branding, media, marketing and PR to help them gain credibility and recognition for their accomplishments. Nick is recognized as the nation's leading expert on personal branding as Fast Company Magazine's Expert Blogger on the subject and lectures regularly on the topic at the University of Central Florida. His book *Celebrity Branding You®* has been selected as the textbook on personal branding at the University.

The CEO of The Dicks + Nanton Celebrity Branding Agency, Nick is a 2-time Emmy nominated television producer and director as well as an award winning songwriter who has worked on everything from large scale events to television shows with the likes of Bill Cosby, President George H.W. Bush, **Brian Tracy**, Michael Gerber and many more.

Nick is recognized as one of the top thought-leaders in the business world and has co-authored 10 best-selling books, including the breakthrough hit *Celebrity Branding You!®*.

Nick serves as publisher of Celebrity Press™, a publishing company that produces and releases books by top Business Experts. CelebrityPress has published books by Brian Tracy, **Mari Smith**, Ron Legrand and many other celebrity experts and Nick has led the marketing and PR campaigns that have driven more than 300 authors to Best-Seller status. Nick has been seen in USA Today, The Wall St. Journal, Newsweek, Inc. Magazine, The New York Times, Entrepreneur® Magazine, **FastCompany.com** and has appeared on ABC, NBC, CBS, and FOX television affiliates around the country speaking on subjects ranging from branding, marketing and law, to American Idol.

Nick is a member of the Florida Bar, holds a JD from the University of Florida Levin College of Law, as well as a BSBA in Finance from the University of Florida's Warrington College of Business. Nick is a voting member of The National Academy of Recording Arts & Sciences (NARAS, Home to The GRAMMYs), a member of The National Academy of Television Arts & Sciences (Home to the Emmy Awards) co-founder of the National Academy of Best-Selling Authors, a 6-time Telly Award winner, and spends his spare time working with Young Life, Downtown Credo Orlando, Florida Hospital and rooting for the Florida Gators with his wife Kristina, and their two sons, Brock and Bowen.

ABOUT JW

JW Dicks, Esq. is America's foremost authority on using personal branding for business development He has created some of the most successful brand and marketing campaigns for business and professional clients to make them the Credible Celebrity Expert in their field and build multi-million dollar businesses using their recognized status.

JW Dicks has started, bought, built, and sold a large number of businesses over his 39 year career and developed a loyal international following as a business attorney, author, speaker, consultant, and business expert's coach. He not only practices what he preaches by using his strategies to build his own businesses he also applies those same concepts to help clients grow their business or professional practice the ways he does.

JW has been extensively quoted in such national media as USA Today, The Wall Street Journal, Newsweek, Inc. Magazine, Forbes.com, CNBC.Com, and Fortune Small business. His television appearances include ABC, NBC, CBS and FOX affiliate stations around the country. He is the resident branding expert for Fast Company's internationally syndicated blog and is the publisher of Celebrity Expert Insider, a monthly newsletter targeting business and brand building strategies.

JW has written over 22 books, including numerous best sellers, and has been inducted into the National Academy of Best Selling Authors. He has also received an Emmy nomination as an Executive Producer.

JW is married to Linda, his wife of 38 years and they have two daughters, a granddaughter and two Yorkies. JW is a 6th generation Floridian and splits time between his home in Orlando and beach house on the Florida west coast.

ABOUT LINDSAY

Lindsay Dicks helps her clients tell their stories in the online world. Being brought up around a family of marketers, but a product of Generation Y, Lindsay naturally gravitated to the new world of online marketing. Lindsay began freelance writing in 2000 and soon after launched her own PR firm that thrived by offering an in-your-face "Guaranteed PR" that was one of the first of its type in the nation.

Lindsay's new media career is centered on her philosophy that "people buy people." Her goal is to help her clients build a relationship with their prospects and customers. Once that relationship is built and they learn to trust them as the expert in their field then they will do business with them. Lindsay also built a patent-pending process called "circular marketing" that utilizes social media marketing, content marketing and search engine optimization to create online "buzz" for her clients that helps them to convey their business and personal story. Lindsay's clientele span the entire business map and range from doctors and small business owners to Inc 500 CEOs.

Lindsay is a graduate of the University of Florida. She is the CEO of CelebritySites™, an online marketing company specializing in social media and online personal branding. Lindsay is also a multi-best-selling author including the best-selling book "Power Principles for Success" which she co-authored with Brian Tracy. She was also selected as one of America's PremierExperts™ and has been quoted in Newsweek, the Wall Street Journal, USA Today, Inc Magazine as well as featured on NBC, ABC, and CBS television affiliates speaking on social media, search engine optimization and making more money online. Lindsay was also recently brought on FOX 35 News as their Online Marketing Expert.

Lindsay, a national speaker, has shared the stage with some of the top speakers in the world such as Brian Tracy, Lee Milteer, Ron LeGrand, Arielle Ford, David Bullock, Brian Horn, Peter Shankman and many others. Lindsay was also a Producer on the Emmy nominated film *Jacob's Turn*.

You can connect with Lindsay at:

Lindsay@CelebritySites.com
www.twitter.com/LindsayMDicks
www.facebook.com/LindsayDicks